LORD HALDANE

SCAPEGOAT FOR LIBERALISM

RICHARD BURDON, VISCOUNT HALDANE

LORD HALDANE

SCAPEGOAT FOR LIBERALISM

STEPHEN E. KOSS

COLUMBIA UNIVERSITY PRESS

NEW YORK & LONDON 1969

Stephen E. Koss is
Assistant Professor of History,
Barnard College,
Columbia University

FOR
RICHARD
AND
JULIET

PREFACE

It is difficult to know where to begin thanking the many individuals who have helped and encouraged me: those who replied to my importunities with invariable courtesy and often copious detail; those who shared in interviews their recollections of Lord Haldane and the events of his lifetime; those who gave me access to family archives and permission to quote from manuscript material. But there are a few to whom I owe a special debt. Dr. and Mrs. A. R. B. Haldane showed me innumerable kindnesses and introduced me to Lord Haldane's other nephew, Mr. Graeme Haldane, who provided an inspirational tour of Cloan, the family's Perthshire estate, and an August afternoon's reminiscences before an electric fire thoughtfully provided for an unseasoned American. Dr. Haldane, a historian in his own right, never sought to restrict or influence my interpretation of his uncle's life. I have come to value his friendship, which I hope will not be prejudiced by anything I have written.

Some acknowledgment, however inadequate, appears in my bibliography for those who allowed me to consult private papers. The list is by no means exhaustive, for there were several collections—whose owners and staffs were no less cooperative—that yielded nothing relevant.

I should like at the outset to record my indebtedness to Her Majesty the Queen for her gracious permission to use materials from the Royal Archives at Windsor Castle. I must further thank Mr. Robert Mackworth-Young, the Royal Librarian, for his efforts on my behalf. I am grateful to the trustees and staffs of numerous public and university depositories, again enumerated in my bibliography, and particularly to Dr. Thomas I. Rae at the National Library of Scotland, who answered many transatlantic queries.

The following individuals and institutions have kindly given me permission to quote unpublished material for which they own the copyright: Mr. Julian Amery; the Army Museums Ogilby Trust (Earl

Roberts correspondence); Mr. Mark Arnold-Forster; Mrs. Katherine Asquith; the Duke of Atholl; the Earl of Balfour; the trustees of the Beaverbrook Foundations (Lloyd George and Bonar Law correspondence); the University Library, Birmingham (Sir Austen Chamberlain correspondence); Mr. Mark Bonham Carter; the Hon. Christopher Brett; the Brotherton Collection, the University of Leeds (Sir Edmund Gosse correspondence); Sir Felix Brunner; the Cabinet Office (Viscount Milner correspondence); Mr. Patrick Campbell; the Viscount Chandos; the late Mr. Randolph Churchill; the Earl of Crawford and Balcarres; the Earl of Dartmouth; the Hon. Mrs. Cecilia Dawson; the Earl of Derby; Professor Myles Dillon; Sir John Elliot; Col. P. V. W. Gell; the Earl Haig; the Duke of Hamilton; the Viscount Harcourt; Sir Geoffrey Harmsworth; Mr. Richard Hewins; Vice-Admiral I. L. T. Hogg; the Hon. Lucy Holland; Lady Mary Howick; Professor Anne Lambton; Mrs. Janet Leeper and Mrs. George Shield; the Baron Lloyd; the Viscount Long of Wraxall; Mr. David McKenna; Mrs. Lucy Masterman; Major J. H. Maxse; the Viscount Mersey; Mr. A. B. L. Munro Ferguson; the Baron Parmoor; the Passfield Trust; Sir R. M. Perks; the Viscount Runciman of Doxford; the Marquess of Salisbury; the Hon. Godfrey Samuel; the Viscount Scarsdale; the Earl of Selborne; the Viscount Simon; Mr. A. F. Thompson; Mrs. Amabel Williams-Ellis; the Baron Willoughby de Broke; Major Cyril John Wilson. In a few cases it proved impossible, despite strenuous effort, either to trace or contact holders of copyright. I humbly beg the indulgence of any who have been omitted.

Bernard Shaw's letters to Lord Haldane are quoted by arrangement with the Public Trustee and the Society of Authors. Hilaire Belloc's "Epitaph on the Politician Himself" is reprinted by permission of Messrs. A. D. Peters and Company.

Sir Max Beerbohm's caricature of Lord Haldane, which adorns a letter to their mutual friend, Sir Edmund Gosse, is in the British Museum manuscripts collection; it is reproduced with the permission of Mrs. Eva G. Reichmann.

Photographs appear by arrangement with the Radio Times Hulton Picture Library, and cartoons from the *Daily Express* with the kind permission of Sir Max Aitken and Beaverbrook Newspapers.

The editors of the *Journal of Modern History* have allowed me to draw upon material that I initially presented in their pages. My travels in the United Kingdom received generous assistance from the Columbia University Council for Research in the Social Sciences and the Barnard College Faculty Research Fund.

In the process of completing this work I established many friendships and deepened others. Among my treasured memories are an interview with the late Dr. G. P. Gooch at Chalfont St. Peters, and a meeting with the Very Reverend W. R. Matthews at the Deanery, St. Paul's. Lord Tweedsmuir, Mr. Hugo Brunner, and Mr. Ian B. M. Hamilton took a lively interest in my project. I have profited from discussions with Mr. A. J. P. Taylor, as evocative in conversation as in print, with Mr. Martin Gilbert, and with Professor R. F. V. Heuston. I have also enjoyed a spirited correspondence with Professor Alfred Gollin. Individual chapters of this book were read and helpfully criticized by Professors Heuston and René Albrecht-Carrié. Professor George Woodbridge subjected the manuscript to careful scrutiny, as did Professor Peter Stansky, who brought to bear his extensive knowledge of Liberal problems and personalities. And Professor Chilton Williamson gave the entire enterprise the warm encouragement and thoughtful consideration that he has accorded each of my undertakings for nearly a decade. The book has been enriched by their various comments and suggestions. Needless to say, I alone am responsible for any errors of fact or judgment.

Lastly, I must express my deep gratitude to my wife, though she will accept no thanks. She has given so generously of her time and talents that to dedicate this volume to her would be a presumption on my part; instead, together, we dedicate it to our son and daughter.

STEPHEN E. KOSS

Barnard College,
Columbia University
8 November 1968

CONTENTS

ILLUSTRATIONS

LORD HALDANE

SCAPEGOAT FOR LIBERALISM

INTRODUCTION

In one respect British wars have all been alike. From Marlborough to Wellington, the Crimea, the Mutiny, Egypt and South Africa, the story is the same. Belated preparation; frantic effort; disappointment; recrimination; scapegoats; followed by inertia.

—THE EARL OF MIDLETON *

On Monday afternoon, May 17, 1915, between lunch and question time in the House of Commons, H. H. Asquith circulated a printed memorandum among his colleagues, requesting their resignations and announcing his intention to reconstruct Britain's Government on a coalition basis. In the process he put an effective end to the Liberal Party he had led for seven years and that had governed without interruption for ten. The Liberals would not again form a Government, though they would participate in future coalitions.

After nine days of bemused speculation, the first wartime coalition was unveiled. Asquith remained to preside over eleven fellow-Liberals, eight Unionists, one Labourite, and Lord Kitchener, who was *sui generis*. Seven members of the old Cabinet had been evicted to make way for the new arrivals. With one exception they were either young men who soon resumed their ministerial careers or party functionaries with little claim to office. The exception was Viscount Haldane, by far the most celebrated victim of the events of May 1915. For a decade he had been one of the most distinguished of ministers, achieving at the war office one of the outstanding successes of prewar Liberalism. He would not return to office until the Liberal Party had been displaced as His Majesty's Opposition and eclipsed as the party of progress.

Various explanations have been offered for Asquith's abrupt action:

* *Records and Reactions* (New York, 1939), p. 138.

that he sought to head off Unionist pressures; that he wanted to bring Italy into the war on the side of the allies; that he expected imminent disaster at the Dardanelles and hoped to stifle criticism; that his hand was forced by Lord Fisher's precipitate resignation from the admiralty or by *The Times*'s shocking disclosure of a shortage in high explosives. These interpretations carry varying degrees of conviction, but none in itself can explain the precise course that the Prime Minister adopted. They will be examined particularly in the seventh chapter of this study.

Various explanations have also been offered for Asquith's decision to exclude from the reconstituted ministry Lord Haldane, to whom he referred as his "oldest personal and political friend": that Haldane's identification with German culture rendered him a liability; that his place was needed to accommodate a newcomer; that the Opposition leaders, believing the infamous press campaign against Haldane, demanded his resignation as the price for their cooperation. These too are explanations, in themselves too simple by half, which require investigation.

The present study attempts to place in perspective a crucial episode in both Haldane's career and British political history. It is an episode that other accounts have either neglected or, for want of information, have treated with clichés. It is not suggested that Haldane's ejection from the Cabinet was the fatal misstep that put the Liberal Party on the road to ruin,[1] or even the central event in the political crisis of May 1915; yet it provides significant testimony to the nature of both developments. Haldane's fate was a by-product of the unedifying events that destroyed the last Liberal Government and, as such, helps to clarify the issues that underlay those events. It was the outgrowth of controversies and recriminations that had accumulated over a decade. It illustrates the gulfs that persisted within each party as well as those between them, the paralysis of leadership on both sides, and the fears and frustrations of a nation at war. Haldane's political fortunes reached their nadir in May 1915 at the same time that Liberalism suffered its deathblow; it is hoped that the first will give insights to the second.

[1] There is a temptation, which should be guarded against, for every chronicler of the Liberal Party to think that the period or event that he is describing was responsible for the death of Liberalism, "strange" or otherwise. Trevor Wilson has some useful remarks and a word of caution in the introduction to his *Downfall of the Liberal Party, 1914–1935* (London, 1966).

The humiliation that Haldane suffered brings into focus the man and his work. At the same time it elucidates the framework that contained him and the complex political relationships of these years. His predicament testifies to the dilemma of Liberalism, forced to repudiate its historic principles in order to achieve the organization of society that was believed essential to military victory. Popularly identified with many of those principles, he consequently shared their disapprobation. His enemies no less than his colleagues knew that in most instances he was identified wrongly; yet it suited their respective purposes to allow him to bear the brunt of public censure. Lord Haldane was the scapegoat for a Liberal leadership that had lost its authority, a Unionist leadership that had lost its self-respect, and a popular press that had lost its sense of proportion. As a result he was sacrificed to the leviathan of war.

Had Haldane better understood the forces at work within political society, he might have shielded himself against them. His silence in the face of hostile criticism reflected not so much nobility of character as irresolution and political miscalculation. Like most leading politicians, he was caught completely off-guard by the convulsions that shook the front benches in May 1915. Unlike some, however, he lacked sufficient public and party support to sustain him. Without either personal defenses or defenders, he perished. Only gradually did he come to appreciate what had happened. The realization deepened his disillusionment with the traditional parties, their leaders and their programs. Still, humility and a sense of propriety kept him from speaking openly on the subject. When he died in 1928, several friends wrote to his sister that he had confided to them privately the "real reasons" behind the creation of the 1915 coalition and his exclusion from it. It is these "real reasons" with which this book is concerned. In its attempt to ascertain them, it will investigate not only the tribulations of an individual, but also those of the party, the Government, and the political order to which he belonged.

The pages that follow are intended to constitute both a chapter in political biography and a commentary upon Liberalism in decline. They make no attempt to provide yet another general life of Lord Haldane.[2] Instead the task of this book is to analyze a crucial episode

[2] Sir Frederick Maurice's two-volume biography (London, 1937–39) says a good many things that modesty and discretion prevented Haldane from saying in

in that life in order to illuminate Haldane's career and the political darkness around it. Successive chapters will deal topically with the diverse factors that combined to deprive him of office in May 1915: his personality, his uncomfortable place among his fellow-Liberals, his military reforms, his 1912 mission to Berlin, wartime hysteria, and the press agitation against him. Because Haldane spent a decade acquiring the reputation that it would take him another decade to live down, it will be necessary to probe his earlier and later experiences.

Haldane is not an altogether sympathetic subject. He lacked the bearing of a tragic hero and the self-possession of a martyr. More often than not, he provoked the reaction against him with a careless word or an air of mannered boredom. As the Archbishop of Canterbury remarked in 1918 after a visit to Cloan, Haldane "manage[d] by his *surface* characteristics to keep up the mistrust which his enemies and critics succeeded in creating." [3] The ambiguities of his character and the shortcomings of his approach denied him the political success to which he constantly aspired. Yet Haldane participated as few did in diverse realms of Liberal thought and activity. This work is not a vindication of him; by this time surely none is needed. It is rather an attempt to see in his experience the destruction of reputations and ideals that accompanied the Liberal demise.

Haldane's predicament was testimony to the debility of early twentieth-century Liberalism, declining as a social ethic and an economic attitude as well as a political force. The pillars of Liberal society began to crumble before the outbreak of war in 1914, in some

his *Autobiography* (London, 1929), but it says many of them sloppily. R. F. V. Heuston, in his inaugural lecture as professor of law at the University of Southampton (*Judges and Biographers,* Southampton, 1967) noted the irony that Maurice, "who in 1918 achieved political immortality by accusing the Government of uttering false statements," took such liberties with his evidence as a biographer. Maurice offers expert analysis of Haldane's army reforms, but his handling of political questions leaves much to be desired.

Dudley Sommer's *Haldane of Cloan* (London, 1960) makes a laudable attempt to supplement Maurice's work with further research and interviews. But it relies too heavily upon secondary sources, many out of date, which it quotes at excessive length. Moreover, it perpetuates a number of Maurice's inaccuracies. Sommer is more successful with narrative than analysis.

By all counts the most successful treatment of Haldane is also the most succinct: it appears in Professor Heuston's *Lives of the Lord Chancellors* (Oxford, 1964) and its focus is upon Haldane's judicial career.

[3] Archbishop of Canterbury to Lord Stamfordham, Sept. 5, 1918, Royal Archives, G.V., O1357/5.

cases before the turn of the century; Haldane's career mirrors this process, for which he shares responsibility. Prewar Liberals did their best to adapt to the conditions of a new age, but the pallor remained beneath Liberalism's rouged complexion. Free Trade, upon which the Liberal world order rested, had been effectively challenged. Confidence in representative institutions had begun to ebb. Theories of progress no longer carried conviction. And there was a widespread rejection of the stolid middle-class values that had been the mainstay of Liberal England. No less than diehard Toryism, orthodox Liberalism was a forlorn creed, spiritually unsatisfying and increasingly irrelevant.

The conflicts and controversies that beset Liberalism were those that plagued Haldane and ultimately drove him from office. He was the incidental victim of what historians have described as the struggle between the forces of Freedom, with their reliance upon the voluntary system and laissez-faire principles, and the forces of Organization, which advocated greater governmental control over society and the citizen to the point of military and industrial conscription. Other, perhaps subsidiary, struggles included the one between those who subordinated their wartime passions to their visions of a better world and those who gave vent to a hatred of Germany that often antedated the war. Another was the struggle to assert civilian control over military affairs. Haldane was also deeply involved in the contest between democracy and reaction that reached its climax in the constitutional crisis of 1909–11 and had yet to be resolved in August 1914; there were those who thought that the forces that had tried unsuccessfully to arrest democracy before the war would destroy it under the pretense of national survival: "The present outcry for conscription is clearly manufactured," F. W. Hirst of the *Economist* wrote to C. P. Scott of the *Manchester Guardian*, "the object being to discipline and enslave the working classes and to keep down Ireland." [4] And Haldane was caught in the crossfire between the back and front benches within both parties. The *Daily Express* professed not to be attacking him on party grounds ("We care not whether Lord Haldane be a Liberal, a Unionist, a socialist, or a Prussian Junker") and, in a sense, this was true. Leo Maxse, editor of the rabidly partisan *National Review*, denounced him as a "Mandarin," an official who placed personal and party interests above those of the nation, and he would have been the last to

[4] May 28, 1915, Scott Papers, Add. MSS. 50, 908, f. 197.

deny that the Unionist Opposition had its share of such creatures. W. A. S. Hewins, an Opposition backbencher who shared Maxse's disdain for old-style politicians and his detestation of Haldane, observed that the leaders of both parties were isolated from their followers and insulated from national opinion, more often a brake upon effective action than the initiators of it. "The wreck of official Conservatism," Hewins wrote in his diary on May 22, 1915, "is as complete as that of Liberalism, and probably none of the so-called leaders of either side will politically survive the war." [5]

Lastly, Haldane's plight reflected the disrepute into which politics and professional politicians had fallen. Hilaire Belloc, who recalled with distaste his own parliamentary experience, gave grim expression to this sentiment:

> Here, richly with ridiculous display,
> The Politician's corpse is laid away.
> While all of his acquaintance sneered and slanged,
> I wept, for I had longed to see him hanged.

War merely exacerbated the nation's contempt for its ruling class. "The distrust of the home Cabinet," Ford Madox Ford wrote in *No More Parades*, "becomes like physical pain. These immense sacrifices, this ocean of mental sufferings, were all undergone to further the private vanities of men who amidst these hugenesses of landscapes and forces appeared pygmies!" Politics, having long lost its dignity, lost the people's respect. Lord Haldane came to understand this as a result of the fate he suffered in May 1915. It is a tribute to him that he dedicated his remaining years to making politics more worthy of the British people and educating them to their privileges and responsibilities as citizens.

[5] Hewins Papers; this extract does not appear in the published version, *Apologia of an Imperialist* (London, 1929).

CHAPTER I

CUSTODIAN OF A LEGACY

Perhaps I was unduly confident in my own capacities. At least, looking back, I think so now. But that is a matter which has ceased to be important.

The Haldane family motto, carved into the wooden panels above the hearths at Cloan and into the marble burial monument at Gleneagles nearby, is "Suffer." The motto, like the family, can be traced to remote centuries of British history: Haldane is a derivative of "half-Dane." No member of this ancient and distinguished line has better fulfilled that motto than the most eminent, Richard Burdon Haldane—Viscount Haldane of Cloan—"statesman, lawyer and philosopher" as he is identified on the commemorative plaque that adorns the house at Queen Anne's Gate that was his London residence.

This is not to imply that Haldane's life was one of anguish and despair. To the contrary, it was marked by proud accomplishments and rare satisfactions. But at the same time it was punctuated by a number of reverses, private and public, of which his expulsion from office in May 1915 was the best publicized but by no means the most deeply felt.

The resigned acceptance of personal and professional misfortune was an integral part of the religious ethic that dominated Lord Haldane's life by its influences, if not by its formal doctrines. His grandfather, James Alexander Haldane, had ended a promising naval career with the East India Company to devote his full energies to evangelical works, including a scheme to convert the Indian multitudes to Christianity. His father, Robert Haldane, had also turned his attention from the

* *Autobiography* (London, 1928), p. 3.

sea to evangelical pursuits. But it was Lord Haldane's mother, *nee* Mary Burdon Sanderson, whose religious influences upon him were most direct. She lived to celebrate her hundredth birthday in 1925 and exchanged daily letters with him in which there passed scarcely a reference to her husband, who had died in 1877 at the age of 72. It was chiefly for purchasing Cloan, their beloved estate in the Perthshire hills, that Haldane remembered his father. Mrs. Haldane, in her youth, had wanted to marry a young man whose "piety was not of the Sanderson brand." Her parents forbade the match, and she had decided to become a missionary when she received a proposal from Robert Haldane, a widower with five children. "I felt it was my duty to obey the nearer call and devote my life to him and his motherless children," she later reminisced to a family friend.[1]

Mrs. Haldane was the delight of her family and those who knew her. Though her memory stretched back beyond the coronation of Queen Victoria, her interests and outlook kept pace with the world around her. To the end her mind remained as clear and forceful as her penmanship. Her faith too remained strong, but not as brooding as that of her forebears. She understood that her son could not share her Calvinistic piety, and took consolation in his assurances that "although the symbols of their belief might differ, yet 'in essentials' they were at one."[2] Although many contemporaries took for granted that Lord Haldane was an agnostic—how could the translator of Schopenhauer, the friend of Einstein, and the author of abstruse tracts on relativity be otherwise?—he remained deeply religious if wholly untheological; in this respect he differed from most intellectuals of his political generation, John Morley and A. J. Balfour among others, who were ardently theological without being religious. It was as a student of philosophy at the University of Göttingen, where he enjoyed long discussions with Professor Lotze and longer walks through the German countryside, that Haldane reconciled the piety of his youth with the religious doubts of his early manhood. Haldane, in the trusted opinion of his intimate friend, Professor Andrew Seth Pringle-Pattison, "philosophized to satisfy a religious need, and the philosophical conclusions in which he rested were held by him with all the intensity which religious convictions possess for the ordinary man."[3] In a conversation with W. R. Inge,

---

[1] Violet Markham, *Friendship's Harvest* (London, 1956), pp. 40–41.
[2] A. S. Pringle-Pattison, *Richard Burdon Haldane* (London, 1928?), p. 27.
[3] *Ibid.*, p. 6.

Dean of Saint Paul's, with whom he often debated the philosophy of religion, Haldane described Christian teachings as "the perfect presentation in a practical form of the completed doctrine to which assent on the theological side has been won by the great philosophers."[4] Cosmo Gordon Lang, then Archbishop of York, considered Haldane's philosophy "a good bridge to religion. He encourages one to cross, but prefers himself to live on the philosophic side."[5] The Biblical texts with which Mrs. Haldane headed her daily letters therefore fulfilled a need in her son's life no less than in hers. "As to yourself," she told him on May 25, 1915, when his exclusion from office became definite,

I feel at rest. My text for you is: "The steps of a good man (or, as your grandfather used to express it, a *justified* man) are ordered by the Lord," and you know that you will be guided aright. As to the wisdom or otherwise of the Government, we can have no means of judging—as outsiders. They may gain or lose, but there is a Power above overruling all.[6]

Haldane might have expressed the matter with greater erudition, but he could hardly have put it in terms more meaningful to himself.

Haldane's relationship with his mother should not be underestimated as a source of his inspiration and resolve. Many of the decisions of his career—his desire to sit upon the woolsack, which had once been occupied by his maternal great-great-uncle, Lord Eldon, and his acceptance of a peerage—can be ascribed to a desire to make his mother proud. He provided her with daily accounts of his London experiences, separate from those he provided for his sister, Elizabeth. Whenever possible he would travel ten hours by railway to visit her at Cloan, usually arriving early on a Saturday morning and leaving late the following afternoon. To pass the time he would immerse himself in Hegel. And he would invariably break his return journey at Edinburgh to dine at the New Club, taking care to write a few lines to his mother so that she would receive something from him in the Monday mail.

The voluminous correspondence that passed between Mrs. Haldane and her eldest son was filled with ritualistic references to events of the past. At the appropriate time each year, both would pause to recall with affection Mrs. Haldane's second son, George, who died at sixteen years of age. Each spring, Haldane would recall his brief engagement to a novelist in 1890, though after twenty-five years he relied upon his

[4] Diary for August 23, 1928, *Diary of a Dean* (New York, 1950), p. 132.
[5] J. G. Lockhart, *Cosmo Gordon Lang* (London, 1949), p. 250.
[6] Haldane Papers [hereafter HP] 6009, f. 120.

mother's extraordinary memory to correct him that it had been in April, not March. His fiancée had broken the engagement after five weeks allegedly on the grounds that she was romantically involved with another woman. This was the most painful of all Haldane's sufferings. For the next seven years he had cherished hopes that she would return to him, while she wrote three romantic novels, each with an ambitious, sensitive hero who in some way resembled Haldane. In September of 1897 she died, providing him with another date to commemorate in his letters to his mother. He never married and never ceased to mourn her. "I never judged her nor blamed her," he told an aunt, who had sent a letter of sympathy;[7] and to Lord Rosebery, who knew them both, he wrote that his "old love . . . remained. . . . It will end, not in her grave, but in mine."[8]

But one must not create the impression that Haldane was sullen and introspective. He was a genial and outgoing person who accepted the misfortunes that befell him and who learned to abide them. Despite his essential loneliness, he had a zest for life and a capacity for gracious living, an unbounding enthusiasm for his work and a warm devotion to his friends. His wine cellar was acknowledged to be among the best in London, and his humidors were stocked with the finest cigarettes and cigars. Lord Hankey recalled that Haldane, eminently a patrician, smoked a cigar "poised delicately on the two prongs of a tiny silver fork, which he always used for this purpose."[9] Haldane had graduated to a gold fork by the time he met Sir Maurice Bowra, then an Oxford undergraduate, whom he told: "You won't mind getting old, except that sometimes after a good lunch you will find that you can't get up."[10] He delighted in the bounty of his table and, unlike some hosts of his generation, always made certain that his guests shared the abundance. Beatrice Webb—whose dinners were described by R. H. Tawney as "exercises in asceticism"—found fault with the "Herculean" appetite

[7] September 17, 1897, HP 5904, f. 122.

[8] September 15, 1897, Rosebery Papers. Beatrice Potter, soon to become Mrs. Sidney Webb, wrote that she received a proposal of marriage from Haldane months after his engagement had ended, but that she refused on grounds that she "could not contemplate an act of *felo de se* for a speculation in personal happiness." Was this another of her romantic fantasies, or could she have misunderstood her friend, whose "woolliness of mind" she often criticized? See Kitty Muggeridge and Ruth Adam, *Beatrice Webb* (London, 1967), pp. 124-25.

[9] *The Supreme Command, 1914–1918*, I (London, 1961), 54.

[10] Bowra, *Memories* (London, 1966), p. 121.

of her portly friend, but this undoubtedly reflected as much upon her puritanism as upon his digestion. Haldane's weight and sallow complexion, which she attributed to over-indulgence, were diagnosed late in his life as symptoms of diabetes, from which he suffered several attacks that inflicted temporary blindness.

The conversation around Haldane's table befitted the high quality of the fare upon it. He invited to his home the leading figures of the political, legal, literary, and social circles in which he traveled: civil servants could meet German metaphysicians, politicians could consult physicists, and playwrights could match wits with archbishops. The atmosphere was graceful, but decidedly masculine, heavy with smoke and great issues. Haldane did not shy away from female company; he simply regarded the dinner table as a sacrosanct institution that was no place for idle chatter. Whenever possible, his sister Elizabeth would serve as hostess, but she—like Mrs. Webb, a frequent guest—was thoroughly at home in the society of men. Miss Haldane was a formidable intellect in her own right, a social reformer and a translator of Hegel and Descartes. She was particularly devoted to her eldest brother, who stood most in need of her companionship and resolution. It was she, often without his knowledge, who inspired attempts to vindicate his name during the wartime years. Yet her pertinacity made her company less congenial than his. There was at least one visitor to the Haldane household who breathed a sigh of relief that "Miss Haldane [had been] happily absent."[11]

Haldane was a man of infinite kindnesses, not all of them paid at the dinner table. "His heart was as large as his head," G. P. Gooch has fondly recalled, "and he was as generous with his purse as with his time."[12] It was Haldane who was first to visit Oscar Wilde in Holloway Gaol, bringing him pen, ink, and something more diverting to read than *The Pilgrim's Progress*. Officials who served under Haldane at the war office were aware that he always made it a point at receptions to converse with those wives least fashionable and most ill-at-ease. Incapable of rudeness, he was inclined to see the best even in those who would see only the worst in him. Bernard Shaw, who admired him as he did few politicians, used him as the model for one of his most endearing

[11] Diary for July 12, 1914, Christopher Addison, *Four and a Half Years*, I (London, 1934), 17.
[12] *Under Six Reigns* (London, 1959), p. 194.

characters, the waiter in *You Never Can Tell,* who is described as an individual

so cheerful and contented that in his encouraging presence ambition stands rebuked as vulgarity, and imagination as treason to the abounding sufficiency and interest of the actual. He has a certain expression peculiar to men who have been extraordinarily successful in their callings, and who, whilst aware of the vanity of success, are untouched by envy.

To boot, Shaw's waiter served his patrons not only the best in food and drink, but ample helpings of the philosophy of Schopenhauer.

Not everyone was as impressed with Haldane as Shaw, whose tastes in any case were idiosyncratic. To most contemporaries—including the majority of his Cabinet colleagues—Haldane appeared ponderous, phlegmatic, and dull. Those who got to know him, like Harold Laski, found a "certain sweet vanity" about the man.[13] Others found him complacent, even insufferable. Among his fellow Liberals he was known as the penguin, Pussy, Schopenhauer, or as Lord Rosebery called him, Justinian. Members of the Opposition referred to him less kindly as the Blimp, the Great Seal (a pun on the lord chancellorship), or Herr Professor. Sir Frederick Maurice's official biography of Haldane attributes this lack of rapport between Haldane and his contemporaries to his subject's preference for dogs instead of horseflesh, and to the fact that Haldane "had none of those little human weaknesses and foibles which often endear a leader to his followers."[14] One might argue that, to the contrary, Haldane's weaknesses were too readily apparent to be obscured by a devotion to the turf. In public addresses, and often in private correspondence, he was wordy to the point of being pedantic. "To follow Haldane into the clouds," Asquith would tease, "needed . . . a special kind of education which he," a Balliol scholar, "had not had."[15] A. G. Gardiner, the distinguished Liberal journalist, observed with affection that a Haldane speech was "a lucid fog"—not in this case a contradiction, he insisted:

The lucidity of his mind is as conclusive as the fog in yours. The clearer he becomes to himself, the more hopeless is your bewilderment. If only one

---

[13] Laski to Holmes, Feb. 26, 1929, M. D. Howe (ed.), *Holmes-Laski Letters* (Cambridge, Mass., 1953), II, 1136.

[14] Maurice, *Haldane,* II, 372.

[15] J. A. Spender and C. Asquith, *Life of Herbert Henry Asquith, Lord Oxford and Asquith,* I (London, 1932), 200.

Lord Haldane as caricatured by Max Beerbohm
on a note to Edmund Gosse

could feel that he himself was getting a little lost in this amazing labyrinth of locution, one would feel less humiliated. But it is obvious that the less you understand him the more he understands himself. He smiles urbanely upon you, and points the fat didactic finger at you with pleasant intimacy. He does you the honour of pretending that you follow him, and self-respect compels you to accept the delicate tribute to your penetration. It is a comedy which saves him a lot of trouble.[16]

Others, it might be presumed, were less sympathetic to Haldane's abstract theories, convoluted sentences, and dry-as-dust exposition. Austen Chamberlain found Haldane's presentation of the 1907 army estimates "ill-arranged" and a third too long. John Morley agreed, and added that he and James Bryce had always found Haldane "very hard to follow. . . . His speeches have no paragraphs. There are full stops here and there, faintly marked, but no paragraphs."[17] The mere prospect of a parliamentary speech from Haldane was sufficient to touch off a minor stampede to the tea-room. Alfred Lyttleton scrawled a note on the back of an envelope to Lewis (Loulou) Harcourt "just before Haldane's army speech" on February 25, 1907: "Submitted: that the House is too hot or is it my inflammation of blood at the prospect of 3 hours from Schopenhauer?"[18] David Lloyd George, the least patient of all politicians, labeled Haldane "the most confusing clever man I have ever met," and noted the irony that such a wordy fellow was, at Cabinet meetings, "almost its most silent member."[19] Lloyd George's observation stands confirmed by the minutes of the Committee of Imperial Defence, to which Haldane belonged but seldom contributed.

Haldane's communication problem—and that was essentially what it was—was caused by something more than his reedy voice, the excessive length of his public addresses, and the halting delivery that resulted in large part from the fact that he often relied upon a typewritten text. He had an unduly hard time adjusting his oratorical style and tailoring the content of his speeches to the particular audience at hand. Unlike politicians of the newer school, he spoke with the same tedious earnestness to colleagues, constituents, even critics. Moreover, he could never manage the feat of being elevated without being elusive. His literary

[16] *Prophets, Priests and Kings* (London, 1914), p. 283.
[17] Austen Chamberlain, *Politics from Inside* (New Haven, 1937), p. 69.
[18] Harcourt Papers.
[19] Diary for July 19, 1913, Lord Riddell, *More Pages from My Diary* (London, 1934), p. 171; also David Lloyd George, *War Memoirs*, I (London, 1934?), 603.

allusions, which were abundant, tended to soar above the heads of his listeners, and created the unfortunate impression that he was flaunting his superior intelligence or, worse, his foreign education. To an extent such an impression was justified, for Haldane, who disdained the vulgar, was apt—no less than Balfour or Asquith—to dismiss minds less cultivated than his own.

And, particularly, Haldane was never able to gauge the adverse effects upon public opinion, even sympathetic public opinion, of his panegyrics to German culture. His assorted allusions to German events and situations, however valid, tended to irritate rather than convince his audiences. Harold Laski liked to tell the story, probably apocryphal, that Haldane, addressing thirteen-thousand miners at Durham on behalf of Sidney Webb's candidacy, quoted at length from Goethe's *Faust*. John Morley complained to H. A. L. Fisher that Haldane "wear[ied] his Cabinet colleagues by long harangues on the contribution of Germany to civilisation."[20] Even when he defended Free Trade—as he did in a letter to the editor of *Spectator* on October 3, 1903—he argued negatively from the German experience, not, as one would have expected of a biographer of Adam Smith, positively from the English experience.

Lord Knutsford, best known as a hospital reformer, worked tirelessly during the wartime years to defend Haldane from unjust imputations. But he had to admit to their mutual friend, Edmund Gosse, that Haldane was little or no help. Unlike either Lloyd George or the seventeenth Earl of Derby (one a "clever" Liberal and the other an "almost stupid" Unionist, but both blessed with the ability to "feel the pulse of the people as their own"), Haldane was wholly unable to "appreciate the feelings of the man in the street." Worse, he was unable to sense the mood of the parliamentary backbenchers. Knutsford likened him to Lord Robert Cecil, another "born lawyer," who possessed "a great mind," but who could never manage to descend "to the level of the ordinary M. P. . . . Haldane," he concluded, "is an exaggerated R. Cecil."[21] The comparison should not be pushed too far, for Cecil had the advantage of invaluable social credentials. Yet it provides a useful reminder that the problem transcended party lines.

Haldane's inability to gauge popular sentiments and to appreciate

[20] Conversation of Sept., 1909, quoted in David Ogg, *Herbert Fisher* (London, 1947), p. 45.
[21] Sept. 8, 1917, Gosse Papers.

the strategic role played by the popular press was a common failing among politicians of his background and tradition; but it rebounded against him more dramatically than against the others. He unwittingly provided the ammunition with which his enemies discredited him. It was this same indifference to public passions, even an ignorance of them, that allowed Margot Asquith and her stepdaughter to pay a farewell call upon the German ambassador, a personal friend, after war was declared in August 1914. One might defend such behavior in terms of personal honor, but hardly in terms of political common sense. The most celebrated of Haldane's indiscretions was his casual remark to a visiting German academic shortly before the war that Germany was his "spiritual home." This was a meaningless attempt at dinner-party diplomacy which his critics pounced upon and exploited. Haldane's attempts to redeem himself on this and later occasions were equally maladroit and fanned the flames of the agitation against him. A gentleman himself, he could never perceive the depths to which his adversaries, let alone his friends, would stoop for political advantage. Indeed, his greatest difficulty lay in determining who his enemies were: a politician might attack him bitterly in the House, but could win his forgiveness by stopping to ask about his mother's health. Flattery of this nature disarmed Haldane, who was too much inclined to credit others with his own standards of propriety. This led him to underestimate the charges against him and the deadly seriousness with which they were leveled. Younger, less principled politicians trespassed beyond the bounds of gentlemanly opposition and had begun to appeal to extra-parliamentary forces that they brought to bear upon the situation at Westminster.

In no sense was Haldane ever a "popular" politician. He was elected to Parliament in 1885 for East Lothian—or the Haddington Division— and retained that seat without difficulty until he left the Commons for the Lords in 1911. His family exerted an appreciable influence over the area, which was in any event steadfastly Liberal in its political affiliations. It was an age in which constituencies on the "Celtic fringe," particularly those in Scotland, were the safe preserve of London-based Liberals; Asquith recorded an account of a climb to the top of a hill in the Scottish lowlands with Haldane and Augustine Birrell and the latter's "grateful thought that there is not an acre in this vast and varied landscape which is not represented at Westminster by a London barrister!"[22]

22 *Memories and Reflections*, I (London, 1926), 105.

Haldane was particularly fortunate in his ability to take for granted the continued support of his constituents, for he was not a politician who could have won over an indifferent crowd from a campaign platform. Even his ministerial accomplishments, however constructive and successful, were not of the nature to fire the public imagination. He understood as well as anyone the limitations of his appeal. "I have no gift of expression," he confessed to Lord Milner, "and no real capacity for managing men—much less leading them. But I seem to see very clearly . . . what needs doing, and I mean to have my try at helping and encouraging others to do what I cannot accomplish myself."[23]

Haldane's reliance upon other, more dynamic politicians, whom he attempted to encourage or stimulate, entitled him to his place at the perimeter of the Fabian Society, to which he belonged more in spirit than in letter. Like the Webbs, he was confident that more constructive work could be accomplished in private consultation, over dinner or a good cigar, than by public agitation or debate. Haldane's tendency to work through others gave rise to frequent accusations that he was a conspirator, a wirepuller. Sir Henry Campbell-Bannerman, to whom the leadership of the ramshackle Liberal Party fell in 1898 and under whom Haldane later served, snickered that Haldane "always prefers the back stairs to the front stairs; but it does not matter, for the clatter can be heard all over the house."[24] Such a view of Haldane was not groundless paranoia, for despite the fact that Haldane sent his nominal chief long, gossipy letters that contained tacit professions of loyalty, he was a party to various attempts to topple Campbell-Bannerman from the Liberal leadership. The profound ideological cleavages within Liberal ranks—which persisted, less openly, after the Liberal revival of 1905— provided an invitation if not an inducement to intrigue which Haldane had neither the inclination nor the position to resist. Like others, he was aware that the disarray of Liberal forces afforded him and his schemes exceptional opportunities. This disarray, which abetted Haldane's rise before 1905, came to distress and ultimately to defeat him in the decade that followed. But given the confusion of Liberal politics in the years before he took office, he cannot be judged too harshly for the variety of his allegiances. Mrs. Webb, who attended "a typical Haldane dinner on the night of the South Africa debate" (July 29, 1897), cited the diversity of her fellow-guests as "typical of Haldane's

---

23 July 6, 1901 [copy], Milner Papers.
24 F. W. Hirst, In the Golden Days (London, 1947), p. 264.

weakness—his dilettante desire to be in every set." At the same time she observed that this was typical of Haldane's "strength—his diffusive friendship which enables him to bring about non-party measures."[25]

With equal perception, Mrs. Webb recognized the fact that Haldane, a friend for decades who ultimately joined her husband in the first Labour Government, was essentially a nonparty politician. His loyalties were to ideas and to friendships rather than to party traditions. Although he fell victim to the most extreme of partisan attacks, he attempted at all times to obtain bipartisan support for his measures and accomplished much of his most creative work in cooperation with Fabians on the one hand and Unionists on the other. Haldane's scheme for the reform and encouragement of higher education was high among these. Working closely with the Webbs, with whom he helped to found the London School of Economics, he enlisted the support of Joseph Chamberlain ("the only man in this Country who has the combination of keenness and power") for schemes to develop provincial universities that would eventually integrate with the older ones. He also proposed an institution, on the model of the German university at Charlottenburg, to provide technical and scientific education. He hoped that Chamberlain would lend his name to a campaign to which he, behind the scenes, would contribute energy and ideas: "Now you are very busy and cannot do more than supervise and exercise influence," he told Chamberlain. "But I can find some time and I have my hand on the experts. I am ready to help you to get together a committee—in and out of the House—and wholly outside politics. . . ."[26]

Why would Haldane have attempted to accomplish his designs in league with his political rivals instead of through normal Liberal channels? Perhaps he realized that Chamberlain, like him, was among the very few prominent politicians without an emotional tie to the traditions of Oxford and Cambridge. Undoubtedly he realized that the Liberals, before 1905 and even after, lacked the viability to handle the vexing problem of education. Any Liberal measure would be a compromise between necessity and nonconformist principles. Haldane vastly preferred the Balfour Government's Education Act of 1902 to any alternative his own party could offer, and he seriously weakened his party standing by saying so. He found his colleagues, particularly

[25] *Our Partnership* (London, 1948), pp. 141–42.
[26] August 14, 1902, Chamberlain Papers.

Campbell-Bannerman, "very stupid in such things,"[27] and concluded that only by working in concert with politicians of other parties could an adequate measure reach the statute book. His activities on behalf of educational proposals revealed Haldane at his most characteristic and his most adept. He was an intriguer, certainly, but as Mrs. Webb strenuously defended him, his "intrigues are always to promote a cause, never to push himself."[28]

Severely critical of Haldane's gastronomic habits, so unlike her own, Mrs. Webb was perhaps too tolerant of her friend's political habits, identical to her own. She recognized in Haldane one of the few Liberal politicians with "collectivist" tendencies, not quite a socialist, but something more than a Radical reformer. Haldane, though he remained faithful to his party's free trade tradition, counted himself among "those who thought that there were great social problems to be solved in this country, and [that] they could only be solved by a considerable amount of interference on the part of the Government of the day with people's liberties."[29] Although he appeared right-wing—particularly on matters of imperialism, foreign policy, and defense—in the eyes of many back-bench Liberals, Haldane was decidedly left-wing in his response to social issues; this was a contradiction that cost him support within his own party and contributed to his downfall in May 1915.

Haldane's undercover activities were not always so creditable nor so constructive as those on behalf of education projects. If Mrs. Webb looked upon them charitably, it was either because she shared his views or Haldane had converted her to them, as he had "manipulated" her and her husband into the Rosebery "clique."[30] Shortly before Gladstone had retired from the premiership in 1894, Haldane pledged his support to Lord Rosebery, in whom he saw the best chance for himself and his policies. Rosebery's leadership promised a more progressive, less doctrinaire approach to welfare legislation, foreign, and colonial affairs; also implicit was the promise that a place might be found for Haldane at the Local Government Board or elsewhere in a Rosebery ministry. The life of the Rosebery Government was too brief and far too unhappy for any of Haldane's hopes to be realized. Haldane had alienated the

27 Haldane to his mother, July 14, 1905, HP 5974, f. 23; see also Sir Almeric Fitzroy, *Memoirs*, I (London, 1927?), 82–83.
28 Diary for Nov. 10, 1902, *Our Partnership*, p. 247.
29 *Parliamentary Debates* (Feb. 8, 1904).
30 Diary for Feb. 28, 1902, *Our Partnership*, pp. 227–28.

"old Radicals" who predominated in the party by his part in the campaign to impose Rosebery upon them. They retaliated by filling the lower rungs of the Cabinet with their own nominees, barring the way to Haldane's entry.

Haldane was disappointed not only by his own exclusion from the reconstituted Liberal hierarchy, but also by subsequent demonstrations of party weakness and Rosebery's ineptitude. Elusive and melancholic, Gladstone's successor led Haldane, once his warmest supporter, to conclude that he "distrusts his own powers—physical or mental."[31] Internecine feuds wracked the Liberal front bench. Suspicions between the supporters of Sir William Harcourt and those of the Prime Minister precluded any far-reaching legislative effort. By the early weeks of 1895, Haldane was convinced that "there is no hope now but to be beaten and then to reconstruct a new party."[32] The parliamentary defeat to which he looked forward came on June 21, and it was followed by an even more emphatic trouncing at the hands of the electorate. But reconstruction failed to proceed as matter-of-factly as Haldane had anticipated and in its deeper sense had yet to be accomplished when the Liberals returned to office a decade later.

For as long as the Liberal Party remained in the political wilderness, Haldane was hopeful that it would achieve its new lease on life under Rosebery's standard. Even after Rosebery had abruptly resigned the party leadership in the autumn of 1896, Haldane continued to believe it possible that his leader might re-emerge when the appropriate moment arrived. Perhaps the most remarkable thing about Rosebery was the expectations he aroused and did nothing to justify. Only after Haldane took office under Campbell-Bannerman in 1905 did he come to the belated conclusion that Rosebery's days as an active politician were over. Until that time he had acted in an unofficial capacity as Rosebery's lieutenant, relaying party news to his chief, who languished at one or another of his country houses. "The process of pulling down the ancient and somewhat dilapidated Temple of Liberalism proceeds apace," he reported to Rosebery on August 24, 1897, "though it is not nearly complete yet."[33] Britain was soon plunged into a long and costly war in South Africa that retarded that process, inflicting new wounds on the Liberal Party and opening some that had begun to heal.

[31] Haldane to Milner, Oct. 6, 1901 [copy], Milner Papers.
[32] Diary for Jan. 20, 1895, Webb, *Our Partnership*, p. 121.
[33] Rosebery Papers.

Lord Rosebery was succeeded as Liberal leader, on a somewhat informal basis, by Sir William Harcourt, who had led the House of Commons during the Rosebery premiership. Harcourt remained at the helm until the close of 1898 when he followed Rosebery into retirement, disillusioned with party prospects and incensed by the recalcitrance of many of his fellow-Liberals, Haldane included. Harcourt's resignation had been long in coming, though the form it took—an exchange of letters with John Morley in *The Times*—was a surprise. Members of the parliamentary Liberal Party gathered at the Reform Club and elected Sir Henry Campbell-Bannerman to the vacant leadership.

Haldane hoped that Campbell-Bannerman would refuse the offer, which would have allowed H. H. Asquith, a close friend and a fellow-Roseberyite, to lead the Liberals in the Commons. The way would then have been open for Rosebery to resume his leadership over the party as a whole. Campbell-Bannerman's election made this a dim prospect. Nonetheless Haldane hastened to give hearty congratulations to the new leader, to whom he wrote an eight-page letter professing delight at the outcome of the Reform Club balloting (". . . I feel as if a pile of featherbeds had been lifted from me. . . ."), assessing party problems, and expressing doubt whether "the movement towards Mentmore [Rosebery's Bedfordshire establishment] will go on at the present pace."[34] Campbell-Bannerman replied cordially in a letter that Haldane reported to Rosebery and forwarded to Asquith. Was Haldane hypocritical in his dealings with the new Liberal leader? One might argue in his defense that Campbell-Bannerman was, strictly speaking, commander of the Liberal forces in the lower house, and that loyalty to him in this capacity was not incompatible with a continued devotion to Lord Rosebery. Perhaps Haldane naively supposed that Campbell-Bannerman would be content to lead the party in the Commons while Rosebery presided over a future Liberal Government. In any event, his support of Campbell-Bannerman was something less than ardent and his behavior something less than loyal.

At the same time that Haldane cultivated Campbell-Bannerman, he made overtures to Sir Alfred (later Viscount) Milner, whom he had come to know through the Webbs. Haldane respected Milner's earlier work as a social reformer and public servant. Both would soon belong to the Coefficients, that "queer diversity of brains" (to use Wells's

[34] Dec. 27, 1898, Campbell-Bannerman Papers, Add. MSS. 41, 218, ff. 141–44.

phrase) that the Webbs gathered for periodic dinners. In 1897 Milner was sent by the Salisbury Government to South Africa, and the imperial policies he pursued split the Liberal Party to which he had once belonged. The so-called Little Englanders within the Liberal camp blamed his provocative diplomacy and unrepentant expansionism for the Boer War, which began officially in October 1899. Haldane, who devoted a month's study to the Transvaal blue-books, told Mrs. Webb that he "was convinced that Milner was right, and that war was from the first inevitable."[35] He wrote to Milner urging him to discount attacks by the Liberal old guard: "I am satisfied that four-fifths of our people really follow and assent. . . ."[36]

For as long as the war in South Africa dragged on, Haldane tried to win Milner's endorsement for the band of Liberal Imperialists, nominally headed by Lord Rosebery, of which he, Asquith, and Sir Edward Grey were the most prominent members. The "Liberal Imps" or "Limps," as they were dubbed by their critics, attempted the delicate feat of supporting the war effort without sacrificing their identity as Liberals. They offered Liberal Imperialism as a more constructive, less hysterical alternative to Joseph Chamberlain's jingoism, although John Morley, notoriously "pro-Boer," scorned their product as "Chamberlain wine with a Rosebery label." Liberal Imperialism, despite the quality of its rhetoric, proved to be a halfway house without a political foundation. The intentions of its spokesmen remained vague and their strategies ambiguous, for aside from Lord Rosebery, none would dare sever his tie to the parliamentary Liberal forces under Campbell-Bannerman. As a result, they aroused Campbell-Bannerman's suspicions without appeasing either Milner or the Unionist Government. Lord Milner received word early in 1900 from one of his numerous confidants, who reported "a recent talk with Haldane" in which the latter urged some conciliatory gesture toward the Boer population, and who derided Haldane's "complicated state of mind."[37] In the summer of 1900, Joseph Chamberlain, the colonial secretary, wanted to send Haldane to South Africa as a judicial commissioner, and both he and Milner were disappointed when Haldane refused on grounds of political expediency. Yet Haldane continued to write Milner affectionate letters of encouragement, intended

[35] Diary for Oct. 30, 1899, Webb, *Our Partnership*, p. 188.
[36] Oct. 11, 1899, Milner Papers.
[37] Philip Lyttleton Gell to Milner, March 23, 1900. Milner Papers.

no doubt to win Milner's prestige and support for a new political grouping that he expected to emerge from the turmoil of wartime under Rosebery's leadership or possibly Asquith's.

Haldane was by no means as certain what would emerge as he was that political alignments within Parliament were due for radical alteration. By July 1900, he, Asquith, and Grey were convinced that Campbell-Bannerman, who fooled them all, was "riding for a fall . . ., that he means to resign and set off for Marienbad on the advice of Maclagan, his good physician." Haldane advised Rosebery that Asquith, who was eager for the chance, would presumably become "the *de facto* leader" of the Liberals in the Commons, "but if you choose to emerge and lead those Liberals who may be called 'Lord R.'s friends,' with Asquith and Grey as lieutenants in the House, I think things will work out."[38] Campbell-Bannerman's refusal to oblige "Lord R.'s friends" forced Haldane to modify his strategy; he counseled Rosebery to mollify Campbell-Bannerman by inquiring after the health of the ailing Lady Campbell-Bannerman. Occasionally Haldane grew impatient with Rosebery, who perversely refused to "come up," and he anticipated that Asquith would eventually lead the reconstructed Liberal Party to victory.

Again Haldane had underestimated the problems that beset his party and had misread the political situation. Animosities ran deeper than he perceived and ideological commitments, for the most part, were more superficial. In October 1903 he and Grey sounded out Rosebery on the prospect of a Liberal reunification under Lord Spencer, who had been Gladstone's personal choice to lead the party in 1894. Rosebery, "expressed the utmost contempt for S." and professed his intention "to work with all his strength for an A[squith] Ministry." At this early date Grey and Haldane were already explicit that they would refuse to serve under Campbell-Bannerman either as premier or as leader of the Commons.[39] It was thought that Campbell-Bannerman, who would never step aside for Asquith, a fellow-Commoner and sixteen years his junior, might be persuaded to defer to Lord Spencer. Despite Rosebery's hostile reception, the idea of a Spencer ministry continued to attract the attention of various Liberals: Lord Tweedmouth devised an elaborate plan to send Campbell-Bannerman to the foreign office, Rosebery to the colonial office, and to allow Asquith to lead the Commons as first lord of the

---

[38] July 25, 1900, Rosebery Papers.
[39] Haldane to Asquith, Oct. 5, 1903, Asquith Papers.

treasury under Spencer; Grey would receive the war office, which Haldane, who was not mentioned, would eventually occupy.[40] According to a piece of "gloomy intelligence" that Edmund Gosse assiduously conveyed to Haldane, Spencer was receptive to these proposals.[41] But the "Red Earl," his beard long since faded from its celebrated hue, fell gravely ill in 1905, and though he lingered until 1910 could take no part in the Liberal revival.

The omission of Haldane's name from Lord Tweedmouth's altogether miscalculated "sketch" was symptomatic. Haldane was the single Liberal Imperialist who could be easily punished for his sins of the past decade. Asquith's place in any future Liberal Cabinet was assured by the fact that he had served so prominently under both Gladstone and Rosebery. Grey had distinguished himself as undersecretary at the foreign office, and even Sydney Buxton's claims to office were recognized. But Haldane had only the devotion of his fellow "Limps"—a questionable asset— to sustain him; he had never sat in any Cabinet, commanded little influence, and had done a thorough job of alienating the powers that be.

Sir Henry Campbell-Bannerman found a way to restore a consensus within his shattered party by condemning not the Boer War, something one wing of the party would never have brooked, but the "methods of barbarism" with which it was waged. The Liberal Imperialists, though they continued to defend the imperial principles at stake in South Africa, more or less agreed that reprisals against civilians, detention camps, and arson left something to be desired. The Liberals were uncommonly united in their opposition to an ordinance, approved by Lord Milner after the restoration of peace, that permitted the importation of Chinese indentured laborers to work the mines of the Rand ten hours a day, six days a week, for a period predetermined by contract; it was only later on that a daily minimum wage of two shillings was set for them. David Lloyd George, displaying his talent for gross exaggerations that summed up what people were thinking, proclaimed that this odious measure brought back slavery to the British Empire. Haldane did not deny that Chinese indentured labor in South Africa, poorly remunerated and quartered in insanitary compounds, posed grave moral problems for the British Parliament; but he deplored the fact that these were being exploited by certain Liberals for parochial advantage.

[40] Munro Ferguson to Rosebery, March 31, 1904, Rosebery Papers.
[41] Note by Gosse on Haldane's letter of Jan. 4, 1905, Gosse Papers.

When the Chinese Labour Ordinance was put to a vote in the Commons on February 19, 1904, Haldane conspicuously abstained, and feeling within the party ran high against him. Grey who, like Asquith, had deferred to party unity, reported to his wife on February 23 "a horrid set being made at Haldane. . . ."[42] A week later Mrs. Webb recorded in her diary that she had heard accounts to the same effect, and she wondered whether the Liberal Imperialist movement would survive. Ronald Munro Ferguson, himself a Liberal Imperialist, expressed the hope "that the Tories should save Haldane's life by appointment to the legal hierarchy,"[43] for his career as a party politician was ruined. But Haldane survived without Tory assistance, and soon after he took his place in the next Liberal Government he was at work to head off a backbench motion to censure Milner.

Why did Haldane take it upon himself to defend Milner while his fellow "Limps" fell into line behind Campbell-Bannerman? First, he was on more intimate terms with Milner and it was through him that the Liberal Imperialists had communicated with the high commissioner. Even more significantly, Haldane, of all the Liberal Imperialists, was most thoroughly committed to the social and administrative programs that Milner advocated. Milner too had "collectivist" tendencies, and while he lacked Haldane's regard for parliamentary institutions, he continued to champion the education schemes that were dear to Haldane's heart. Grey, preoccupied with foreign affairs, was not nearly so impressed by Milner's social policies. Asquith, a reformer of a different stripe, was anyhow guided by more personal considerations: he had no intention of sacrificing his political future at this point, when office and possibly the premiership were within reach. As L. S. Amery wrote to Milner, "the temptation" had proved "too much" for Asquith, "with office looming so near and wall paper for 10 Downing Street already selected by Mrs. A.. . . ."[44] Haldane had no such inducements to keep silent.

By this time Haldane's name was invariably mentioned in the same breath as those of Asquith and Grey. The three had entered the House within months of one another and had since shared pretty much the same political outlook. The differences in their tastes were at least as

---

[42] Quoted in G. M. Trevelyan, *Grey of Fallodon* (Boston, 1937), p. 87.
[43] Munro Ferguson to Rosebery, April 25, 1904, Rosebery Papers.
[44] Feb. 26, 1904, Milner Papers.

pronounced as those in their backgrounds: Asquith relaxed upon the golf links, Grey knee-deep in a trout stream, and Haldane on marathon hikes through Perthshire. Haldane had a passion for Wagnerian opera, whereas Asquith drew the line at Gilbert and Sullivan. Of the three Grey was, by all odds, most prosaic in temperament, most rural in his pastimes, most Whiggish in his political views, and least energetic: "A great Member of Parliament," Gladstone had once said of him, "but then, no one knows when he will not be going fishing."

Asquith, Grey, and Haldane were linked by their common activities on behalf of Liberal Imperialism. It was understood by all concerned that Haldane could obtain a major post in the next Liberal Government, regardless of its head, only if his comrades exerted pressures in his behalf. But Haldane, always least successful of the three, was not simply riding the coattails of the other two. He was in many ways the mainstay of the triumvirate, and his contributions, subtle and indirect, should not be discounted. It was he who had persuaded Asquith to launch his parliamentary career in 1886, and Grey, four years later, wrote Haldane: "If it were not for you, I do not think I should have even the hold on public life which I have now. . . . I should say . . . that Asquith owed some of the very best in himself to you. . . ."[45] Asquith readily agreed and later described his friendship with Haldane as "one of the most intimate and valuable . . . of my life."[46]

The relationship of Haldane, Asquith, and Grey constituted considerably more than a political alliance. It was a source of strength to each of them in times of emotional stress. G. M. Trevelyan, Grey's biographer, has concluded that "it would be difficult to overestimate what Haldane did for Grey" when the latter's wife died in February 1906; Grey, newly appointed to the foreign office, came to live for a time at Whitehall Court with his bachelor friend, to whom he unburdened his soul, and he returned to Haldane's new address at Queen Anne's Gate for periodic visits until he remarried in 1922. Haldane, in turn, came to Asquith distraught and shaken when his own engagement was broken in 1890. He went to live in Hampstead with Asquith, married at the time to his first wife, and the five Asquith children took delight in his lavish attention and roly-poly figure. Asquith required no comparable consolation from either Haldane or Grey when his wife died of typhoid a year later. The future premier was already caught up

---

[45] Quoted in Trevelyan, p. 66.   [46] *Memories and Reflections*, I, 83.

H. H. Asquith

cr. Radio Times Hulton Picture Library

in his own ambitions, political and social. In 1894 he married the ebullient Margot Tennant, and his subsequent relations with Haldane reflected the change in his manner and outlook.

Haldane was not enthusiastic about either of his friends' second marriages, though he had in fact introduced Sir Edward to the second Lady Grey and was best man at Asquith's wedding to Margot. It was not that he, a bachelor, was jealous, so much as the fact that on both occasions he lost a degree of the contact and intimacy he had come to rely upon. The loss was far greater in the case of Asquith, a less settled individual, who remarried earlier and who chose Margot for his wife. Haldane, who had been so fond of the first Mrs. Asquith, preferred to blame Margot for distracting Asquith rather than to recognize how much Asquith, who had not been born into society, yearned to be distracted. In his *Autobiography*, published posthumously in 1929, Haldane explained that "London society came . . . to have a great attraction for him [Asquith], and he grew by degrees diverted from the sterner outlook on life which he and I long shared." This passage was based upon an autobiographical memorandum that Haldane had written three years earlier from which he tactfully expurgated the phrase "particularly after his second marriage."[47]

Haldane strongly disapproved of the social whirl into which his friend had plunged. Asquith was too often out of reach, off learning how to ride or making the rounds of aristocratic country houses. Haldane complained to Rosebery that Asquith had become slothful and that he "does many thing *per incuriam*."[48] Asquith's impressive gifts, Haldane felt, were wasted upon members of Margot's meretricious social set, and his time was wasted at her incessant luncheons and dinner parties. And Haldane was too much a Scotsman to approve Margot's extravagance which sank her husband, a strict Gladstonian in matters of public finance, deeper and deeper into debt. Asquith was forced to rely increasingly upon the generosity of his father-in-law, Sir Charles Tennant ("the Bart"), a wealthy Glasgow businessman and Liberal M. P. It was Haldane whom Asquith entrusted in 1898 with the discreet task of asking Rosebery and Balfour to put in a good word with "the Bart" so that the latter would increase his son-in-law's allowance.[49] Asquith's income was consumed in the maintenance of a fashionable London residence that required fourteen servants and a less pretentious Thames-side retreat near Abingdon. The Asquiths, in Haldane's opinion, "would have done better to let or sell 20 Cavendish Square, and move into a smaller house. But Margot wants many things."[50] Haldane was not unreceptive to Margot's wit and vitality, but he could forgive neither her failure to "live in contact with realities,"[51] nor her corruption of her husband's Hampstead values. When a wartime inquiry into the Dardanelles fiasco censured Asquith for negligence, Haldane, without doubting the verdict, cited extenuating circumstances: "the household at Downing Street, and the social engagements there, made things even more difficult than they ought to have been. The unfortunate Margot is responsible for a good deal of the want of concentration."[52]

It is important to appreciate the precise nature of his relationship with Asquith if one is to understand Haldane's twentieth-century political career, its achievements, and, particularly, its reverses. The two

[47] P. 108; HP 5923, f. 3.   [48] Sept. 27, 1901, Rosebery Papers.
[49] Haldane to Balfour, Dec. 18, 1898, Balfour Papers.
[50] Haldane to his mother, Jan. 27, 1917, HP 5997, ff. 28–29.
[51] Haldane to Gosse, March 23, 1918, Gosse Papers.
[52] Haldane to his mother, March 10, 1917, HP 5997, ff. 88–89.

Sir Edward Grey

cr. Radio Times Hulton Picture Library

remained fond friends, but out of a common respect for memories of the past more so than any common approach to the problems of the present. Each remained close to Sir Edward Grey, but no longer through one another. Contacts between Haldane and Asquith after 1905, which might otherwise have been cool, were warmed in the afterglow of their earlier intimacy. Asquith rarely came to Cloan during these years (although the signatures of Margot and his daughter Violet, who came to see Haldane's mother, appear in the guestbook), and Roy Jenkins, in his research for his biography of Asquith, found no record that Haldane visited the Asquiths during 1913 or the first half of 1914. The indifference was not all on one side: Haldane, invited to a dinner in May 1914 to celebrate Asquith's twentieth wedding anniversary, offered the feeble excuse—which Asquith repeated incredulously—that "a stepbrother . . . had just passed away in the Shetlands at the ripe age of 80!"[53] Occasionally the two would dine together as of old at Grillions Club,

[53] Roy Jenkins, *Asquith* (London, 1964), pp. 270 ff.

but their meetings were usually coincidental, the atmosphere public, and the conversation restrained. Others might have been impressed when Asquith referred to Haldane as his oldest friend, but Haldane realized better than they that the length of a friendship was no measure of its strength.

CHAPTER II

WAR LORD IN A SOFT HAT

The General [Sir John French] is in uniform and booted and spurred, but the Secretary of State is in a tweed suit with a soft hat.

—HALDANE[*]

To the delight of a good many people (including the King), the dismay of at least a few (including the backbench Radicals), and the surprise of virtually everyone (including themselves), all three Liberal Imperialists—Asquith, Grey, and Haldane—took office in the Liberal Government of 1905. This was less a tribute to any power they wielded within the party than a further indication of Sir Henry Campbell-Bannerman's astute appreciation of political talent, his shrewd bargaining power, and, most of all, his rare ability to forgive if not quite forget.

A. J. Balfour's Unionist Government, its parliamentary majority dating from the "khaki" election of 1900, staved off electoral defeat by clinging to power until the last possible moment. This gave Liberal politicians ample time—perhaps too much time—to contemplate the succession. Each entertained his own ideas about the distribution of places in the next Liberal Government; the longer they waited the more excessive their expectations became. John Morley revived designs dormant for a decade on either the foreign office or the exchequer; James Bryce was known to covet the India office, and David Lloyd George the home office, while Sir Charles Dilke hoped in vain to resume his ministerial career, interrupted two decades earlier when he was named correspondent in a sensational divorce scandal.

The Liberal Imperialists were no less self-seeking than most. For years, ever since Balfour's capitulation was first expected, Asquith, Grey,

[*] Letter to his mother, Feb. 10, 1906, from Aldershot, HP 5975, f. 59.

and Haldane had proclaimed their refusal to take office in any government in which Campbell-Bannerman served either as premier or leader
of the house. In September of 1905 the three met informally at Relugas,
Grey's fishing lodge in the remote northeast of Scotland, to formalize
their position. This became known as the Relugas Compact and rumors
of its contents circulated widely as its participants had intended. It is
doubtful whether knowledge of this agreement influenced Campbell-
Bannerman, whose amiable exterior concealed a core of iron; but it
undoubtedly prompted Balfour, eager to exploit this division in opposition ranks, to resign rather than seek a dissolution.

The terms of the Relugas Compact,[1] strong as they seemed, were a
retreat from the earlier position that the three colleagues had occupied.
By this time they were obliged to concede that Lord Rosebery would
not emerge to take the place to which they believed him entitled.
("One longs for Rosebery," Haldane told Lord Knollys. "Had he been
coming to his place at the head of affairs we could have gone anywhere
with the confidence that the tone would be set.") Illness had taken
Lord Spencer, too, out of the running. Asquith and, more grudgingly,
Haldane and Grey were now prepared to accept a Campbell-Bannerman
ministry provided that its head removed himself to the upper house,
leaving the leadership of the Commons and the exchequer to Asquith,
the foreign office (or at least the colonial office) to Grey, and the lord
chancellorship to Haldane. The "compact" also contained provisions
to defend the interests of such lesser "Limps" as Sydney Buxton and
Henry Fowler. It was written off by Haldane a decade later as "a private
agreement of a purely defensive character,"[2] but the frequency with
which the phrase "putting a pistol to C. B.'s head" appears in his
correspondence leaves no doubt that it was nothing of the sort.

It was Asquith's assignment to negotiate with Campbell-Bannerman
on behalf of the triple alliance. The choice was appropriate: Asquith
was most persuasive, strongest politically, and knew Sir Henry best. But
it was nonetheless unfortunate: Asquith was most susceptible to personal
blandishments. It fell to Haldane to keep alive a spark of interest on
the part of Grey, who spoke longingly of the ducks at Fallodon, and
to acquaint the King with their strategy. This choice, too, was appro-

---

[1] The following paragraphs have been based in large measure upon Haldane's
letter to Lord Knollys, Sept. 12, 1905 (a copy exists in the Asquith Papers) and
Knollys's reply, both printed in Sommer, pp. 145–48; also Haldane to Asquith, Oct.
6, 1905, Asquith Papers.
[2] HP 5919, f. 23.

priate, for Haldane was already on excellent terms with Edward VII, who had honored him with a privy councilorship in 1901 and, more recently, with invitations to Windsor. Haldane communicated the terms of the Relugas Compact to Lord Knollys, the King's private secretary, on September 12. The King was at Marienbad until the 25th, but soon after his return he summoned Haldane to Balmoral for discussions. His Majesty, according to Knollys, was anxious to see these "most able and moderate men" in the Cabinet as a counterbalance to "men holding extreme views." Yet Edward VII took a more proper view of his constitutional powers than his three petitioners, and agreed to go only so far as to express to Campbell-Bannerman his royal doubts, "from recent observation, whether anyone but a young man can be both P. M. and leader in the H. of C." When the time came, Campbell-Bannerman listened patiently, then dismissed the King's advice, which he recognized as the work of "that ingenious person, Richard Burdon Haldane."[3]

Asquith acted more slowly and even less successfully. Campbell-Bannerman, too, was at Marienbad, and after his return he managed to put off Asquith until November 13. All the while, Haldane wrote anxious letters reminding Asquith that the advantage would be lost if Campbell-Bannerman caught wind of the intrigue. He was particularly afraid that the King would disclose the affair to Lord Esher, who would inform Lord Rosebery ("His interest would be to wreck it") or, still worse, J. A. Spender, editor of the *Westminster Gazette* and the future biographer of both Campbell-Bannerman and Asquith.

Campbell-Bannerman had girded himself for his confrontation with Asquith. Margot Asquith provided a polished account of the encounter, as she heard it that morning from her husband while her hair was being washed. Its conclusions, if not its details, stand corroborated by the correspondence that followed. Asquith, as planned, advanced his own claims to the exchequer and his friends' claims to the foreign office and the woolsack. Campbell-Bannerman made clear his resolution to remain a member of the Commons and his preference for Sir Robert Reid, a longtime friend, for the lord chancellorship. Asquith came away convinced that at any rate he had impressed upon Campbell-Bannerman Grey's genius for foreign affairs; but it was only after Lord Cromer refused the foreign office that it was offered to Grey.

The Relugas Compact achieved only what would have been achieved in any event. It did not obtain the leadership of the front bench for

[3] Margot Asquith, *Autobiography*, II (London, 1922), p. 66.

Asquith, nor the woolsack for Haldane, and, strictly speaking, it was not responsible for Grey's subsequent appointment to the foreign office. It is often explained that Sir Robert Reid, attorney-general in the last Liberal Government, had an indisputable claim to the woolsack in the next; but the claims of another attorney-general, Sir Rufus Isaacs, were passed by (not without comment) when Haldane became lord chancellor in 1912. The failure of the Relugas Compact resulted not from the fact that its demands were so high, but that they were pressed so halfheartedly. Campbell-Bannerman knew from the start that Asquith, who stood next in line to lead the party, would not jeopardize his position for the sake of his friends' ambitions. He gave no ground to Asquith at their November 13 meeting; nor did he have to, for Asquith, after a perfunctory defense of Haldane and Grey, agreed unconditionally to take office in a Campbell-Bannerman ministry. His place at the exchequer assured Asquith the deputy leadership of the house, and there was the added consolation of knowing that the leader was a tired man, old at the age of sixty-nine, who did not expect to retain power very long. In the spring of 1908, which had not been too long to wait, Asquith inherited from Campbell-Bannerman immeasurably more than he could ever have pressed for in December 1905.

Asquith defended his repudiation of the Relugas Compact by arguing that the situation had altered to such an extent since early September that the strategy he helped to frame had become obsolete. At that time he, like Grey and Haldane, had presumed that Balfour would follow the usual procedure of dissolving Parliament, leaving the next Government to be formed after a General Election. Balfour, aware of discord among the Liberals, had decided instead to resign, forcing Campbell-Bannerman to form a Government before going to the people; with few hopes at this point, Balfour calculated that his opponents might discredit themselves by parading a decade's soiled linen before the electorate. Asquith proclaimed that he could not, in good conscience, weaken the party by standing aside at such a crucial time: "If the election were over, and Free Trade secure, different considerations would arise," he assured Haldane.[4] But as A. M. Gollin has pointed out,[5] Asquith's argument ignores chronology: he had accepted Camp-

[4] Dec. 7, 1905, quoted in Spender and Asquith, I, 174–75.
[5] "Asquith: a New View," in M. Gilbert (ed.), *Century of Conflict* (London, 1966), p. 111.

bell-Bannerman's offer of the exchequer on November 13, three weeks before Balfour tendered his resignation to the King.

In the lengthy autobiographical memorandum he prepared in 1916, Haldane made it clear that he regarded Asquith's *volte face* in 1905 a fatal blow to the Relugas policy that rendered his position and Grey's untenable. This criticism of Asquith's behavior was not simply the product of subsequent disappointments Haldane had suffered at his friend's hand. There can be no doubt that neither he nor Grey had suspected Asquith's withdrawal until the last moment, for each wrote him letters of gratitude for his continued efforts on their behalf. Haldane's letters to his mother and sister during these weeks imply that he expected Asquith to stand aloof should their terms be rejected; and Grey, as late as December 4, wrote in this sense to Asquith. On the same day, Haldane advised his mother that he and Grey "completely understand each other. So does Asquith," he added rather ambiguously and not too convincingly, "but the former's character shines out at such a time."[6] Grey, who urged his wife not to blame Asquith (". . . it was hard for him, cruelly hard") was rhapsodic in his praise for "R. B. H., dear man, [who] stays with me."[7]

Asquith's defection left Haldane and Grey pretty much to their own devices. Grey had little to worry about: he could easily obtain high Cabinet rank, if not the one to which he aspired, on the basis of past service. Campbell-Bannerman had in fact suggested him for the war office when he met with Asquith on November 13. Haldane was quite another matter, for there are ample indications that Campbell-Bannerman would have been glad to dispense altogether with his services. And Haldane's absence from the new Government, unlike Asquith's or even Grey's, would have raised few eyebrows. Anything that Haldane received at this point was an act of charity, and Campbell-Bannerman made it clear that the woolsack was not among the alms he was prepared to bestow.

The office of lord chancellor had always exerted a special appeal for Haldane. It was not only the highest attainment of his profession, but also an object of family pride. His mother's great uncle was Lord Eldon, and he hoped to reward her by following in those distinguished footsteps. This was not egotism so much as something that his family had expected of him since his youth. The story is told by each of his

[6] HP 5974, f. 177.   [7] Dec. 7, 1905, quoted in Trevelyan, *Grey*, p. 114.

biographers that Haldane, visiting London at the age of six, was seated (with the help of a compliant guard) on the woolsack by his Scottish nurse, who prophesied: "One day the bairn will sit there as of right." Her prediction proved true, but not in 1905.

There were other less personal reasons for Haldane to seek the lord chancellorship in the impending Liberal Government. For one thing, the Liberal Imperialists would require a spokesman in the House of Lords, as prominently situated as possible, if they were to defend themselves and their principles from diehard Tories on the one hand and fire-eating Radicals on the other. They knew they could no longer depend upon Lord Rosebery, who was too unpredictable and who was unlikely to affiliate himself in any capacity with the new Government. Asquith could hardly leave the Commons, for that would effectively remove him from the succession. Grey was a possibility; he sat in the upper house during his last six months at the foreign office, but a decade earlier such an arrangement was considered, with good justification, unsatisfactory. But Haldane was not nominated by his friends simply by default. He took a keen interest in the legal relationships between Britain and the dominions, so strenuously debated during the early years of the century. ". . . The precarious state into which the Supreme Court of the Empire has got," he explained to Lord Knollys, made the lord chancellorship even more strategic than it would normally be.[8] R. F. V. Heuston, in a brilliant assessment of Haldane's judicial career, pays tribute to his subject's contributions to dominion constitutional law as a privy councillor and, later, as lord chancellor. This was Liberal Imperialism in its least conspicuous but most constructive form.

Haldane made no attempt to conceal from Lord Esher, whom he met at Balmoral in early October, either his fervent desire to be chancellor or his premonition that he would be passed by. Like his royal confidant, Esher's "only wish" was to see Haldane upon the woolsack.[9] Asquith brought Haldane news from his November 13 interview with Campbell-Bannerman that Sir Robert Reid would have first choice between the lord chancellorship and the home office, and that Haldane could take what remained. Against his better judgment, and without suspecting that Asquith had pledged himself to Campbell-Bannerman,

[8] Sept. 12, 1905 [copy], Asquith Papers.
[9] Esher to Rosebery, Oct. 27, 1905, Rosebery Papers.

Haldane went on hoping that the greater prize would be his. "It is still uncertain what will be done with the woolsack," he wrote to his mother on December 2. "One must just take these things coolly."[10] And two days later he professed continued uncertainty whether he would get his wish, "go elsewhere," or "stand out" of the new Government.[11] Finally, on Tuesday the 5th, Haldane learned along with everyone else that Asquith had surrendered unconditionally to Campbell-Bannerman. There was no longer any chance of the woolsack and, instead, a very good chance that he would be completely excluded from the new ministry.

In any event, he would share his fate with Grey; that much was decided. The two friends, living at Haldane's flat in Whitehall Court, waited (impatiently in Haldane's case) for Campbell-Bannerman to make the next move. Asquith, much to Haldane's annoyance, had left London with Margot to keep an engagement at Hatfield House, hardly an appropriate address for a Liberal chancellor of the exchequer to make his debut. On Thursday morning, Asquith motored back to London to confer with Campbell-Bannerman, who instructed him to offer the foreign office to Grey and the war office to Haldane. Asquith wrote a letter that reached Haldane at the same time as one direct from Campbell-Bannerman that offered not the war office but merely the attorney-generalship, which "involve[d] what are practically Cabinet responsibilities, though not Cabinet rank. . . ." The Prime Minister took care to point out that "a proposition of a different nature" would be forthcoming should Haldane find the attorney-generalship unsatisfactory.[12] Perhaps Asquith had misunderstood that morning, but it is more likely that Campbell-Bannerman—quite uncharacteristically—was rubbing salt in wounds before, for the party's sake, he would attempt to heal them.

The attorney-generalship, as Campbell-Bannerman knew very well, was not in the least satisfactory. But Haldane was nonetheless encouraged to learn that something better, if not the lord chancellorship, remained available. Even before he consulted Grey, he went to see Lady Horner, a close friend since the early 1890s with whom he spent his Christmasses at Mells Manor in Somersetshire.[13] She counseled that

---

[10] HP 5974, f. 175. [11] HP 5974, f. 177. [12] HP 5906, f. 274.

[13] Haldane dictated a memorandum on these events to Lady Horner during a visit to Mells in 1906; it is reproduced in his *Autobiography* (pp. 173 ff.) and it is upon this account that this paragraph is based.

it was his duty not only to the King but also to the cause of Free Trade to lend his weight to the new Government. This was essentially the same argument that Asquith had presented in his letter and the one to which Asquith had himself succumbed earlier. From Lady Horner's, Haldane returned to Whitehall Court, where he found Grey "lying on a sofa in the library," contemplating the sunlit days of leisure that awaited him. He acquainted Grey with the letters he had received that afternoon. At seven o'clock they left for dinner, stopping on the way to keep a prearranged meeting with Arthur Acland, an ally of Boer War days who had retired from active political life and implored them not to follow. Acland repeated the familiar arguments about Liberal Party unity that they had heard from everyone else. All the while, Haldane and Grey were subjecting themselves and each other to intense soul-searching, and the former insisted that it was this and not Acland's "moral earnestness" that changed their minds. During dinner at the Café Royal, Grey agreed to retract the *nolo episcopari* he had handed to Campbell-Bannerman, provided that he and Haldane could enter the new Cabinet as colleagues. Meanwhile Asquith, who had no inkling of this development, took time out from the festivities at Hatfield House to suggest Lord Crewe for the foreign office.

The Times, too, took for granted that Grey's decision was irrevocable, and it cited this as proof that the new ministry and the policies for which it stood were doomed. This "deliberate attempt" on the part of *The Times* "to smash the credit of the new Government" has been cited as the stimulus that brought Haldane and Grey into the fold.[14] But Haldane was explicit that *The Times*'s jibes merely added to their determination to come to the aid of Liberalism in distress; after all, electoral victory lay ahead, its magnitude unsuspected. No one was more appreciative of Haldane's and Grey's chivalry than Asquith, who wrote a glowing tribute to Haldane: "by your action during the last two days you have laid the party and the country and myself (most of all) under an unmeasured debt of gratitude." Asquith should indeed have been grateful; he was now absolved of having sacrificed the interests of his friends in his haste to insure advantages for himself. ". . . More could not have been accomplished," he assured Haldane.[15] This was extremely doubtful, and no one knew it better than Haldane, who was on his

[14] Fitzroy, I, 271.   [15] Dec. 8, 1905, HP 5906, f. 255.

way to the war office at the same time that Sir Robert Reid (now Lord Loreburn) was mounting the woolsack.

Why the war office, of all places? Initially Campbell-Bannerman had proposed it for Grey, but when he saw Asquith on the morning of the 7th, the prime minister had suggested it for Haldane. A secretaryship of state was infinitely preferable to the attorney-generalship; but Haldane knew that he could have the home office (which Herbert Gladstone subsequently filled so poorly) for the asking. In many respects, education was the most suitable portfolio, although that appointment would have been a red flag to the nonconformists within the party. Later on, he conveniently recalled that he had once told Asquith that the war office "was the only office, apart perhaps from the colonial office (with the exception of the lord chancellorship) that attracted me."[16] It was true that he had occasionally spoken in the house on army matters, but it remains doubtful whether previous interest was itself sufficient to account for his assignment. Rather, Haldane took this office, knowing of its reputation as a political graveyard, to prove the extent of his sacrifice for party and national welfare. As Grey put it, they were entering the new Government "not for pleasure's sake, and . . . must take the most beastly things."[17] There was no telling at this point how long Haldane would lie buried in this particular graveyard, for the Liberal Government might not survive the general election early in the new year.

In the jocular account of the 1905 deliberations that he provided on October 18, 1912, for an audience of cadets at Bristol University, Haldane related Campbell-Bannerman's amazement when he requested the war office: "Is it full?" Haldane asked, to which Sir Henry exclaimed "Full? No one will touch it with a pole!" Other accounts agree that Campbell-Bannerman could hardly believe that Haldane would go by choice to such a destination. A former secretary for war himself, he knew first-hand its frustrations, particularly for a Liberal. But if any Liberal had to take this thankless assignment, Campbell-Bannerman was glad to let it be Haldane: it would be a just penance for Haldane's transgressions against his leadership during recent months. "We shall now see," the Prime Minister was widely quoted in the closing weeks of 1905, "how Schopenhauer gets on in the kail-yard."

On the following Monday, Haldane—accompanied by Henry Fowler and Grey—traveled through dense fog to Buckingham Palace to kiss

---

[16] *Autobiography*, p. 177.   [17] *Ibid.*, p. 180.

hands and receive the seals of office. Seated at his desk at the war office, his first act was to write a letter to his mother in which he described the "curious feeling" of being an "absolute ruler" over a vital department of state: "The Cabinet and Parliament are my only masters."[18] He might have reflected, even at this inspiring moment, that his subservience to the Cabinet and to Parliament cut significantly into his "absolute" powers. Participating with him in the royal ceremonies that afternoon were an assortment of personalities who represented every conceivable variety of Liberal thought.[19] That they were brought together in the first place was a tribute to Sir Henry Campbell-Bannerman's resourceful leadership and to Herbert Gladstone's tireless negotiations behind the scenes. Their respective talents and intellectual abilities are undeniable, but it is debatable whether in all the years they worked together they ever surmounted their parochialisms and fused into a cohesive body.

Haldane's place in the Liberal Cabinet was in many respects typical. Like others, he felt loyalties to men and, particularly, ideas that the new Government did not embrace. "Watched at the door or not," he wrote to Lord Rosebery,

I am coming to try to see you. Grey and I have accepted office and we mean to be loyal to Campbell-Bannerman in spirit as well as in letter. But we told him *why* we joined him and that we were nonetheless of our old opinions, and attached to you by ties of the deepest affection. My decision was bound up with Grey's. Neither of us would have gone in without the other. Neither of us had a personal wish to join. When we decided that we ought—late in the day—we competed for the worst burdens to carry. It has fallen to me—the war office.

Now you will see why—even if prudential motives could arise—and they do not—I cannot let them prevent me from coming to see the Chief of my choice—whom I would fain be under at this moment.[20]

Rosebery understood better than most this contradiction in Haldane's political position; when a mutual friend reported shortly afterward that Haldane had "changed his views," he brusquely replied: "If this means that he was determined to give a wholehearted allegiance to his present

---

[18] Dec. [11], 1905, HP 5974, f. 192.

[19] In addition to the Liberal Imperialists mentioned above, the new ministry contained such staunch Gladstonians as John Morley, James Bryce, and Herbert Gladstone; the Whiggish Lords Crewe and Elgin; John Burns, once "the man with the red flag"; the fiery Welsh Radical, David Lloyd George; and, in an undersecretarial capacity, the young convert from Conservatism, Winston Churchill.

[20] Dec. 10, 1905, Rosebery Papers.

chief, I think that that is a clear matter of duty."[21] Few individuals in public life, inside the Cabinet or out, could appreciate nearly so well Haldane's loyalties and motives. Radicals tended to be put off by his manner and to suspect his past imperial views along with his present military designs. Other political factions—among them certain Liberal Imperialists, the Milnerites and the Chamberlainites—never forgave him for throwing in his lot with the Radical riffraff and the Pro-Boers, and for conferring his respectability upon a Government capable of such villainies as the People's Budget and the Parliament Act. Such suspicions, coming simultaneously from both extremes of the political spectrum, undermined Haldane's position during his half-dozen years at the war office; they were largely responsible for the fact that, although his invaluable services have since been recognized, in the short run the war office added Haldane's reputation to its infamous graveyard.

In a letter to Sir John Simon on May 26, 1915, days after his ejection from office, Haldane recognized the fact that he had "lived in an atmosphere of heated controversy since I set my hand to Army reforms nine years ago, and it has extended to European politics."[22] He rightly observed that had he not made so many enemies by his war office policies, his later activities—even his 1912 mission to Berlin—would not have been so suspect. It was, however, impossible for an early twentieth-century war minister, particularly a successful one, to avoid such pitfalls.

Haldane's two immediate predecessors, St. John Brodrick and H. O. Arnold-Forster, had proved unequal to the task. The unhappiness of their experiences at the war office accounts in large part for their subsequent hostility to Haldane: they could not bear to see someone (a Liberal, no less!) succeed where they had failed so dismally. Arnold-Forster replaced Brodrick in 1903, when the latter was transferred to the India office. Three years earlier, he had denied premature rumors that he was headed for the war office: "As a matter of fact, I can think of no more unlikely occurrence. Indeed I fear I should be as unwelcome as a lyddite shell in that tape-bound rabbit warren (simile doubtful, I fear)."[23] Eventually, Arnold-Forster's performance as secretary of state for war proved as doubtful as his simile.

Virtually everyone, including his colleagues on the Unionist front

---

[21] Rosebery to Munro Ferguson, Feb. 23, 1906, Rosebery Papers.
[22] Simon Papers.
[23] Arnold-Forster to Philip Gell, Jan. [1], 1900, Gell Papers.

bench, recognized Arnold-Forster as a failure except Arnold-Forster himself, who boasted to an audience of Glasgow volunteers that "at the end of two years of office" he had "left the British Army better manned, officered, and equipped . . . and organised than for fifty years." He greeted his successor with a ten-page letter of recommendations, which he took for granted Haldane would accept. When it became clear that Haldane did not subscribe to his views, Arnold-Forster wrote polemics for any editor who would print them. He headed the "old fogey brigade"—Arthur Lee and Leo Maxse were other members— that met from time to time to denounce the new order. Failing health and an early death prevented Arnold-Forster from being even more vexatious. He was convinced, from all indications without justification, that had he been permitted more time, he could have solved the perennial problems of British defense. No one could deny that he had ideas; the question was their efficacy. Haldane, who did not overestimate his predecessor's capabilities, saw at once that the root of the trouble was that "he launched reckless schemes without consulting his officials."[24] Determined not to repeat the mistake, Haldane cleared his mind of preconceptions and initiated a fresh study of the problems at hand. He was not ashamed to admit that he arrived at the war office with a "virgin mind," which, he told his commander-in-chief, "is better than Arnold-Forster's immaculate conceptions."[25]

The Boer War had demonstrated the imperative need for an overhaul of the military system. At the same time it had made equally clear the pressing need for retrenchment. Any Government would have had a difficult time reconciling these two criteria. Indeed Balfour, shortly before he left office, admitted to Lord Roberts that "one of the greatest disappointments I have had to submit to in the last two or three years [has been] the failure to find, or to get adopted, some new organisation which would give a greater power of military expansion in time of war, and, if possible, bring with it greater economies in time of peace."[26] It was Balfour who instituted the Committee of Imperial Defence and who appointed a committee under Lord Esher to consider war office problems.

Haldane, whose interests ranged far and wide, had also pondered

[24] Haldane to Campbell-Bannerman, Jan. 5, 1906, Campbell-Bannerman Papers, Add. MSS. 41,218, f. 165.
[25] Laski to Holmes, Sept. 27, 1925, Holmes-Laski, I, 789–90.
[26] Aug. 12, 1905, Roberts Papers.

these problems, if not their details. His projects for educational and bureaucratic reform often touched upon military matters and brought him into contact with army reformers, some of whom in time became his advisers, some his critics. Among them was Sir George Clarke, later Lord Sydenham, whose eleven-page memorandum of February 6, 1905,[27] pointed up the problems that Haldane would soon face. By this time it was as obvious to Clarke as it was to others that it would fall to a Liberal to effect the long-overdue changes at the war office, changes comparable to those that Sir John Fisher, later Lord Fisher, had accomplished at the admiralty. And, he predicted, the next war minister—whoever he might be—would occupy an unenviable position: ". . . In matters of national defence, a Liberal Government would not—on taking office—command great confidence. . . . Of course this feeling is unjust, but it constitutes a factor to be taken into account." Clarke explained that the Liberals would be suspected of weakening the army in their attempt to pinch pennies. "Am I not right in thinking," he asked Haldane prophetically, "that success at the W. O. may very probably be the crux of the next Government?"

Haldane assumed his duties with unbounded enthusiasm and, within days, he had made up his mind that the war office posed greater challenges and therefore provided greater rewards than the lord chancellorship: "I would not change this for the woolsack," he averred to his sister on December 11.[28] To Edmund Gosse, he offered "a confession of fickleness" on the 17th: "I thought I loved the law. But out of sight is out of mind. I am enjoying myself simply hugely. . . . It is the best of fun—though my solemn predecessors, not being Scotsmen, never saw it. You never saw such a band of Reformers as I am trying to hold back. If I could only get three years here I could do something. It suits my habits of mind."[29] No well-wisher could have been more pleased than the King, who anticipated that Haldane's "sound common sense and great powers of organising ought to make [him] an excellent War Minister, which is much needed as his predecessor was hopeless."[30]

No sooner had he come to the war office than Haldane encountered in full measure the problems that Sir George Clarke had anticipated. The huge majority that the Liberals obtained in the January General Election—only 157 Unionists had survived the avalanche, Balfour not

[27] HP 5906, ff. 145 ff.   [28] HP 6011, f. 17.   [29] Gosse Papers.
[30] King to Prince of Wales, Dec. 15, 1905, Harold Nicolson, *King George the Fifth* (London, 1952), p. 93.

among them—proved, curiously enough, more a liability than an asset. Gone were a number of moderate Tories who might have been expected to support Haldane; in their places sat Radicals and Labourities to many of whom a Liberal Imperialist, especially one who carried a military portfolio, was the devil incarnate. Haldane was not the only minister whose policies were obstructed by his own backbenchers: Morley and Grey were among those who suffered similarly. But the others were compensated with support from both front benches to an extent Haldane was denied.

Sir Almeric Fitzroy, clerk of the Privy Council, told Haldane, whom he met at the Webbs' on April 4, 1906, that he "had incurred the wrath of my Tory friends by saying that I was prepared to run the risk of ten years of Radical Government so long as Haldane could be made secure at the War Office for six." Haldane surprised him with the rejoinder that "there are numbers of 'our friends' who would wreck the Government in these years to get me out of it."[31] He spoke without exaggeration. "Scarcely one of his colleagues and very few of his party actively supported Mr. Haldane," Colonel Repington observed. "They trimmed their sails to profit by his success if he succeeded and to drop him if he failed."[32] Haldane, in his wartime memorandum, described with bitterness how certain "Liberal newspapers even kept demanding my resignation as a person who was breaking faith with pledges alleged to have been given by other of the party leaders at the General Election." It was Campbell-Bannerman and Asquith who gave him the "quiet support . . . that enabled me to hold on." But, he recalled, "neither they nor my other colleagues took much active part in fighting for my plans. . . ."[33]

There was no reason for Campbell-Bannerman to suppose that Haldane's tenure at the war office would be any more venturesome than his own had been under Gladstone and Rosebery. Not that Liberalism was a bar to success. Edward Cardwell, war secretary in Gladstone's first administration, had so thoroughly transformed the military structure that his reputation continued to daunt his successors for a generation. Liberals, particularly, were reluctant to amend the Cardwellian system, even when it showed signs of running down. Campbell-Bannerman, who began his career as financial secretary to Cardwell, had since lost his enthusiasm for war office reform, a pursuit that appeared to him

[31] *Memoirs*, I, 288–89.   [32] *Vestigia* (Boston, 1919), p. 275.
[33] HP 5919, *passim*.

only slightly less costly than war itself. "Leave the army alone and don't make war," he instructed the House of Commons on February 5, 1904, and as late as the General Election campaign of 1906 he affirmed his determination to curtail armaments. There was an early clash between him and Haldane when the latter assured an audience of City businessmen on January 4, 1906, that he recognized "an obligation higher even than that of economy" and that contemplated cutbacks would not impair efficiency.[34] Fisher applauded the speech as a much-needed clarification of the Government's intentions. But Campbell-Bannerman thought that Haldane had spoken out of turn and he protested to Asquith, whom he regarded his brother's keeper, that "our philosophic friend has not yet learned the trick of accurate and guarded official language."[35]

And yet, as time passed, Campbell-Bannerman came to value Haldane as a trusted colleague and Haldane saw in him a valuable ally. The Prime Minister, who held his interventions to a minimum, warned "against talking and speaking in public too much, and above all against dogmatism and swagger," and he urged Haldane that "whatever he does to give the credit of it to the soldiers and never to seem to be making capital for himself. In short, to be as unlike his predecessors as he can."[36] It was sound advice, well taken. Haldane made superb use of the talents, military and civilian, at his disposal and knit them into a brilliant team. As his principal private secretary he took Colonel (later General) Gerald Ellison, who had served the 1904 Esher Committee in the same capacity and had drawn up its report. Sir Charles Harris was an equally happy choice as permanent head of the financial department. They headed a long list of loyal and dedicated administrators. In addition, Sir Ian Hamilton, an old friend, was available for consultation, Lord Esher could be depended upon for backstairs support, and the assistance of the King, sometimes grudgingly given, should not be underestimated.

On March 8, 1906, three months after he had taken office, Haldane made his parliamentary debut as war minister, delivering the first of his speeches on army estimates. It was a triumphant occasion and congratulatory messages poured in. "Curiously," he wrote to his mother,

[34] Haldane to Campbell-Bannerman, Jan. 5, 1906, Campbell-Bannerman Papers, Add. MSS. 41, 218, f. 163.

[35] Jan. 5, 1906, Asquith Papers.

[36] Campbell-Bannerman to Lord Haliburton, Feb. 27, 1906, Campbell-Bannerman Papers, Add. MSS. 41, 218, f. 356.

"old Sir. H. C.-B. is about the most enthusiastic and warmest."[37] The *National Review,* soon to exhaust its supply of kind words, applauded this "conspicuous . . . success: Though the speech lasted two hours it did not contain a dull sentence." True, Haldane had "cleverly avoided anything very definite," but he had "disarm[ed] criticism by his candid confession that for the moment his ideas are in a nebulous condition." For the time being, Haldane could get away with pious platitudes and professions of earnestness. But the time was soon upon him when something more concrete was required. There was a growing impatience among the zealots for economy on the one hand and the old guard on the other. One of the former went so far as to introduce a private motion on May 9, expressing the "opinion that the growth of expenditure in armaments is excessive and ought to be reduced." Several of the latter expressed forebodings privately to the King and publicly to *The Times.*

On July 12, Haldane rose in the Commons to deliver a speech to which *The Times* had "look[ed] forward . . . with great interest and with no small anxiety." It lasted nearly three hours and confirmed what was widely rumored, that the Government was entertaining major proposals for military reorganization and retrenchment. "Rarely has a reputation for sagacity in opposition been so rapidly falsified by six months' tenure of office," the *National Review* proclaimed in disgust. Haldane insisted that his reforms were designed, first and foremost, to streamline the army for greater fighting efficiency. Wasn't any successful business operation, he asked, carefully budgeted? His critics saw reductions only as a sop to the pacifists and Little Englanders, upon whose votes the ministry depended. Had this been Haldane's intention, however, it was entirely unsuccessful: the savings he managed to effect were too meager to satiate the wild men of the left. And at the same time, he had completely alienated the wild men of the right.

Haldane's army reforms are not easy to summarize: that, in itself, explains much of the difficulty they encountered.[38] It was wartime experience that ultimately clarified his intentions and vindicated his theories.

---

[37] March 10, 1906, HP 5975, f. 109.

[38] The present study is concerned with those aspects of Haldane's army policy that elicited subsequent attacks upon him. More extensive treatment of the reforms is to be found in the first volume of Sir Frederick Maurice's biography and Sir Charles Harris's *Lord Haldane* (London, 1928). H. T. Baker, financial secretary to the war office from 1912 to 1915, contributed a useful essay to the *Army Quarterly* (October, 1928); and Ellison's reminiscences, serialized in his regimental magazine, the *Lancashire Lad* (1935–6), are invaluable.

Briefly, Haldane tried to create order out of the chaos he had inherited. This he attempted in two ways, by revitalizing the war office and by transforming the various fighting forces. In both areas he obtained a coordination and cohesion that had previously been lacking. The need for far-reaching reform had long been apparent. Others had diagnosed the problem and had prescribed remedies along many of the same lines. But they had lacked Haldane's determination and his over-all view of the nation's requirements. The fact that much of what he instituted had been mooted for years does not detract from his achievement. Operating under far less auspicious circumstances than his predecessors, he demonstrated that a man of theory, given the opportunity, could prove a man of action.

Like most ingredients in Haldane's reforms package, the idea of a General Staff was not new. Steps had been taken in this direction before he came to the war office, but it was left to him to carry them through. To do this, he had to overcome a latent hostility to change in many quarters ("If you organise the British Army," Sir Evelyn Wood, then quartermaster-general, had once warned Ellison, "you'll ruin it"[39]). Haldane took his inspiration not from an academic reading of Clausewitz and Moltke, as Germanophobe critics maliciously charged, but from army reformers nearer at hand, particularly Lord Esher. He successfully extended the General Staff system, hitherto confined to the war office, to the whole of the army, and he had ambitions to extend it further to cover the fighting forces of the empire. It was a brain trust—he stored immense faith in such groups and belonged to many—that would, in the event of war, supervise and conduct operations.

With the invaluable assistance of his army council, Haldane set about reorganizing the British army on a more rational basis. The Regular Army was shorn of eight battalions of the line and two battalions of guards, much to the King's distress, but the troops and functions concerned were reassigned elsewhere. It was refashioned as an expeditionary force, consisting of one cavalry and six infantry divisions, kept in constant readiness for service abroad. Appended to it was a special reserve from which it would feed in time of emergency. The expeditionary force was regarded by its creator "in point of quality the finest army for its size on the earth."[40] But what about its size? The most vocal members of the Cabinet, Lloyd George and Churchill,

---

[39] Ellison, "Reminiscences," *Lancashire Lad* (Jan., 1935), p. 8.
[40] *Autobiography*, p. 197.

thought it far too large and expensive, while the Unionist Opposition and foreign observers considered this lilliputian force of 160,000 men no match for the huge conscript armies of continental states.

Even greater controversy surrounded Haldane's scheme to reshape the second-line or auxiliary forces: the militia, the yeomanry, and the volunteers. These were incorporated, as tactfully as possible, into a new army, the Territorial Force, designed for home defense or voluntary service abroad. It consisted of fourteen divisions and fourteen mounted brigades, each administered by a Lord Lieutenant through a county association. This throwback to Cromwellian organization won it the nickname the New Model. Haldane, knowing very well that this would be only a skeletal structure, rightly anticipated that sufficient recruits would step forward when and if the need arose. His critics, including some who knew better, accused him of building a phantom army that existed only on paper.[41] But within weeks after war was declared, the County of London Association, responsible for more units than any other association in the kingdom, proved able to get all of them, including those 30 per cent below establishment, up to full strength.[42] The Earl of Dartmouth, chairman of the Council of Territorial Associations, later recalled similar experience: the effective mobilization of the Territorial Force in the early days of August 1914 had made possible the prompt despatch of the Expeditionary Force. Yet Dartmouth was hard pressed to "remember any far reaching scheme so riddled with criticism when it first saw the light, that in the end justified the intentions of its Inventor."[43]

The special reserve sapped the militia's supply of manpower and usurped the greater part of its functions. Although Unionist critics decried Haldane's decision to abolish this age-old institution, it is extremely doubtful whether it would have been permitted to continue much longer regardless of the party in power. It was the respected opinion of Lord Esher that the militia had been dying "a slow death,"[44] and Arnold-Forster had spoken of merging the militia ("a decaying

---

41 ". . . You should not be too much alarmed," Arnold-Forster had counseled Haldane, "by the figures purporting to show the falling off of men in the Army during the next few years. All the Estimates have been taken on an absurdly unfavourable basis, and without any regard to the reasonable possibilities of the case." Dec. 18, 1905, HP 5906, f. 274.

42 Letter to *The Times*, by Sir Assheton Pownall, Aug. 30, 1928.

43 Dartmouth to Haldane, April 12, 1926, HP 5917, ff. 22–23.

44 Note by Esher on letter from Arnold-Forster, July 28, 1904, Esher Papers.

force which every soldier knows is useless, if not dangerous") into the Home Army.[45] Balfour, who knew the furor that would result, had doubted whether Arnold-Forster would succeed, but he frankly admitted that "there must be a large reduction of men in some direction or another if any economies are to be effected; and, unless economies are effected, the whole system will break down."[46] Arnold-Forster, recalling "all the abuse I received" for similar proposals, could only "rub my eyes" when Haldane proceeded to convert the militia into "short service Territorial Regulars."[47] Yet rather than applaud his successor's initiative, he joined those who deprecated change and romanticized the "Old Constitutional Force" into something it had never been.

Haldane's most inexorable critics were diehard Tories who viewed his army policies as an integral part of the attack upon privilege that culminated in the 1911 Parliament Act. To an extent that is not often realized, they were defending vested interests by opposing Haldane. Colonel Ellison perceived that his chief was pitted "against the individualistic influences and beliefs of the nineteenth century"; more than this, Haldane was pitted against the vestiges of fifteenth-century bastard feudalism. As Ellison explained:

Each unit had come to be regarded, in a sense, the property of the Commanding Officer who conceived it to be his duty to preserve intact its status and its financial stability. Accordingly the prospect of drastic changes . . . was far from being popular. More distasteful however were the financial provisions of the New Model. The idea of their units being placed financially at the mercy of County Associations filled many C.O.s with genuine despondency and alarm. Hitherto all Government grants for maintenance and training had been paid directly to the C.O. who often supplemented them by gifts from his own pocket and by subscriptions raised locally. He thus possessed autocratic powers in all matters that concerned his unit.[48]

The list of those who were deprived of their commands or otherwise denied authority by Haldane's reforms contains many names of those most bitterly opposed to the war minister.

Had Haldane occupied a stronger position within the Liberal Party and Cabinet, he could have replied to his various critics with greater

[45] Arnold-Forster to Roberts, July 19, 1904, Roberts Papers.
[46] Balfour to Roberts, July 12, 1904, *Ibid.*
[47] Arnold-Forster to his sister, July, 1907, quoted in Mary Arnold-Forster, *The Rt. Hon. H. O. Arnold-Forster* (London, 1910), p. 327.
[48] "Reminiscences," *Lancashire Lad* (Feb., 1936), p. 9.

conviction and authority. Each time he gave way to Radical demands for economy, he unleashed the fury of Unionists. Each time he stood firm, he brought the wrath of Radicals upon himself. On nonmilitary matters, including the problem of education in which he took such keen interest, Haldane's influence upon his colleagues was negligible. These were, for the most part, thankless years, redeemed only by the devotion of those who worked beside him and by the knowledge that he was achieving what no other major politician of either party would risk his reputation to attempt.

In August 1906 Haldane paid a brief official visit to Berlin to inspect the setup at the German war office and, generally, to foster better relations between the countries. The day before his departure, he described the assignment to J. A. Spender as a "nuissance" that would take him away from pressing business: ". . . I doubt very much coming out of these foreign visits in a definite form. The most to be hoped for is that they may smooth matters gradually."[49] At the end of the year, when the war office left its outgrown quarters in Pall Mall for more commodious lodgings in Whitehall, Haldane delivered the text of his Territorial and Reserve Forces Bill to Campbell-Bannerman. The Prime Minister was receptive; the Cabinet less so. "The dangers to the *Cabinet* and its solidarity," Morley wrote to Campbell-Bannerman on the first day of the new year, "seem to be Ireland and Haldane." Morley reported that he had found Haldane in an "extraordinary depression" after a recent meeting of the Defense Committee: "The W. O. at sixes and sevens; the army council divided; probable divisions in Cabinet; thought it more likely than not that he would fail, and if so would gladly return to bar."[50] Lord Esher, who had chaired the committee that framed the proposed legislation, learned from Morley that while "the Cabinet Committee were not hostile to Haldane's scheme, there was no enthusiasm about it. What really frightens them is the length of the Bill, and the *bother* which drastic proposals always entail."[51]

Haldane's spirits had revived by the time he wrote to Campbell-Bannerman on the 9th:

[49] Aug. 24, 1906, Spender Papers, Add. MSS. 46, 390, ff. 150–51.
[50] Campbell-Bannerman Papers, Add. MSS. 41, 223, f. 208.
[51] Esher to M. V. Brett, Jan. 9, 1907, in M. V. Brett (ed.), *Journals and Letters*, II (London, 1934), 215.

You may think me over-sanguine, but I am really getting very hopeful. . . .
It seems to me from indications which come from important quarters, that
the feeling, professional and public, is becoming very friendly. . . . At all
events I have confidence enough in myself to be keen to try if you and the
Cabinet will let me. You have given me every help, and if you and my
colleagues will take the amount of risk of reputation and credit which a
failure on my part would involve, I will gladly do my part to the utmost of
my capacity.

The main obstacle, as Haldane saw it, was opposition within the party:
"It seems to me that what would require care would be the mode of
presentation to our own people, for it is our own people who count
most in this case." In closing, he appealed to Campbell-Bannerman
by stressing the thoroughly Cardwellian nature of his proposed reforms.[52]
Haldane also made an effort to canvass support outside the Cabinet
and, not unnaturally, he sought out Lord Milner. The result was not in
the least encouraging. "I listened to Haldane for nearly 20 minutes the
other night," Milner reported to L. S. Amery on February 11; "[it
was] a private conversation, so that he might have said something if
he had a mind to. It was all *blather*. If that is *the best* we can expect
from these fellows, Heaven help us."[53] On February 25 Haldane took
the occasion of his speech on the army estimates to reveal to the
Commons his intention to introduce legislation to create the Territorial
Force. "I am under no illusion," he assured J. A. Spender a day later.
There would be "keen fight" from the Militia and Yeomanry, who
would resist to the death. "But, as C. B. said to me today, 'Beat them
we must, for an agitation for Compulsion is the inevitable result of
failure.' "[54]
Like Asquith at the exchequer, who candidly admitted to protec-
tionist friends that the Free Trade system was on trial for its life,
Haldane knew that the continuation of voluntary recruiting depended
upon the success of his army reforms. In 1901 Lord Roberts had returned to England from service in South Africa, convinced that compulsory military service was a prerequisite to national survival. In 1905
he became president of the National Service League and for the rest
of his life led the agitation for conscription. Roberts, if not many of
his supporters, respected Haldane's work as far as it went, but urged

[52] Campbell-Bannerman Papers, Add. MSS. 41, 218, ff. 182–83.
[53] Quoted in A. M. Gollin, *Proconsul in Politics* (London, 1964), p. 133.
[54] Feb. 26, 1907, Spender Papers, Add. MSS. 46, 390, f. 152.

that it be carried further: "You and I both desire to see the Army recognized by the people of this country as a part of their national life. We only differ as to the means by which that object can be obtained."[55] The pressures were considerable, but Haldane withstood them, justly confident that, at least at this point, conscription would create more problems than it would solve. Gradually, the conscriptionists grew more truculent if no more persuasive. But it was not until after Haldane had left the war office in 1912 that their full fury was vent upon him.

The Territorial and Reserve Forces Bill, introduced in February, did not have its second reading until after the Easter recess. Meanwhile, as Sir Almeric Fitzroy noted, there were "auguries of no great promise" for its success.[56] Labourites and Radicals deprecated its cost and feared that it would pave the way for conscription. Unionists tended to doubt whether adequate recruits would come forward to bring the scheme to life. "Where are the men to come from?" John Buchan asked. "There will be small inducement to enlist in battalions which are not units with any substantive character of their own, but merely storehouses for the first line to draw upon."[57] Austen Chamberlain confessed to his diary on March 3 that he was no more impressed when he read Haldane's speech in *Hansard* than he had been when he heard it in the House: "It seems to me that he will never get his new voluntary force and, meantime, he begins by destroying what exists instead of building up the new."[58] Two days later, Chamberlain relayed word that Balfour, too, "regards [Haldane's] scheme as already dead."[59] Arnold-Forster predicted more cautiously to his sister that the Bill would eventually pass, but only after the provisions regarding the Militia, Yeomanry, and Volunteers had been modified beyond recognition.[60]

The prophets of doom were mistaken. The controversial Bill passed

[55] Roberts to Haldane, June 27, 1907, HP 5907, f. 171.

[56] April 14, 1907, *Memoirs*, I, 319.

[57] "Lord Haldane's 'New Model' ", March 7, 1907, reprinted in *Comments and Characters* (London, 1940), p. 5.

[58] *Politics from Inside*, pp. 54–55; Chamberlain added in a footnote: "I never understood till the Great War came what a magnificent achievement Haldane's army reorganization was. Confession of my error is the only amends I can offer to his memory."

[59] Sir Charles Petrie, *Life and Letters of Austen Chamberlain* (London, 1939), I, 208.

[60] April, 1907, quoted in Mary Arnold-Forster, p. 326.

the Commons in June by a resounding vote of 283 to 63. For this, Haldane gave credit neither to his party nor his colleagues ("Not a good Parliament," he complained to the Webbs on May 3, "no constructive ideas, merely objections to other people's ideas"), but exclusively to A. J. Balfour, with whom he was in close communication.[61] But the measure had still to face the House of Lords, where its fate was uncertain. At this point, only one Government measure had been safely piloted through the upper house. And here Haldane's enemies were most firmly entrenched. Colonel Repington, at Haldane's behest, sounded out Lord Lansdowne, leader of the Unionist majority in the Lords, and found him "sympathetic and reasonable." Lansdowne, who admitted that he could offer nothing better, declared that despite certain reservations he had "no intention of wrecking your Bill."[62] This assured the scheme of easy passage and the Territorial Army was born.

In a superficial sense, 1907 was a year of unmitigated success for Haldane: the General Staff was developed, the Expeditionary Force was launched, and legislation creating the Territorial Force was lodged upon the statute book. And yet his work remained, at year's end, in a precarious state. Critics continued to deride the reforms as over-theorized and under-capitalized. J. A. Spender, in a November 21 *Westminster Gazette* editorial that won him Haldane's gratitude, noted the irony "that the very people who predicted failure for Mr. Haldane are ready to turn about and attack him on the ground that he is spoiling a brilliant success by excessive parsimony." Spender assured his readers that the Liberal Government was "too much concerned with the success of this scheme to risk it for a few hundred thousand pounds." But was this really the case? Haldane pared two million pounds from his 1907 estimates without satisfying certain members of the Cabinet who demanded additional economies. ". . . I have cut everything as closely as I dare," he informed his colleagues in a November 11 memorandum: "Unless the Cabinet decides to withdraw troops from overseas I cannot go further without breaking heavily into the efficiency of the Army."[63] Once again, he was sustained by Campbell-Bannerman, but it soon became doubtful how much longer he could rely upon this support.

By November 1907 the illness was evident that would bring Campbell-

61 Webb, *Our Partnership*, pp. 379–80.
62 Repington to Haldane, April 19, 1907, HP 5907, ff. 144 ff.
63 Campbell-Bannerman Papers, Add. MSS. 41, 242, f. 275.

Bannerman's resignation and death the following April. It was equally evident that Asquith would succeed to the premiership, a prospect not contemplated with universal satisfaction. Morley and the Gladstonians could not forgive him his turnabout on Irish Home Rule, the Roseberyites for sanctioning Radical proposals for House of Lords reform and land redistribution; several of the latter expressed hope that Rosebery would head off Asquith by forming a Center Party with Lord Cromer. Ronald Munro Ferguson thought anything worth trying, even Lloyd George, to keep out Asquith, "a raw middle-class radical, with a character deteriorated by a vulgar society of another sort and by a free use of wine which he cannot carry." He was particularly concerned with the fate of Haldane, who, he predicted, "will be in trouble before long." He speculated that Haldane, "if he gets kicked out," would help reactivate the Liberal League as "the center of his operations, for however unsuccessful he will always be indefatigable." Sir Edward Grey, he reported to Rosebery, "regards [Haldane] as *the* Prime Minister. I said he would get as much support as the Cities of the Plain."[64]

Grey was not the only one to see in Haldane the makings of a first-rate Prime Minister. Bernard Shaw regarded him "C. B.'s only possible successor" and wrote him a puckish letter of encouragement: "Do not lie low and be modest merely because the thing is inevitable. . . . You must seize the crown; and when you have got it let the first acts of your reign be to give me that pension for Ashton Ellis (who is pawning his spare scarf-pins) and to abolish the Censorship of Plays."[65] Haldane did not give a second thought to the suggestion, for he knew that Asquith's succession was assured. But he was not without misgivings on that score. He knew that his friend could never inspire the confidence and devotion of his predecessor: men might respect "Mr. A.'s" penetrating mind and envy his parliamentary skills, but they had come to love "good old C. B." The passionate loyalties that Asquith commanded were, by and large, the product of later years and, at this time, Margot Asquith was not entirely mistaken when she described her husband, with typically Margot-esque hyperbole, as "a cold hard unsympathetic man, loved by none, admired by a few."[66] For his part, Hal-

---

[64] Munro Ferguson to Rosebery, Dec. 21 and 26, 1907 and Jan. 13, 1908, Rosebery Papers.

[65] Nov. 16, 1907, HP 5907, ff. 256–57.

[66] Margot Asquith to Leo Maxse [April 24], 1908, Maxse Papers.

dane doubted whether Asquith could maintain discipline within the party and Cabinet. "C. B. is the only person who can hold this motley crew together," he told his sister on February 1. "I should like to liquidate the concern and start afresh. That is just what I fear H. H. A. will never do."[67] A few days later he reported an impending crisis over military and naval expenditure. Lloyd George, who referred to him as "the Minister for Slaughter," had launched an attack upon the army estimates which Haldane repulsed with the help of "the wonderful old P. M. and H. H. A." But Haldane anticipated that "a split will come sooner or later" ("the fissure is deeper than the mere matter of army estimates"), and he did not expect to survive it without Campbell-Bannerman.[68]

On April 6 Haldane wrote the dying Prime Minister an affectionate letter of farewell: "There is no member of your Cabinet who has realized more what he has learned and gained from you than myself."[69] At this point, storms broke upon him from all directions. The April *National Review* noted "with satisfaction that the Opposition, who had hitherto made no serious effort to expose 'the great Haldane humbug' are at last stirring in their slumbers." Lord Roberts's National Service League intensified its efforts and emboldened its rhetoric. Sir John Fisher, whose relations with Haldane had cooled, incited politicians and journalists against the war minister, who had claimed for the army appropriations which might otherwise have gone to the navy. And Arnold-Forster, who could not long hold his peace, denounced Haldane and his scheme in letters to the *Observer* and *The Times*. Had he lived, Campbell-Bannerman could not, of course, have warded off these attacks. But his continued leadership would have been sufficient to prevent another that threatened far greater mischief.

For reasons wholly unrelated, Asquith raised Haldane's leading Liberal critics to positions of greater authority—Lloyd George went to the exchequer, Churchill to the board of trade—and at the same time provided them with less supervision. The result, as Haldane later complained, was that soon after the change in the premiership,

there came an attack on my estimates from within the Cabinet, one of whose members put forward an army scheme of his own, and the Chancellor of the Exchequer insisted on having a committee to see whether it could

[67] HP 6011, ff. 40–41.   [68] Feb. 5 and [7], 1908, HP 6011, ff. 42, 44.
[69] Campbell-Bannerman Papers, Add. MSS. 41, 218, ff. 200–201.

not be carried out. The scheme would have meant ruin and confusion to the Expeditionary Force, and I fought against it tooth and nail. If I had not succeeded we could have rendered little assistance to France in the year 1914.[70]

The unnamed colleague who launched the attack was Winston Churchill, who was working hand in hand with Lloyd George for purposes best known to themselves. John Burns, president of the local government board, who had his own reasons to resent their collusion, called them "the two Romeos."[71] Mrs. Webb, who came to lunch with Haldane on May 19, ascribed his fulminations against Lloyd George and Churchill to a fear of "the young generation knocking at the door."[72] But she had little idea of the fierce struggles taking place within the Cabinet.

On May 14 Haldane announced to his sister that "Ll. G. has opened fire—wants to cut down the Army. My reply has been a point blank refusal."[73] Churchill rushed to the fray with an alternative army scheme that he boasted was more effective and less costly than Haldane's. Leo Maxse, who detested Churchill ("the cynical adventurer at the Board of Trade who 'ratted' from the Unionist Party") even more than he did Haldane, reported on good authority in the August National Review that Churchill had been "turned loose in the War Office, where he was given a room and a staff, [and] . . . has been permitted to masquerade as a sort of deputy war minister behind Mr. Haldane's back." Balfour confirmed this story on June 30 to Austen Chamberlain, who heard "that all the Cabinet, with the possible exception of Grey, is against Haldane."[74] Morley and Esher, who examined Churchill's brief on army estimates on June 22, thought that Haldane had no reason to worry, but Haldane apparently thought otherwise. Esher found him "agitated and nervous" on the 25th: "he was well supported by Morley, and he relied on Grey, but he did not speak with the confidence of a few weeks ago."[75] A committee was appointed to review Churchill's criticisms. It consisted of Lloyd George, Charles Hobhouse, then financial secretary to the treasury, and Maurice Headlam, a war office official who claimed credit for bringing down "the egregious Hobhouse" on the

[70] HP 5919, f. 132.
[71] Runciman to McKenna, March 27, 1910, McKenna Papers.
[72] Our Partnership, p. 411.   [73] HP 6011, f. 63.
[74] Politics from Inside, pp. 126–27.
[75] Esher to Lord Knollys, June 26, 1908. In M. V. Brett (ed.), Journals and Letters of Reginald, Viscount Esher, II (London, 1934), 324–25.

cr. Radio Times Hulton Picture Library

Winston Churchill with Lloyd George in Whitehall

right side: "There is no knowing what that House of Commons might
have done," Headlam later reminisced, "if an anti-Haldane report had
been laid before them."[76] Still, Haldane was kept on edge by rumors
that he would be made lord chancellor in order to create an opening for
Churchill at the war office. He notified Asquith that he did not covet
the woolsack under such conditions and wished to remain where he was.
He confided to Esher his belief "that Churchill wants to get rid of *him*
and that Ll. George backs him." Esher's own thought was "that Win-

[76] Headlam to Harris, April 10, 1935, Harris Papers.

ston wanted to push to the front of the Cabinet. He thinks himself Napoleon."[77]

There can be no doubt that Campbell-Bannerman would never have abided such a state of affairs. But Asquith began his premiership as he ended it nearly nine years later, unable to control his subordinates and to reconcile the views among them. The prolonged crisis over naval expenditure was another case in point. Although Asquith admitted private doubts about Dreadnought construction, he defended an expanded shipbuilding program and threw his weight to Reginald McKenna, the first lord of the admiralty, as he had never done to Haldane. By this time Lord Fisher, father of the Dreadnought policy, had come to look upon Haldane as a rival for budgetary appropriations. As leading spokesman for the Blue Water School—so called because it preached an exclusive reliance upon naval defenses—Fisher considered a large standing army a useless extravagance for an island nation and concluded that "every penny spent on the army is a penny taken from the navy." Inclined to see personal enemies lurking behind every corner, he suspected Haldane ("a soapy Jesuit") of ambitions to embroil Britain in continental struggles ("suicidal idiocy"), and he unreasonably accused him of intriguing with Lord Charles Beresford to effect a palace revolution at the admiralty. In particular, Fisher bridled at Haldane's proposals to set up a naval war staff that would work in conjunction with the general staff at the war office.[78]

The Agadir crisis in the summer of 1911 made obvious the need for more extensive cooperation between the services and for a thoroughgoing reform of admiralty procedures. At very least it brought Lloyd George and Churchill round to Haldane's view on defenses. The crisis passed, but Haldane was left with the conviction that had there been a European war, the navy would not have been prepared to carry the Expeditionary Force across the Channel. He did not feel that he could remain a member of any Government that did not take immediate steps to rectify this situation, which nullified all that he had accomplished in six years at the war office. If necessary, he announced, he would go to the admiralty to carry out reforms.

The Prime Minister quietly conceded the need to replace McKenna,

---

[77] Journal for July 8, 1908, *Journals and Letters*, II, 327.
[78] See Alfred J. Marder, *Dreadnought to Scapa Flow*, I (London, 1961), particularly 103, 205, 387–88.

an able administrator but not the man to impose a solution upon his departmental officials. He invited Haldane to join him for a day's discussion at Archerfield House, where he was enjoying a Scottish holiday in late September. Haldane was greeted at the door not by his host, but by a fellow-guest, Winston Churchill, who had come north with with his own designs upon the admiralty. Asquith listened to both men and eventually decided upon Churchill on the grounds that he had to have a first lord in the Commons (Haldane had by this time taken a peerage), and that Haldane's appointment would seem a punitive measure to the admirals. And Churchill had the backing of Lloyd George, another visitor to Archerfield. Haldane initially had grave doubts whether Churchill had sufficient tact to handle the assignment, but he was eventually satisfied by the arrangement. McKenna, however, was not consoled with the home office and fought bitterly to remain where he was. He would always hold Haldane more responsible than Churchill for instigating his transfer.

Despite the serious thought he had given to the situation at the admiralty, Haldane remained preoccupied with the affairs of his own department. His position grew more difficult as political acrimonies grew more intense. It proved impossible to keep army reform, essentially a nonpartisan subject, out of the mire of party politics. An anonymous article in the October 1909 *National Review* asserted that the peers had rejected the People's Budget as a national service to force out the present Government which had "done the Kaiser's work" and to bring in "men of character and patriotism" who would restore the nation's defenses. Haldane was not entirely convinced that a change in administration would be a bad thing. The Liberals were losing ground in the country and were badly divided. ". . . No ministry does any good to its reputation by remaining in office through a second Parliament," he told Sir Almeric Fitzroy, whom he met on the parade-ground on March 14, 1910, and he professed his readiness "to take his dismissal as soon as it comes." He had accomplished nearly all he could at the war office, and he postulated that the Unionists, "in combination with the County Associations, could at this stage do more to develop the territorial organisation than it is in his power to do."[79]

Haldane was deeply pained by the political situation, particularly

[79] Fitzroy, I, 399.

that within the Cabinet, where more truculent colleagues pressed for a war to the death against the House of Lords. "We are drifting towards the rock of a split," he wrote to his sister on March 21, "and cannot go on much longer."[80] Outsiders, unable to perceive the moderating influences that Haldane and Grey were attempting to exert, condemned them for allowing themselves to be swallowed up. The *National Review* scorned them as "the two most broken reeds in public life." Austen Chamberlain admitted that he had come to "feel such a profound contempt for Haldane as a politician that I am unable to speak of him without showing it." When he replied extemporaneously to Haldane's April 6 speech in the Commons, he "received many congratulations" from those who shared his indignation.[81]

The constitutional crisis brought a recrudescence of Opposition attacks upon matters long settled, including Haldane's army reforms. The diehard Tories, threatened with the extinction of their privileges, made maximum use of their ancient chamber to denounce the enemy at the gates. All aspects of Liberal policy, particularly those Balfour had supported, were condemned. Through the summer of 1910, Haldane continued "toiling like a camel," acutely conscious of the renewed agitation against his work, but determined to "work harder than ever to get rid of all the points they can hang any attacks onto."[82] With the encouragement of Asquith and Lloyd George, he contemplated moving to the local government board, where he might carry through the poor law reform that had eluded John Burns. But that would take time, and he doubted that the Liberals would remain much longer in office.

On March 5, 1911, Haldane heard from a *Times* reporter, who intruded upon him at twenty minutes to midnight, a rumor that he was to take a peerage in order to bolster the beleaguered Liberal forces in the House of Lords. "Of course it is not true," he assured his mother the next day,[83] but on the 10th he wrote to tell her that Asquith had made a strong appeal to him. Within a week it was "settled that . . . I should go to the House of Lords as Viscount Haldane of Cloan. I rather hate it. But the public interest necessitates the step." There would be no need to commemorate the occasion with "a bonfire at Cloan. It

80 HP 6011, f. 110.
81 Diary entries for April 7 and 11, *Politics from Inside*, pp. 244 ff.
82 Haldane to his mother, July 27, 1910, HP 5984, ff. 41–42.
83 HP 5985, f. 83.

is not wholly a matter for rejoicing."[84] He was offered the secretaryship of state for India, held at the time by the ailing Lord Crewe,
but preferred to retain the war ministry.

It was a logical decision. The India office would have been an interim assignment—it was evident that the lord chancellorship would
soon fall vacant—and after Morley's recent tenure, little could have
been accomplished there. And a new hand at the war office would
have had a difficult time with the following year's estimates. Haldane's
elevation to the peerage and his continuation as war minister were
generally applauded, even by many of those who had criticized details
of his scheme and who would participate in the wartime agitation
against him. ". . . He has accomplished more in five years [at the
war office] than any of his predecessors since Cardwell," the *Morning
Post* declared in a March 25 tribute. "Although we are at the present
moment as acutely in political antagonism as men can be who have
not got rifles in their hands," Lord Selborne wrote affectionately, "yet
I hope that we shall not allow that fact to mar our personal relationship. Let mey say then how very glad I am that you are coming to
my House and that you are not leaving the W. O."[85] The *National
Review* stood out as an exception. It was, if nothing else, consistent,
and disdained "the paeans of Unionist journals" for Haldane. ". . . If
he had been an honest man," Maxse argued, Haldane "would have
assumed the title Viscount Humbug." Haldane did not endear himself
to Maxse by proceeding to take an active part in forcing the Parliament
Bill upon the Lords.

But Maxse's sharpest barbs were reserved for A. J. Balfour, under
whose leadership the Unionist Party had suffered this ultimate ignominy.
He had often chided Balfour for lack of contact with public opinion
and with the party machine, but the constitutional crisis convinced
him that "Balfour Must Go." Haldane's peerage occasioned a by-
election for the seat he had held since 1882. Balfour, a resident in the
constituency, ceremoniously traveled seven-hundred miles to cast his
vote for the Unionist candidate. "Had he shown a tithe of such energy
on previous occasions," the *National Review* snickered, "he would have
been spared the shame of being represented for a quarter of a century
by Haldane." Maxse proclaimed what a good many more dignified

Unionists had come to believe, namely "that the Unionist leader has not fought the Parliament Bill as it should have been fought, as he would have fought it some years ago when Mr. Chamberlain sat by his side to keep him up to the mark. . . ." But this was only the most recent of many shameful retreats under Balfourian leadership: ". . . He has prevented his party from adopting and pressing a coherent Naval policy. . . . He has likewise given his sanction to the Territorial sham of his friend, Viscount Haldane, and has protected that humbug from attack in the House of Commons. . . ." The cooperation Haldane and Balfour had given one another worked to their mutual disadvantage as politicians. Arthur Lee, Unionist M. P. for Fareham, reflected that Haldane's only success had been "in bamboozling our people, and notably Arthur Balfour, who has perhaps been too intimate with him socially. To do Balfour justice, however," Lee felt obliged to admit to Andrew Bonar Law, "he may well have found a difficulty in contrasting Haldane's performance unfavourably with those of Unionist War Ministers of recent date."[86]

The movement to oust Balfour achieved its aim in the autumn of 1911. Haldane sent a tactful letter to his friend: "No one who knows you in the least will imagine that in your case attacks, whether from in front or from behind, would have made the least difference, except possibly to increase your determination to fight."[87] Haldane's loss was considerable. Balfour, never averse to giving the Liberals a chance with problems that had confounded the Unionists, had given him valuable encouragement and support. Bonar Law, the new leader of the Opposition, was determined never to compromise himself by abetting a Radical Government in any capacity. On January 12, 1912, he delivered a major address at the Albert Hall that was guaranteed to appease the rebels to whom he owed his position. He provided a systematic attack upon the Government, department by department, and lingered longest over the war office. "Mr. Haldane—I beg his Lordship's pardon—Lord Haldane," he began facetiously,

has many merits and he has had great difficulties. His greatest difficulty is that . . . to a greater extent even than the Prime Minister, he is suspected by the dominant faction in his own party. . . . He is very industrious. I don't think any War Secretary ever made so many speeches, and long speeches. . . . He has endeavoured to impress upon the country the need for clear think-

[86] Jan. 21, 1912, Bonar Law Papers.   [87] Nov. 8, 1911, Balfour Papers.

ing. He has taught the lesson by precept but he has taught it much more effectively by his own example. But, ladies and gentlemen, neither his merits nor his difficulties should conceal from us the extent of his failure. The cost of the Army is much the same as when he took it in hand, but he strengthened the Regular Forces—that is his description of it—by reducing them to the extent of 20,000 men, and he has strengthened in the same way the Auxiliary Forces, another reduction of 30,000 men. But this is not the worst of it. Our Regular Forces are armed with weapons—and that is still true of the Auxiliary Forces—which are utterly inferior to the Armies of other nations, and if the time ever comes when our soldiers are brought face to face with Continental armies they will suffer from the inferiority of their weapons, a handicap which no courage can overcome.

Bonar Law's remarks were particularly damaging in one respect. Coming from the leader of the Opposition and not from an irresponsible back-bencher, they gave credence to imputations that the Liberals relied upon obsolete weapons and too few of them. The *Scotsman*, usually slow to lose its composure, accused the Government in a January 30 editorial of "starving the army." Haldane was infuriated, but hesitated to make the question of armaments a political issue. "As a matter of fact," he advised his mother, "they are very fine weapons—the guns the best in the world, and the rifles only defective in points which the stupidity of Lord Roberts and the Unionist war minister overlooked. These we have rectified in every way we can."[88] But it was only the testimony of German commanders at Mons and Ypres that finally dispelled suspicions that British weapons were inferior.

Haldane spent his remaining months at the war office devising replies to critics who would not under any circumstances allow themselves to be convinced. Industrial disputes were a constant headache, taxing his departmental resources and leading to strong words with certain colleagues. "Winston violent for the Masters against the Men," Loulou Harcourt jotted on a scrap of paper during a February 29 Cabinet on the coal strike; "Haldane has troops all ready, but will not use them at present."[89] It was more to Haldane's liking to employ powers of persuasion. A London dockers' strike threatened on May 21, when Asquith and Lloyd George were away and Haldane was left in charge. He summoned a Cabinet and "ordered an entirely new experiment—a

---

[88] Feb. 1, 1912, HP 5987, ff. 41–42. Sir Frederick Maurice made short work of Bonar Law's criticisms regarding manpower in an appendix to the appropriate chapter of his first volume, pp. 320–21.

[89] Harcourt Papers.

public enquiry into which was right—the employers or the men." Both sides accepted this solution, and the Cabinet went along.[90] Industrial crises provided sufficient distraction for Haldane to present his 1912 army estimates directly to Parliament without first submitting them for Cabinet approval. He assured Harcourt, who twitted him good-naturedly, that the estimates "had been about for some time," to which Harcourt replied, "about where?"[91]

The political situation remained depressing, and there was continual debate whether the Government, in its seventh year and "losing moral authority," should resign. Haldane strongly favored such a course, but he was overruled by colleagues who agreed with Lord Loreburn that they "must stay and go down fighting."[92] Social problems remained acute. Financial pressures continued to weigh heavily upon the Government. And the Irish situation grew increasingly desperate. The one bright spot in the spring of 1912 was, curiously enough, international affairs. Here, too, Haldane's energies were engaged. His visit to Berlin in February and the negotiations in London that followed gave promise of better relations between Britain and Germany. But to those convinced that Haldane had weakened British defenses, his diplomatic activities betokened further betrayal. He would henceforth be the scapegoat not only for the military policy he had shaped, but also for the foreign policy that he did his best to influence.

[90] Haldane to his mother, May 22, 1912, HP 5987, ff. 198–99.
[91] Notes of Cabinet, Feb. 29, 1912, Harcourt Papers.
[92] Notes of Cabinet, March 6, 1912, *Ibid.*

CHAPTER III

MINISTER FOR GERMANY

I find myself in Germany more popular than in England. It reminds me of the sort of reception Lloyd George gets when he travels in Wales.
—HALDANE[*]

A century after British and Prussian troops had joined at Waterloo to put down the first Napoleon, the two allies were locked in fierce combat against each other upon nearby battlefields. To many contemporaries on both sides of the North Sea the confrontation was one that had been long in coming and that statesmen had been powerless to avert. War had been prophesied since 1870, when Prussia single-handedly defeated another Napoleon, completing the process of German unification. With Austria and France thrust aside, and Russia removed by Bismarckian diplomacy, Britain seemed to remain the final obstacle to German world power. The inevitability of Anglo-German conflict was seen in a succession of diplomatic incidents, colonial disputes, and, particularly, commercial and naval rivalries. It appeared that the young German empire, restless and expansive, could not obtain her place in the sun without eclipsing to one degree or another that older empire upon which the sun never set.

Haldane, for one, did not share this apocalyptic vision of Armageddon: "The strained relations" between Britain and Germany, he later maintained, "did not occur till the last moment and they were due to outside causes."[1] As a student of German literature and philosophy, he detected no incompatibility between the two cultures. As a Free Trader, he anticipated that German industrial growth would exert a

[*] Letter to his mother, May 31, 1912, from Göttingen, HP 5987, f. 216.

[1] Haldane to Sir Charles Harris, Nov. 20, 1916, Harris Papers.

salutary influence upon the more mature British economy. As a legalist, he was confident that conflicts of interest could be settled as they arose by patient negotiation. He did not deny the existence of tensions between the two countries, but in true Hegelian fashion believed that these would evolve a more valuable partnership; these differences, he was convinced, were superficial, the product of mutual misapprehension. Imperial Germany, like any parvenu, was quick to take offense and quicker to give it. And the popular press of both societies, much to his regret, emphasized the few sources of discord rather than the wide areas of sympathy and interdependence. Haldane took it upon himself to call attention, whenever possible, to the affinities between Germany and Britain. For this reason he often went to extravagant lengths to extoll German thought and to apologize for German statecraft. He implored Lord Northcliffe to discount the fulminations of the Kaiser, "an impulsive and rather excitable man," and pointed out that had newspapers reported "all that Edward VII said in private. . . , there would be rows galore."[2] Better able than most of his contemporaries to attach a proper value to royal chatter, Hohenzollern or Hanoverian, Haldane proved less qualified to gauge its incendiary effects upon public opinion in either country.

Long before the phrase had acquired a pejorative connotation, Haldane had earned himself a reputation as a pro-German. This meant that he admired German cultural attainments, sought to emulate certain German organizational techniques, and strove for improved relations between the two governments; in no way did it imply lack of patriotism on his part, nor for that matter infidelity to the 1904 entente with France. Even Lord Charles Beresford, who reportedly began each day with the greeting "Good morning, one day nearer the German war," came to applaud the festival of German opera that Sir Thomas Beecham presented at Covent Garden in 1913. It had for decades been common practice for British literary and political figures, especially those of Liberal orientation, to identify themselves as pro-German or pro-French. Few, like G. P. Gooch, could maintain a judicious balance between the two traditions. In most cases such allegiances were sentimental and politically meaningless. Leo Maxse, as usual an exception to the rule, had a predilection for French culture that extended to French foreign

    [2] [June], 1912, cited in Reginald Pound and Geoffrey Harmsworth, *Northcliffe* (London, 1959), p. 434.

policy. But Lord Morley, no less devoted to French letters, vigorously opposed Britain's entry into war on France's side in August 1914. Like Morley, who was pro-French short of an active military alliance, Haldane was pro-German short of sacrificing vital British interests.

Seeing no reason to conceal his sympathies, Haldane often made remarks, public and private, that were open to misconstruction. At least part of the misfortune that befell him during the war was due to the looseness with which he had spoken and with which some of his close friends continued to speak. His enemies merely exploited—they did not invent—the notion that he was pro-German. He was constantly referred to in such terms by friends and colleagues, many of whom described themselves the same way. Margot Asquith confessed to Lord Rosebery when war broke out that "heaps and heaps" of her acquaintances had been willingly deceived by the Germans, and she expressed pity for "Poor Haldane and all the other pro-Germans among whom I have always counted myself."[3] Morley, who resigned from the Cabinet when war was declared, wrote a touching letter of farewell to Haldane, for whom he knew "it must be more than personal pain to find yourself the enemy of Germany and the friend of Russia."[4] When the two friends met that autumn, Haldane "repeated again and again" that he found "this quarrel with Germany . . . a 'deep personal sorrow.' "[5] After the war Haldane appeased his hunger for news about Germany, which he dared not visit, by avidly questioning Gooch and other friends as soon as they returned.

By no means was Haldane a lone crusader for Anglo-German understanding, though he emerged the most prominent. And by no means was this an exclusively Liberal tendency, though it took on that color. Politicians of both parties, among them Andrew Bonar Law, had sent their sons to German universities. The Unionist press had tried as long as possible to keep alive Joseph Chamberlain's ideal of Teutonic solidarity. The situation changed after 1905, partly because the Unionists went into opposition, partly as a result of the first Morocco crisis, partly because of Chamberlain's incapacitation, and not least of all because the Germans embarked upon Dreadnought construction. After this date there continued to be those within both political parties who

[3] Aug. 28 and Sept. 1, 1914, Rosebery Papers.
[4] Aug. 5, 1914, HP 5910, f. 253.
[5] Morley to Rosebery, Nov. 13, 1914, Rosebery Papers.

counseled moderation, but those who dared to advocate accommodation were overwhelmingly Liberal. An Anglo-German friendship committee, founded in the autumn of 1905 by British businessmen, rapidly lost its bipartisan character. The National Liberal Federation, inspired by the venerable Sir John Brunner, passed repeated resolutions to divert funds from the naval race to welfare programs. To allay German fears of Britain's agreements with France and Russia, J. A. Spender contributed innumerable articles to his own *Westminster Gazette* and to various English and German journals. Seven members of the Asquith Government, including Haldane, opened 1912 by sending pledges of good will toward Germany to the *Arbitrator,* the official publication of the International Arbitration League.[6] Incidents of this type were legion, making it no small wonder that the Liberals acquired a wartime reputation as the party that had been "soft on Germany."

There were acute differences among the pro-Germans in the Liberal camp, even those within the Cabinet. Haldane, unlike most others, based his position upon intellectual and not budgetary considerations. Aside from a determination to arrest the drift toward war, he had little in common with the pro-German Radicals who crowded the Government backbenches. They tended to be internationalists in their approach to foreign affairs and orthodox Cobdenites in their approach to commerce; for both reasons they were inclined to conciliate Germany. Many of them, A. J. P. Taylor has observed, "were more hostile to the Foreign Office," that ally of Tsarist autocracy, "than favourable to Germany."[7] Some were impressed by German experiments in social welfare. Little Englanders themselves, they did not begrudge Germany imperial and naval power, though they trusted that she would outgrow such adolescent pursuits. Dedicated to Gladstonian principles of finance, they hoped, as Spender put it, that both Germany and Britain would "be brought to a more reasonable frame of mind when they come to count the cost" of competition.[8] Not wholly without justification, these dissentient Liberals looked upon Anglo-German antagonism as one of the bitter fruits of the previous Unionist administrations, whose acts of jingo rapacity had undermined political morality at home and respect for Britain abroad. And they considered the Liberal Imperialists

---

[6] The others were McKenna, Harcourt, Buxton, Samuel, Pease, and Hobhouse.
[7] *The Trouble Makers* (London, 1964), p. 115.
[8] Spender to Brunner, April 13, 1909, Brunner Papers.

who now led their party accessories to those crimes. Long after 1905, Radicals continued to regard Haldane with suspicion, if not distrust, as a militarist. His work at the war office, by its very nature, did little to mollify that judgment. Until it was too late, they played into the hands of their common enemies, reflecting in their recriminations the internal weaknesses of the Liberal Party.

Leo Maxse, whose *National Review* was among the most acrimonious of the anti-ministerial journals, was quick to bracket Haldane with the pro-German Radicals. Although he had welcomed Haldane's appointment to the war office in December 1905 as a bulwark against the forces of pacifism and disruption, within a year he attacked Haldane— along with Lord Loreburn and James Bryce—as a member of the "Potsdam Party" within the Cabinet. These "Germanophile Ministers," Maxse subsequently explained, were backed by a "miscellaneous assortment . . . of ex-Ambassadors on the stump, Cocoa Quakers, Hebrew journalists at the beck and call of German diplomats, soft-headed Sentimentalists, cranks convinced that their country is always in the wrong, [and] Cosmopolitan financiers domiciled in London in order to do 'good work' for the Fatherland." With Bryce's early departure for the Washington embassy and Loreburn's retirement in June 1912, Haldane was left in sole command of the "Potsdammerung." But long before this time, he had established his pre-eminence in Maxse's eyes by setting himself "up as an authority upon Germany on the strength of his having been annually bamboozled by German professors in his earlier days."

Others, less biased, had also come to look upon him as the foremost sympathizer with German aspirations. Shortly before Haldane had taken his place in the Campbell-Bannerman ministry, Count Metternich, the German ambassador to London, enlisted his support in attempts to heal the rift between the Kaiser and Edward VII. No sooner was he installed in office than he became "the recipient of the woes and lamentations of the German ambassador," much to the amusement of Sir Edward Grey, who considered him "quite sound about foreign policy nonetheless."[9] The foreign secretary did not hestitate to entrust incidental diplomatic assignments to his pro-German friend; nor is there any reason why he should not have done so. Fond of his leisure, Grey

---

[9] Grey to Munro Ferguson, Oct. 31, 1905, quoted in Trevelyan, p. 105.

was grateful for assistance, and Haldane, who sought relief from war office routine, was glad to oblige. He spent the evening of January 18, 1906, reviewing the international situation with Count Metternich: "Foreign affairs are very difficult," he told his mother, "and some of the responsibility has come on me."[10]

Grey's confidence in Haldane was not misplaced, though it came to evoke heavy criticism. Within weeks after he had become minister for war, Haldane was preparing to assist France in the event of German aggression; this was something, he later admitted, that even most of his Cabinet colleagues "hardly knew." Looking back a decade later, he cited January 1906, the Liberal Government's first month in office, as the "really critical moment" in international affairs: in the wake of the first Morocco crisis and Delcassé's resignation, "a decision had to be taken. For the ways were parting." However much he might consort with the German ambassador, Haldane took his decision in favor of France. He did not anticipate "a breach with Germany," but nonetheless created his Expeditionary Force to "provid[e] against" such an "emergency."[11]

For reasons of security, Haldane's diplomatic work could be neither publicized nor defended. At the same time his name was associated with a variety of projects and activities that invited distortion. A frequent visitor to Germany since his youth, he found it increasingly difficult to travel in a private capacity. He could no longer retrace the footsteps of Goethe nor engage in other academic pastimes without inciting speculation in the chancelleries of Europe and along Fleet Street. To the same extent, his public position conferred new meaning upon his platform addresses and after-dinner remarks. His continual pleas for mutual understanding and forebearance were laudable, but coming from a minister of the Crown they acquired a significance that was often largely unintended. Unable to perceive the drift of public opinion, Haldane also failed to appreciate the image that he projected.

The plaudits that Haldane received from German sources were sufficient to insure that he would incur the resentment of certain groups and individuals at home. And concentrating as he did upon the German reaction, he often lost sight of the domestic situation. It gave him great

[10] Jan. 19, 1906, HP 5975, f. 73.
[11] Haldane to Rosebery, Aug. 14 and 17, 1916, Rosebery Papers; also Haldane to Harris, Nov. 20, 1916, Harris Papers.

pleasure that his address at Oxford on August 3, 1911—designed, he told Lord Northcliffe, "to show that the misinterpretation of each other's ideas by Germans and Englishmen arises out of differences of tradition and education"[12]—was praised by German professors and by the "secretary of the German Embassy who came down specially."[13] He was even more elated when the Kaiser, during a visit to London in May 1911, accepted his invitation to luncheon. Ever the gracious host, Haldane provided a guest list as distinctive as his bill of fare: space was at a premium at Queen Anne's Gate—a "Dolls' House," the Kaiser called it—but he managed to crowd around his table, among others, Lords Morley, Kitchener, and Curzon, Sir Arthur Wilson, J. A. Spender, Ramsay MacDonald, Sir John French, Sir Ian Hamilton, Edmund Gosse, J. S. Sargent, and R. S. S. Baden-Powell. One of Haldane's proudest moments before the war, this occasion caused him considerable embarrassment later on, when malicious journalists, conveniently forgetting the military and naval officials who were present, recalled it as an opportunity for the guest of honor to make converts to pacifism.

Haldane's intrusions into diplomacy, a realm that held endless fascination for him, were neither as constructive as he liked to believe nor as destructive as his enemies alleged. They might have contributed to a general lessening of tensions, but could have done little if any harm. This holds true even for his most celebrated venture, his mission to Berlin from February 8 to 11, 1912, which was the culmination of less formal exchanges.

Controversy continues to shroud the negotiations that Haldane conducted with ranking German government and naval officials two and a half years before the outbreak of war. Was the venture a serious undertaking or an empty gesture? If the latter, whom was it meant to impress? Was it a qualified success or an unmitigated disaster? With whom did the proposal for talks originate? Would more have been achieved had the assignment fallen to other hands? Did Haldane convince the Germans of Britain's pacific intentions and if so, did he encourage their ambitions? Did he convince them of Britain's resolve,

[12] [June], 1911, quoted in Pound and Harmsworth, p. 417.
[13] Haldane to his mother, Aug. 4, 1911, HP 5986, ff. 98–99; the address was published the following March by the American Association for International Conciliation.

and if so, did he dash the hopes of rapprochement? Did he obtain a slowdown of the German shipbuilding program, or did he leave his hosts more determined than ever to contest Britain's command of the seas? Had he proposed himself for the assignment or was he nominated by others? Did he receive the unanimous support of his colleagues, or was he used by one faction within the Cabinet to embarrass another? Did he learn anything from the experience, and did he convey that lesson to his associates? In short, was Haldane qualified to speak for his Government, his party, his nation?

Until the German violation of Belgian neutrality in the early days of August 1914 and the consequent British declaration of war, feeling had never run as high between the two countries as it did in the months that preceded Haldane's visit. What had begun that July as a German maneuver to impede the projected French annexation of Morocco ended in a prolonged enmity between Germany and Britain. Chastened by the arrival of the German gunboat *Panther* at the Moroccan harbor of Agadir, the French negotiated a settlement with Germany, leaving the British, who had hastened to give Paris more support than she wanted or required, on uneasy terms with Berlin. In order to leave no doubt in any mind, German or French, that Britain intended to stand by the entente, David Lloyd George, long an advocate of Anglo-German reconciliation, delivered a stern warning at London's Mansion House on July 21 that Britain would not stand idly by when her interests were "vitally affected." And to back up this threat, the Royal Navy was alerted for unspecified action.

In her hasty effort to extract concessions from France, Germany had come up against the implacable resistance of Great Britain. The encounter was all the more resented because it was completely unexpected. German statemen were no better able to apprciate the "vitally affected" interests to which Lloyd George alluded than the British foreign office could discern the German interests that the *Panther* had allegedly been sent to protect; both of course were euphemisms. Many Germans, particularly naval authorities, blamed British naval superiority for their country's failure to emerge from the crisis with greater gains. This provided all the more incentive for Germany to increase the size of her fleet. The British were accused of seeking to encircle Germany by land and sea, maintaining a balance of power that had long ceased to benefit anyone but themselves. The Kaiser subsequently complained to the Russian foreign minister that Britain had acted "disloyally" during the Agadir crisis, preparing her navy for an offensive against Germany.[14] The impression persisted in Berlin well into the following winter that Britain had been on the verge of war. Haldane's mission was designed in large part to dispel lingering suspicions that in her "military and naval preparations last summer" Britain had "meditated an unprovoked attack on Germany, even if she herself took no warlike step."[15]

Haldane was dispatched to Berlin in response not only to the international situation, which in most respects had begun to improve, but also to increasing parliamentary and party pressures. This is a factor too often overlooked, for it alone accounts for the urgency of the undertaking. The left and right wings of the Liberal Party, hastily united in shotgun style in 1905, continued to divide on many issues, past and present. Perhaps the most long-standing of disputes was that regarding naval appropriations: elder statemen recalled that this subject had broken Liberal unity as far back as Gladstone's fourth administration. In the intervening years Radical M. P.s and journalists had campaigned for a reduction of British naval estimates in the hope that Germany would reciprocate with comparable cuts. These activities were stepped up in the months following the Agadir crisis. Unlike those within the Cabinet, Haldane among them, who saw the 1911 crisis as a warning to put naval defenses in order, the Radicals regarded the incident as a warning against further intensification of the naval race.

Lord Morley, the most eminent of the Gladstonians, confessed to his friend F. W. Hirst that the Agadir crisis had left him "very anxious about foreign affairs." Hirst, closer to the radicalism of Cobden than that of Lloyd George, anticipated that "there will be a big reduction in naval expenditure if only friendly negotiations can be opened up with Germany." He imagined that the Germans, too, would be glad to abate naval construction, so long as they did not lose face. He appealed to Sir John Brunner to pressure the Government through the National Liberal Federation, which the latter headed and in whose counsels he exerted great influence.[16] On January 17, 1912, Brunner moved a resolution at a meeting of the executive committee of the

[14] Hugh O'Beirne to Grey, July 10, 1912, printed Cabinet memorandum, Harcourt Papers.

[15] Grey to Sir Edward Goschen, Feb. 12, 1912, CAB 37/109/19.

[16] Dec. 5, 1911, Brunner Papers.

Federation "in favour of a friendly understanding with Germany, with the object of procuring substantial measures of retrenchment." Accepted by the members of the committee with "perfect unanimity," the resolution was forwarded to Liberal leaders in each constituency, with a request for their endorsement "at as early a date as possible."[17] Brunner's appeal was dated February 8. At 7:30 that morning Lord Haldane reached Berlin.

Contrary to the view propounded in wartime years by Haldane's political enemies, he did not travel to Berlin, hat in hand, at the bidding of tightfisted, shortsighted Radicals. The initiative for his mission came from another quarter. It was true that the Liberal Government, burdened by its commitments to social reform and defense, would have welcomed financial relief. It was also true that the Government knew, as did its critics, of strong backbench agitation for some overture toward Germany. Colonel Repington, military correspondent for *The Times* and a familiar figure in the precincts of the war office, was correct in perceiving that Haldane's mission had a double-edged function: on the one hand, he explained to his editor, "the tension between us and Germany" had reached sufficiently dangerous proportions to make it necessary "to see whether any arrangement of a amicable character was open to us"; on the other, the Liberal leaders—Asquith, Grey, Lloyd George, and Churchill—hoped to convince the party's "Radical tail that all possible had been done to come to such an arrangement, so that, if it failed, the party might stomach the national consequences, namely increased [naval] estimates—or at all events not decreased naval estimates as [it had been] promised by McKenna." According to Repington, "the inner circle of the Cabinet," despairing of Haldane's chances, was nonetheless obliged to go along "to humour their followers"; this, he pointed out, was "as good a way" as any. "Personally," he concluded, "I do not anticipate any result from the mission except possibly some increased reasonableness among the Radical Left, whom Haldane will purr to sleep when he returns."[18]

By sending Haldane to Berlin, the British Government stood to achieve considerable gains at virtually no risk. He was authorized "not to make any agreement or to bind his colleagues," but simply to conduct conversations "*ad referendum*, . . . to ascertain whether there were

17 Circular letter of Feb. 8, 1912, *Ibid.*
18 Repington to Buckle, Feb. 8, 1912 [copy], Northcliffe Papers.

materials on the two sides for a possible agreement."[19] If the mission succeeded, it would insure substantial savings for the exchequer and presumably the European peace. If it failed, it would at least rally Radical and Labour support for projected military and naval increases.[20] In either case, the Government's critics, no less than its leading members, would find cause for satisfaction. Why then was the Haldane mission so much resented at the time and so maligned thereafter by those who might have been expected to most appreciate its value?

The fault rested partly with the sponsors of the mission, including Sir Edward Grey, and partly with the missionary himself. However skillfully Haldane might have put his case to the Germans, it cannot be denied that he put it to the British public in a way that was highly unfortunate. He agreed "thoroughly" with J. A. Spender "that to have conducted the negotiations publicly would have been to invite great risk of a preventive war."[21] He therefore traveled secretly, telling reporters who intercepted him at Dover that he was on his way to Berlin to investigate "university affairs." To lend a modicum of credence to his story, he brought along his brother John, known to share his interest in educational reform. "You may tell the *Daily Mail* unequivocally," he told the Berlin correspondent for that paper, "that my trip . . . is of an entirely non-political character. I am here for quite private reasons. I have many friends in Berlin, as you know, and I shall see them, I hope, as well as other interesting persons, but I am not here for politics." Repington, urging Buckle of *The Times* to "play the game as Grey has arranged it" and avoid disclosure of Haldane's real objectives, deplored the fact that the Government considered it necessary to deceive "the public whose intelligence [it] seems to rate rather low."[22]

British public opinion, considerably more astute than its elected leaders seemed to realize, was antagonized by the Government's failure to confirm the obvious. It was neither impressed nor amused by such

[19] Draft Memorandum for communication to the German Government, March 15, 1912, CAB 37/110/50; according to Lewis Harcourt, this was "not communicated—re-written by Ld. Haldane."

[20] Churchill, the first lord, calculated that his position would "be all the stronger in asking the Cabinet and the House of Commons for the necessary monies, if I could go hand in hand with the Chancellor of the Exchequer and testify that we had tried our best to secure a mitigation of the naval rivalry and failed." *World Crisis* (New York, 1923), I, 95.

[21] Haldane to Spender, Oct. 10, 1919, Spender Papers.

[22] Feb. 8, 1912 [copy], Northcliffe Papers.

charades as Haldane's reception for British journalists in a Berlin hotel room strewn with educational pamphlets. By February 10 the Berlin correspondent for the *Daily Mail* was able to report that "the fiction that Lord Haldane's presence is connected with 'University affairs' or any other non-political business is now no longer maintained in any responsible quarter. It has never been seriously entertained in any intelligent quarter, despite the smiling assurances of the distinguished visitor himself." With the Liberal Government distrusted by wide segments of British society, it is understandable why the Haldane mission generated such forebodings. Was Haldane sent to sell out imperial holdings as his pro-Boer, Home Rule comrades appeared to advocate? Was Perfidious Albion planning to repudiate her agreements with France and Russia? Was Haldane prepared to barter maritime supremacy for reciprocal Free Trade? Austen Chamberlain was typical in his refusal to accept as "the whole truth" the few facts that dribbled from the Government.[23] The Labour Party continued to demand that treaties be debated and approved by Parliament. The difficulty, as it was seen most clearly by the historian, Sir Charles Firth, was that the British Government was conducting diplomacy in the interests of a nation to which it dared not appeal. The foreign office had never awoken to the fact, he told Haldane in 1918, "that the British empire is a democracy and must be persuaded and convinced by being informed." For the most part, he noted, it had directed its publicity not to citizens at home so much as neutrals abroad. "It is not democratic control of foreign affairs which is needed in [the] future, but a new method of managing foreign affairs—a system by which the nation is efficiently and continuously informed about them in order that statesmen may be intelligently supported and policy consistently presented."[24] Six years before Woodrow Wilson articulated the demand for "open covenants, openly arrived at," the Haldane mission demonstrated the need for a fundamental rethinking of the public presentation of foreign policy.

The facts of Haldane's Berlin visit, long withheld from the public, are by this time readily available and well known. His cordial conversations with the Chancellor, Bethmann Hollweg, were followed by less encouraging interviews with the Kaiser and Admiral Tirpitz. Haldane

23 Feb. 21, 1912, *Politics from Inside*, p. 422.
24 Sept. 26, 1918, HP 5914, ff. 88–89.

provided his most straightforward and certainly his most succinct definition of his assignment not in any of the books he authored or inspired, but in a letter he wrote a decade later to assist Asquith, at work on his memoirs. The impetus for his 1912 journey, he reaffirmed, had come from Britain's determination to avoid estrangement from the continental powers and thereby retain her naval superiority over them. France's capitulation to German demands at the time of the Agadir crisis, followed by a Franco-German colonial agreement, had left British statesmen fearful of being isolated by a rapprochement between her partners in the entente and Germany.[25] "Put shortly," Haldane reminded Asquith,

my cardinal principle—settled before I left London—was that the size of the German navy made it impracticable to quit the Entente. As Grey always said among ourselves, the real reason for the Entente is that it was one way of retaining command of the sea. If we could not at least neutralise the navies of France and Russia, Germany could add to the power of a smaller fleet by making naval alliances. Thus we must stick to the Entente. But Grey, as I told Bethmann, was willing to try—if Germany would check her shipbuilding— . . . to enlarge this Entente [so] as to bring it to the form of a real Concert of Great Powers and so secure Germany as well as France and Russia.[26]

Haldane learned that this did not suit the purposes of the German government, which was unwilling to sacrifice its naval program and sought nothing less than a promise of British neutrality in continental affairs.

The voluminous literature on the Haldane mission and the gradual publication of diplomatic and political documents has not precluded vast discrepancies in historical interpretation. Haldane has been praised as a sincere and resourceful emissary who did the best anyone could under difficult circumstances, and who, at very least, achieved a more relaxed interchange between the two governments; on the other hand, his efforts have been written off as a complete failure to which he contributed by preparing insufficiently and speaking too freely. It is not the purpose of the present study to recount in any detail Haldane's

[25] As Grey took pains to point out to the French ambassador, "France had made her agreement with Germany as to Morocco; Russia had made hers as to the Baghdad Railway; but . . . we had not made any agreement with Germany as to any of the difficulties between us." Quoted in Grey to Bertie, Feb. 7, 1912, CAB 37/109/16.
[26] Sept. 1, 1922, Asquith Papers.

Berlin experiences nor to assess in any depth the effects of his visit upon international relations; both tasks have been attempted many times, with varying degrees of success.[27] Haldane's performance at Berlin will concern us only in connection with the suspicions and accusations to which it gave rise.

The Haldane mission was received through a haze of outraged emotion that made it difficult to distinguish shadow from substance. News that the secretary for war had crossed the Channel, bound for Berlin, diverted the London dailies from the Bertrand Stewart case that had in recent weeks dominated their front pages. Days before Haldane's departure, Stewart, a London solicitor, had been convicted of espionage by a Leipzig tribunal meeting in closed session. The *Daily Express* decried the "savage sentence" of three and a half years handed to Stewart, who joined three other British nationals imprisoned in Germany as spies. Even after the arrival of the new year British nerves continued to be jarred by the echo of the saber that the Kaiser had rattled the previous summer. Nor was German opinion any less agitated over recollections of the Agadir crisis. "One has only to refer to the German newspapers in the end of 1911 and the beginning of 1912," Haldane recalled after the war, "to see how excited German opinion was."[28]

The origins of the 1912 negotiations were sufficiently obscure to

---

[27] Most of the participants in the 1912 Anglo-German discussions provided personal accounts. Haldane, reviewing them for Asquith's benefit (letters of Sept. 1, 15, and 19, 1922, Asquith Papers), found Albert Ballin's version, quoted in Bernhard Huldermann's biography (Berlin, 1922), "pretty accurate." He also recommended the translations of Tirpitz's *Memoirs* (2 vols., London, 1919?) and Bethmann's *Reflections* (London, 1920) as "authoritative statements on what actually passed" during his visit a decade earlier. He cautioned Asquith not to accept the word of the Kaiser (*Memoirs*, London, 1922), who "is sure to have coloured his narrative unduly, though probably without intending to take liberties with his facts." In his opinion, the classic statement was of course his own. He had written a "dossier" after leaving office in 1915 which he allowed Harold Begbie to paraphrase in his *Vindication of Great Britain* (London, 1916); this document was used more extensively and to far greater advantage in Haldane's *Before the War* (London, 1920). His *Autobiography*, published posthumously in 1929, adds little of consequence. A diary that he kept in Berlin, printed as a Cabinet memorandum upon his return, appears as an appendix to Maurice's life of Haldane. Among the secondary accounts, both the Maurice and Sommer biographies cover the mission exhaustively. Lamar Cecil has recently written a life of Ballin (Princeton, 1967) with a firm grasp of German sources. Sir Ernest Woodward's *Great Britain and the German Navy* (Oxford, 1935) is encyclopedic, but lacks the incisiveness of the relevant chapter in the first volume of Arthur J. Marder's masterful chronicle of the Royal Navy, *From the Dreadnought to Scapa Flow*.

[28] Haldane to Spender, Oct. 10, 1919, Spender Papers.

allow both parties to presume that the other had taken the initiative. As a result, excessive expectations were aroused on both sides that were doomed to frustration. The suggestion came in fact from neither government but from two private but well placed individuals. Sir Ernest Cassel was a German-born London financier who had been a close friend of Edward VII and who knew Churchill and to a lesser extent other ministers. Albert Ballin, head of the Hamburg-Amerika Line, moved with equal ease in the upper reaches of German political society, so much so that the Kaiser was willing to overlook his Jewish extraction. Ballin, expecting a visit from Cassel in March, wrote early in 1912 to suggest that he bring along Churchill who might discuss naval problems with his German counterpart. Churchill, who declined the invitation, referred it to his colleagues, who delegated Cassel to travel to Berlin and sound out German authorities regarding more formal negotiations. With Ballin's help, he met Bethmann and the Kaiser on January 29, who approved the memorandum that he delivered and who extended an invitation for a British minister to visit Berlin.

The assignment fell to Haldane more or less by default. There are ample indications that the Germans held out hopes of a visit from Churchill or, better still, Grey. To send the first lord of the admiralty would have advertized the precise nature of the talks, and moreover would have entrusted a volatile situation to an intemperate individual. To send the foreign secretary, Asquith told the King, was felt to be "premature," and in the event of failure would be regarded a prognosis of war. There were not many ministers of adequate stature who at the same time were considered sufficiently dependable: the irascible Lord Loreburn, the petulant Lord Morley, the meandering Lord Crewe were all clearly out of the question. Haldane's qualifications were several. He could be trusted by Asquith and Grey as few of their colleagues could. In addition, he was *personna gratissima* in Berlin: he spoke the language and knew those with whom he would have to deal. He was better equipped to discuss naval matters than most people assumed, having recently entertained designs upon the admiralty and having given considerable thought to its needs and strategy. And best of all Lord Haldane had a pretense for a visit to Berlin that would allow him to cover his tracks. As chairman of the London University Commission, he had gone several times to discuss technical education and had intended another visit about this time. Grey proposed, and the members of the

Cabinet agreed, to commission Haldane "who had occasion to go to Germany" to open negotiations with the German government "at the same time."[29]

Haldane, who did not campaign for the assignment, saw the humor of having "the War Minister . . . transformed into the Peace Minister."[30] Others, on the whole, were less amused. The Radicals who had pressed for Anglo-German discussions were dismayed by the aura of secrecy and had mixed feelings about the selection: Morley, who soon "removed his scruples," initially raised doubts "as to the wisdom of Haldane's mission."[31] Permanent officials at the foreign office, including Sir Arthur Nicolson, considered the procedure highly irregular and Haldane insufficiently steeped in the arts of diplomacy. Austen Chamberlain summed up the feeling of his fellow-Unionists when he described the affair as "singularly ill-timed and the representative ill-chosen": the German government, so far as he could tell, had not provided adequate assurances of its good intentions to warrant talks, let alone concessions on the part of Great Britain.[32] While the Liberal press responded with cautious optimism, the Unionist journals treated the matter either with silent disapprobation or outright hostility. Most Opposition editors had long feared a Liberal sellout to Germany and they now came to look upon Haldane, whom few had particularly liked, as the personification of that shameful policy.

The little that was known about the arrangements for Haldane's visit to Berlin produced immediate misgivings among those who later demanded his removal from office. The *National Review*, always in the forefront, looked with scorn upon Cassel, who accompanied Haldane, and upon Ballin, who welcomed him to the German capital: "Germans doubtless approve the intervention of financiers in international affairs and know well how to make use of them in German interests, but Englishmen prefer that their Government should keep clear of the Cosmopolitans of *la haute* finance." It had surely not escaped the attention of Maxse, editor of the *Review*, that both Cassel and Ballin were of Jewish birth. "What is the use of having a Foreign Office or an Embassy," he asked, "if international affairs are to be transacted by the Ballins and the Cassels?" Maxse implied inside knowledge that the ordinary diplomatic channels had been circumvented because the

[29] Prime Minister to Sovereign, Feb. 3, 1912, CAB 41/33/34.
[30] Haldane to his mother, Feb. 19, 1912, HP 5987, f. 64.
[31] Fitzroy, II, 477.   [32] Feb. 13, 1912, *Politics from Inside*, p. 412.

foreign office disapproved so strongly of the mission. Haldane had traveled to Germany, he alleged, against the better judgment, even against the wishes of Sir Edward Grey, who was being elbowed aside "by his intimate but treacherous friend." The supposition was absurd, given the fact that Haldane and Grey continued to share the same roof; yet it convinced many who thought they detected two competing British foreign policies, one decently pro-French, the other insidiously pro-German. When a Garter was conferred upon Grey in mid-February, the *Daily Mail* chose to regard it "as a sign that his foreign policy . . . commands the complete approval of the King, and has no relation to Lord Haldane's 'conversations.' "

In the absence of any official explanation, rumors abounded, nearly all to Haldane's disadvantage. To many critics he appeared not only the executor but also the author of the Government's misguided policy. Perhaps his visit was something he had planned the previous August over luncheon with his imperial guest. Had he been propelled by his "colossal vanity, love of publicity and passion for intrigue" (to quote Maxse) or had he been handpicked by the Kaiser who recognized in him an accomplice or dupe? "Not long ago," the *Daily Express* recalled, the German emperor had told Lord Lonsdale that "Englishmen would see things in a different light if British Ministers would take the trouble to come and see us personally. The man whom I consider best qualified," he added, "is my friend Lord Haldane." This was praise that damned. In 1915 F. S. Oliver, who numbered many influential Unionists among his friends, looked back upon the Haldane mission and "guessed" that Haldane had sold the idea and himself to his colleagues: "the desire of the Kaiser that Lord Haldane should be sent was met half-way by the desire of Lord Haldane to go forth. . . . Ready on the shortest notice to mind everybody else's business, he was allowed to mind too much of it; and he appears to have minded most of it rather ill than well. He was no more suited to act for the Foreign Office than King Alfred was to watch the housewife's cakes."[33]

At first Haldane was only vaguely aware of the aspersions cast upon him. The applause he received from those closest to him ("The Cabinet thanked me for a 'success as brilliant as it was unexpected,' " he proudly reported to his mother on February 14[34]) drowned out the murmurs of those who stood further back. Later, when his critics grew more

[33] *Ordeal By Battle* (London, 1915), pp. 289 ff.   [34] HP 5987, f. 58.

vocal, he consoled himself that most of them would have been hostile in any case. Diffident by nature, he thought it best "to maintain silence and leave all speaking to others."[35] There were several considerations that prompted this decision. In the weeks after his return, he was sanguine that an Anglo-German naval formula, which he expected any day, would speak for itself. When that hope had evaporated, he still hesitated to defend himself for fear that he might cause Grey additional effort or embarrassment. Nor did he wish to jeopardize the diplomatic work that his mission had initiated and in which he continued to take an active hand.

When Haldane's wartime assailants denounced his diplomatic activities, they referred not only to his brief visit to Berlin but also to the months of secret negotiations that followed. During the spring and summer of 1912, he met frequently with the German ambassador, alone or with Grey. It gave him inestimable pleasure to play a vital role in attempts to keep the peace, knowing what a "comfort" it was to his mother that her "son is able to do something to help all these millions of people to a better understanding of each other."[36] For her sake he remained optimistic. "You will be rejoiced to hear that I had a very private and personal communication from the German ambassador last night," he told her on March 13. "Despite threatened difficulties the Berlin mission promises to bear its fruit. But it is premature to be certain."[37] A week later, he expressed disappointment that "for the moment Germany should not be responding as fully as we wish to our overtures, but I still think that good results may come."[38]

It is not difficult to see in retrospect where misunderstandings—and willful distortions—arose. As negotiations dragged on without achieving tangible results, both sides took Haldane to task. The German authorities broadly hinted that he had made promises that his colleagues refused to honor. There were those within the Cabinet who began to wonder as much as their Unionist opponents whether Haldane had dispensed concessions too freely. Lewis Harcourt, the colonial secretary, marked with an indignant question mark his copy of a Cabinet document citing German reports that Haldane had offered generous helpings of Belgian and Portuguese Africa. Harcourt, who reveled in

[35] Haldane to his mother, Feb. 15, 1912, HP 5987, f. 60.
[36] Haldane to his mother, March 3, 1912, HP 5987, f. 79.
[37] HP 5987, ff. 100–101.   [38] Mar. 20, 1912, HP 5987, f. 110.

his reputation as a pro-German, was authorized to notify the German ambassador that there could be no territorial changes without Belgian or Portuguese approval, but Count Metternich remained firm "that this was not the impression created by Haldane in Berlin."[39] A month after he completed his mission, Haldane felt the need to defend himself in a tersely worded memorandum to the Cabinet. He denied insinuations that he had assumed "full powers to conclude a binding agreement" on the part of the British Government, that he had offered "unconditionally" Belgian or Portuguese colonies to the Germans ("I merely stated that these were places which might very well come into a general bargain"), or that he had accorded his approval to the Novelle, the German naval bill.[40] It was Grey's opinion that the Germans were "trying to make out that Haldane offered a complete bargain," so that they could ascribe to British backsliding their decision to persevere with naval increases.[41]

Discussions between Germany and Britain regarding the economic development if not the parceling out of Portugal's African colonies were terminated only by the intercession of war. Contemporaries entertained exaggerated notions of what was at stake. Although Haldane was barely involved, he nonetheless incurred full opprobrium. Lovat Fraser, whose pieces usually appeared in the Northcliffe press, wrote numerous articles on the abortive Anglo-German colonial negotiations for the *National Review*. In the issue for November 1917, he threw "Fresh Light on Haldaneism" by linking proposals to reallocate the Portuguese colonies with the Anglo-German Baghdad railway agreement of June 1914. He assured his readers that the terms of that agreement, fortunately negated by the war, were "amazingly detrimental to British interests," for they had allotted Germany "an immense belt of tropical Africa, stretching from sea to sea, including almost all of the Belgian Congo, the French Congo territory, and much of Portuguese West Africa." Prodded by Fraser, Maxse implored Unionist politicians to press the Government for the complete text of the Baghdad railway agreement so that "Haldaneism" might be discredited once and for all.

Not only was Lord Haldane, the Liberal Imperialist, accused of insufficient regard for imperial values, but he was also reputed to have

---

[39] Memorandum by Harcourt, March 9, 1912, CAB 37/110/44.
[40] Memorandum by Haldane, March 11, 1912, CAB 37/110/46.
[41] Grey to Goschen, March 11, 1912 [copy], FO 800/62.

been willing to concede Germany naval parity. His own ambiguities fostered this impression. On his return journey from Berlin he disingenuously denied to a *Daily Mail* reporter any knowledge "of the impending increases of the German Army and Navy" (these were "in preparation," he explained, and not yet available), neglecting to mention the fact that a confidential "copy of the bulky print of the impending fleet law" weighed down his luggage. He later strenuously maintained that he had resisted any urge to thumb through the document, delivering it unopened to Winston Churchill, who promptly laid it before British naval experts. It was only on February 14, when the admiralty furnished its report, that he learned the provisions of the bill.[42] Others, including the Kaiser, disputed Haldane's disclaimer and argued that he had not only been fully informed of Germany's projected naval increases, but that he had taken no exception to them.

Taking Haldane's word that he knew no more about Germany's naval intentions when he left Berlin than he did when he had arrived four days earlier, namely that she was planning a third squadron to increase the size and mobility of her fleet, his subsequet letdown appears all the greater. Churchill reported to his colleagues "that the most serious feature of the new German proposals is, not so much the addition of three battleships to their present statutory programme; or even the creation of a third Battle Squadron; but the contemplated increase in the personnel of the fleet . . . amounting by the year 1920, to 15,000 fresh naval recruits."[43] Without a knowledge of these auxiliary provisions, Haldane's discussions at Berlin could only have been superficial and self-delusive. He nonetheless managed to extract a promise which Churchill cited as the one "tangible result of the Haldane mission,"[44] that Germany would delay indefinitely the construction of one of the three ships for which the Novelle provided. However significant in strategic and economic terms, this cutback was overshadowed by attendant increases.

Greater concessions could have been bought from Germany, but only at the price of formal assurances that Britain would observe unconditional neutrality in the event of European war. In effect, this would dismember the entente, clearing the way for either German aggression

---

[42] Haldane to Asquith, Sept. 19, 1922, Asquith Papers; also *Before the War*, p. 60.
[43] Prime Minister to Sovereign, Feb. 15, 1912, CAB 41/33/36.
[44] *World Crisis*, I, 111.

upon France and Russia, or the possible combination of those powers with Germany against Britain. For more than a month after his journey, Haldane remained hopeful that a mutual declaration of peaceful intentions—without the so-called neutrality clause—would be sufficient to retard, if not halt, the German naval program. Either he, Harcourt, or Grey[45] met daily with the German representatives in London, Count Metternich and Baron von Kuhlmann, to devise some sort of verbal compromise. Harcourt visited Kuhlmann in the early evening on March 14, and went to see Haldane at eleven o'clock. That afternoon Metternich had led Haldane to believe that the issue of British neutrality was not crucial to the proposed political formula. Harcourt's impression from Kuhlmann was quite the contrary. It was only when Grey returned to Queen Anne's Gate close to midnight that Haldane learned of "a note from Metternich saying the formula was not wholly satisfactory and required the neutrality clause."

Harcourt saw no stumbling block. He took the line that a " 'neutrality' declaration was no more than we had put in our formula" and posed no impediment to Britain's continued participation in the entente. According to the pencilled minutes he took of a Cabinet meeting on March 16, McKenna and Haldane joined him in "press[ing] for [an] extension of [the] formula," presumably to cover an offer of conditional British neutrality. Grey, who related Germany's "amazing" offer to Haldane to "withdraw Novelle on our giving a 'formula,' " agreed to go only so far as to advise Berlin that Britain contemplated "no unprovoked attack or aggression," and would "pursue no aggressive policy towards her." He hastened to add that "aggression upon Germany is not the subject and forms no *part of* any treaty, understanding, or combination, to which England is now a party, nor will she become a party to anything that has such an object." Harcourt continued that Haldane recounted an interview that day with Count Metternich, who had revealed that Tirpitz and Bethmann Hollweg were engaged in a "desperate fight," the former demanding immediate publication of the full naval law and the latter preaching restraint. Haldane prophesied that "one or other must win this week," and he urged the Cabinet to do nothing that would weaken the hand of the German moderates, led by Bethmann, in their struggle against the irreconcilables.

[45] Except where otherwise noted, I have based these paragraphs upon Harcourt's personal memoranda of March 14 and 16, Harcourt Papers.

On the following day, word reached Haldane that the tug-of-war between Bethmann and Tirpitz had ended in the Kaiser's decision to heed the admiral's advice. Ballin had telegraphed Cassel, who contacted Haldane immediately, that "the Emperor is of opinion that the simple and otherwise 'very insufficient Neutrality treaty' cannot make any difference" to German naval requirements.[46] It therefore came as no surprise to Grey on the 19th, when Metternich informed him that because Britain's "promise not to make or join in an unprovoked attack upon Germany was so elastic as to be valueless," Germany was forced to persevere with her program as outlined in the Novelle.[47] "Things do not promise well," Haldane wrote his sister on the 18th. "The new Fleet Law will go on. . . . Nothing but an *alliance*—which we dare not think of—would now stop the Law." Still, he expressed his "hope to lay the foundations of better things, this notwithstanding."[48] Discussions continued long after either party had ceased to expect anything to come of them. By April 10 Asquith was ready to "confess" to Grey that he was "becoming more and more doubtful as to the wisdom of prolonging these discussions with Germany about a formula. Nothing, I believe, will meet her purpose which falls short of a promise on our part of neutrality: a promise we cannot give. And she makes no firm or solid offer, even in exchange for that."[49]

During the spring of 1912 Haldane strengthend his claim to the dubious honor of being the Cabinet member for German affairs. Although formal contacts had passed to the foreign and colonial secretaries, it was he who continued to appear in the public eye the statesman most concerned. In early May rumors circulated that he would leave the war office to succeed Sir Edward Goschen as ambassador to Berlin. The *Daily Express* warmly endorsed the idea, but Haldane told his mother it was completely out of the question. Uncertain of the diplomatic projects afoot—the staunchly Liberal *Daily News* bluntly requested a declaration of intent from the Government on April 22— the British press grabbed at any straw. When Lord Morley visited Germany in mid-May, Fleet Street mistakenly surmised that this was a follow-up to the Haldane mission. On May 21, when Haldane left

[46] Cassel to Haldane, March 17, 1912, HP 5909, f. 207.

[47] Grey to Goschen, March 19, 1912, printed Cabinet memorandum, Harcourt Papers.

[48] HP 6011, f. 201.   [49] Grey Papers, FO 800/100.

for his annual German holiday, there was speculation that he went to complete the work he had begun in February. He was annoyed to have his "quiet peaceful holiday" turned into a "public affair," and vowed that he would "not come again to Germany while I am in office except on business."[50] The German newspapermen, who followed him everywhere, struck him as "ridiculous," going so far as to report that his brother, who accompanied him, was "Mr. Asquith in disguise, and that we are here to make a treaty."[51] Yet whether the German papers were any worse than the British was debatable: the June *National Review* derided Haldane's latest pilgrimage to Germany, "where we devoutly wish he would take up his permanent abode"; a month later, it featured a full-scale diatribe against "the chief instructor and mis-leader of the Cabinet upon German policy."

Haldane returned after a fortnight, exhilarated by the mountain air and genuinely touched by the welcome he had received from the academics and townspeople of southern Germany. More than ever he saw himself the interpreter of Britain to the German people and of Germany to the British. He established a working relationship with the new German ambassador, Baron Marschall von Bieberstein, and delivered a series of sententious speeches, often in German, on behalf of Anglo-German friendship. Once again, and with no greater success, he appealed personally to *The Times* for support. Even so, he noted an improvement in the tone of British and German journals alike. That autumn he was offered an honorary doctorate by the University of Göttingen, more in recognition of his diplomatic services than a compliment to his scholarship. It was conferred in June 1913, on the occasion of the twenty-fifth anniversary of the Kaiser's accession.

Not expecting to work miracles, Haldane nonetheless believed that individuals could make valuable contributions to international understanding. He did not underestimate the gravity of the situation, nor the forces arrayed against him. Not the least of the difficulties, he realized, was an absence of tact and prudence on the part of the German government. He perceived at once the implications of a speech made by Bethmann during the Balkan crisis of late 1912 "about Germany backing Austria through thick and thin";[52] this would not only have an

[50] Haldane to his sister, June 1, 1912, HP 6011, f. 207.
[51] May 27, 1912, HP 5987, f. 208.
[52] Haldane to his mother, Dec. 4, 1912, HP 5988, ff. 217–18.

unsettling effect upon east European affairs, but would also impede Anglo-German cooperation by posing an implicit threat to Russia. It was precisely this unleashing of Austria in the Balkans that paved the way for the world war of 1914–18.

Members of the Cabinet, caught off guard by the events of early August 1914 wondered like other Englishmen how they could have been so blind to German intentions. Charles Hobhouse, the postmaster general, described to Lord Buxton the Government's shock to learn "from America that for three months before last August the Chicago 'packers' were working night and day for the German Government, and in the face of this and other corroborative evidence it seems impossible to believe that the whole of this terrible suffering is not the outcome of a deliberate plan of Tirpitz and Moltke to crush Europe at an opportune moment."[53] To outsiders the explanation appeared simple: Lord Haldane had deceived his countrymen out of irresponsibility, vanity, love of Germany, party interests, or a combination of any of these factors. Lord Midleton recalled that Haldane had returned from his mission to Berlin "profoundly convinced of the imminence of war," but had hesitated to speak his mind at a time when "the utmost tension existed between the parties on the Home Rule Question, and the fear of rebellion in Ulster was nearing its height." Unwilling to sacrifice party advantage by diverting attention from Irish affairs, Haldane— according to Midleton—defeated Unionist proposals in the House of Lords to accelerate recruiting and munitions production with facile assurances "that nothing was needed." Midleton insisted that it was this event which prompted eventual Unionist demands for Haldane's exclusion from office.[54]

The truth of the matter is that Lord Haldane had been neither blind nor clairvoyant. He had hesitated to take any public step that might endanger the secret negotiations that continued in London. At the same time, he had hesitated to upset the precarious balance of political forces within Germany and diplomatic forces within Europe. Belonging to a political breed that saw government as an instrument to restrain rather than manipulate public passions, he had taken for granted that if enlightened statesmen were permitted to operate in a calm atmosphere they could remove the sources of friction between Britain and Germany

[53] Dec. 4, 1914, Buxton Papers.   [54] *Records and Reactions*, pp. 283–84.

as they had earlier in the century removed those between Britain and France and Britain and Russia. His only fear was that irrational forces would intervene, forcing statesmen into intractable positions. For this reason, he had said as little as possible to as few people as possible so as not to provoke a vindictive spirit in British society that would give substance to the arguments of German Anglophobes.

Haldane found himself with two alternatives: he could admit that he had thoroughly miscalculated German intentions, knowing that this would raise embarrassing questions about the numerous times he had postured as an expert on German affairs; or, if he liked, he could insist that he had clearly foreseen the German peril, knowing that this would raise embarrassing questions about his failure to alert his country-men. Either was self-incriminating. But he made matters worse by vacillating between the two. In a public address on November 17, 1915, he denied that his knowledge had ever been "as great as that of many wise people who talk now," and assured his audience that whatever information came his way was relayed "not to where it would con-ceivably lead to mischief, but to the minds of my colleagues," who had quietly acted upon it.[55] But on other occasions he implied quite the contrary. Lord Grey, Sir Edward's Tory cousin, was incensed by a piece Haldane had contributed to the August 7 *Nation* ("Democracy and Ideas") from which he inferred "that the reason why he [Haldane] did not convey to the British Democracy the real nature of the German Peril was because Demos was in an unreflecting mood"; writing to Munro Ferguson, he likened Haldane to the proverbial "Foolish Virgin whose lamp was untrimmed," and added that Haldane had gone "one better than the Foolish Virgin, for he was busily employed in blowing out everybody else's lamp."[56]

Haldane trusted that his name would be cleared as soon as the foreign office opened its files. Unfortunately, those upon whom he relied for rehabilitation were men of declining power and growing reticence. At the behest of Grey and Asquith, F. D. Acland asked Austen Chamber-lain's advice on December 1, 1914, about a memorandum on pre-war Anglo-German negotiations drawn up in September, but still unpub-lished; since that time, much of the material it contained had been

---

[55] *Glasgow Herald*, Nov. 18, 1915.

[56] Dec. 1, 1915, Novar Papers, National Library of Australia; copy courtesy of G. C. L. Hazelhurst.

"duplicated" in a twopenny pamphlet by Sir Edward Cook, *How Britain Strove for Peace*. (The November *National Review* had cited Cook's pamphlet as confirmation of its charges against Haldane.) Acland confided to Chamberlain his personal "feeling that while any proof that we made genuine efforts towards reductions of armaments may do good with the pacifists—who are not now a very influential section in the Country—it might expose us to attack . . . from the opposite section." Chamberlain replied that he, to the contrary, considered publication of all pre-war diplomatic documents overdue. But Grey, who had the last word, decided (Acland told Chamberlain) "that we should not at present give the Germans fresh opportunities for misinterpretation and attack by any publication of new material." Nor did Grey "wish to give himself or his department the extra strain of preparing papers and having to deal with all the questions which would at once be raised here and in neutral countries" by the publication of this twenty-page memorandum.[57] Haldane was disappointed, but took heart from reports "that the information about negotiations was asked for" by Chamberlain.[58]

Even after he had been dropped from the Government, Haldane continued to rely upon the foreign office to make clear the facts and purpose of his Berlin mission. He was convinced, he told Lord Mersey, to whom he unburdened his mind ("my life is uncertain and I should like to feel that I had told the story to someone who could in case of need repeat it") that "it was mainly if not entirely out of that visit that the difficulties which led to his retirement had arisen."[59] Yet it was only when the *Norddeutsche Allgemeine Zeitung*, a semi-official German publication with a large American circulation, featured an account of the 1912 deliberations that Grey felt impelled to act. He announced his intention in a Cabinet memorandum on August 13, 1915, and in a letter to *The Times* on the 26th. But the white paper that appeared five days later was a grave disappointment to Haldane, who appeared in it fleetingly as a glorified messenger sent to receive terms from the German government; colonial questions were ignored, and there were only cursory references to such controversial topics as naval reductions

---

[57] Acland's letters of Dec. 1, 1914 and Jan. 20, 1915, and a copy of Chamberlain's reply of Dec. 7, 1914, are among the Chamberlain Papers, AC 13/1/2 ff.

[58] Haldane to Gosse, Dec. 24, 1914, Gosse Papers.

[59] Memorandum by Lord Mersey, Nov. 16, 1915, Mersey Papers.

and the issue of British neutrality. The *Glasgow Herald*, after its "perusal" of the document, voiced surprise that Haldane could have nursed his "uneasiness in silence," knowing as he did what was in the offing; it repeated "vain regrets" that he had not warned his countrymen so that "we should have been better prepared for the struggle that we were in August of last year." *The Times*, evaluating this latest disclosure about the Haldane mission, declared that nothing "now published, or ever likely to be published, will justify that unfortunate experiment in diplomatic intercourse." After looking forward to the white paper with more than casual interest, Haldane wrote a firm but well-mannered protest to Grey, pointing out that the document implied that he had accepted the German formula that the Government later rejected; this, he explained, "has enabled the hostile press to suggest that I was ready . . . to lower the flag of my country. The result is the usual shower of abusive letters and articles. . . . Between the reproaches of having failed to organise the Army and of having interfered with and embarrassed your foreign policy, I have not now many rags of character left."[60]

On July 14, 1916, feeling that he could wait no longer for redemption Haldane "sent for" Grey "and asked him to clear my character." He described the scene in a letter to his sister: Grey was "quite nice, tho' I told him some plain things." He agreed to "raise debate at once in the H. of Lords [he had just taken a peerage] and make a statement." Haldane gave him "the points I wanted put." Grey remained "averse to publishing any papers," but Haldane thought that a public declaration would do nearly as well. And this time, he confidently predicted, Grey "will . . . move."[61] Again he waited in vain. Churchill wrote "an admirable article" in his defense that Haldane considered "very courageous and generous of him." But Grey, "*per contra*, . . . is showing signs of running away from the debate he proposed in the H. of Lords. I think he fears that the French may not think him sufficiently *acharné*."[62]

Asquith was no better. When a backbencher asked that summer whether material pertaining to the Haldane mission could now be published, he skirted the issue. "I feel strongly," he advised Haldane, "that our previous decision against publication is still right. Publication will involve disclosure of the negotiations with regard to the

---

[60] Haldane to Grey, Sept. 2, 1915, HP 5912, ff. 94–95.
[61] July 15, 1916, HP 6012, f. 144.
[62] Haldane to his sister, July 31, 1916, HP 6012, f. 146.

Portuguese colonies and to the Baghdad railway and to my mind during the war at least this cannot be contemplated. In view of this consideration, do you not agree?"[63] Haldane was not quite sure that he did. He replied that he was willing to defer to the public interest, but pointed out that recent German publications contained "a full account not only of my visit but of Grey's subsequent negotiations about the Portuguese colonies." In any event, he beseeched Asquith to take care not to reply to the question "in such a fashion as to suggest that it is in my interest that these conversations should not be published."[64]

By this time Haldane had come to realize that Asquith and Grey were struggling too hard to save themselves to worry about a third reputation which they looked upon, not without regret, as a lost cause. From the materials in his possession, he assembled a personal narrative of the past decade that he dictated to "a stolid lady shorthand-writer" whom he had sworn to secrecy.[65] She produced several typewritten copies of the one-hundred-fifty-page document, strictly for private circulation. (There was great anxiety until he recovered the copy, returned by Lord Rosebery, that was stolen in a mail shipment at Euston Station.) With Edmund Gosse's help, the dossier—as they called it—was brought to the attention of a wide range of public figures, including Lords Morley, Selborne, Lansdowne, and Islington, the Archbishop of Canterbury, Lord Robert Cecil, Balfour, Sir Arthur Nicolson, H. A. L. Fisher, Gilbert Murray, Jan Christian Smuts, such civil servants as Sir Robert Morant and Sir John Sankey, and such journalists as John St. Loe Strachey, C. P. Scott, and H. W. Massingham. Lord Derby found it "a very striking vindication of your conduct."[66] John Buchan loaned a copy to F. S. Oliver, who, "after a very careful reading," had "a much warmer personal regard for my fellow-Scotsman than I had when I began it." Oliver professed his inability to "conceive how Lord Haldane was able to carry such a colossal burden of work on his shoulders. Frankly, I think he attempted more than any human creature could hope to accomplish and that this is the explanation of a great deal"; for this, he blamed Asquith.[67] Others came away from the dossier with much

[63] Aug. 8, 1916, HP 5913, ff. 50–51.
[64] Aug. 9, 1916 [draft], HP 5913, ff. 52–53.
[65] Haldane to Gosse, April 25, 1916, Gosse Papers.
[66] Derby to Haldane, Feb. 22, 1918, HP 5914, f. 10.
[67] Oliver to Buchan, June 16, 1916, HP 5913, f. 22.

the same impression. Lord Knutsford, converted by what he had read, wrote Haldane that his "blood boils at the F. O. refusal to you to be allowed to publish now all that took place, especially as Grey and Asquith never speak up for you. You helped them as no other man in England could have or did—and they sit and let you be abused. Both men are personally attractive to me, but I cannot understand their conduct to you."[68] It was "clear" to Sir Charles Firth that Haldane had given his superiors "exact and adequate information," and "equally clear that they did not adequately appreciate its significance. . . . If I were Lloyd George or Asquith," he postulated, "I should be glad to have as little said on the subject as possible."[69]

Haldane was uncertain what more he dared do with his dossier. He declined an offer to have it published in the *Edinburgh Review*, but allowed Harold Begbie, a well-meaning journalist, to borrow heavily from it for his *Vindication of Great Britain*, largely a vindication of Haldane. Critics were therefore not entirely mistaken when they suspected that Begbie's book had been ghostwritten by its subject. Haldane's friends regretted that he dissipated the arguments in his defense in such a haphazard, anecdotal fashion. The Archbishop of Canterbury agreed with Elizabeth Haldane that Begbie had not "written in the way which will carry most weight."[70] Haldane was aware that some of his supporters "resent its tone a little, but that does not matter."[71] More important to him was the fact that it sold handsomely ("W. H. Smith and Sons sent for 1,000 copies straight off, as soon as they had looked at it"), and at last his case was being heard. For this he was "very grateful" to Begbie, who had, as the situation required, wielded "the weapon of a trained bruiser who is encountering a furious mob."[72]

Begbie's *Vindication*, as Haldane well knew, was no substitute for an authorized edition of diplomatic documents. That, however, had to await Ramsay MacDonald's government, which redeemed Haldane in many ways. As many had feared, Begbie merely took the edge from Haldane's own account of prewar diplomacy, *Before the War*, that appeared early in 1920. This was essentially the complete dossier, minus its appendixes, and it pleased its author by selling more copies in its

[68] Sept. 10, 1917, Gosse Papers.
[69] Firth to Haldane, Sept. 26, 1918, HP 5914, ff. 83 ff.
[70] Oct. 17, 1916, HP 6026, f. 95.
[71] Haldane to his sister, Oct. 21, 1916, HP 6012, f. 157.
[72] Haldane to Gosse, letters of Oct. 14, 17, 19, 1916, Gosse Papers.

its first week than any book at Selfridge's "excepting a fashionable anti-German novel."[73] By this time, Haldane had witnessed a strong reaction in his favor that came with the armistice. In the closing weeks of 1918, he found the British press "full of my efforts in preparing the country for war," and he noted that Asquith had paid an oblique tribute to him in a campaign speech at Hull on December 5 and another, more pronounced, six days later at Fife. He could barely contain his amusement when he told his mother that "the Liberals," in their bid for electoral support, were "now clinging" to his prewar record "as a defence of themselves."[74] It was in vain. In the "khaki" election of December 1918, a straight line of Asquithian Liberals went down in defeat, and their leader, already evicted from the premiership, lost the seat Haldane had helped him obtain in 1886.

[73] Haldane to his sister, Jan. 20, 1918, HP 6013, f. 79.
[74] Dec. 6 and 12, HP 6000, ff. 202–203, 212.

CHAPTER IV

THE UNEASIEST SEAT IN THE REALM

Ah, my Lords, it is indeed painful to have to sit upon a woolsack which is stuffed with such thorns as these!

—THE LORD CHANCELLOR, *Iolanthe*

Four months passed between Lord Haldane's return from Berlin in February 1912 and his appointment to the lord chancellorship. The announcement came as no surprise. Every since Asquith had become premier, it was assumed that at the first possible moment he would bestow upon his friend the prize that he was unable to extract from Campbell-Bannerman in 1905. At the same time, it was expected that Lord Loreburn, whom Campbell-Bannerman had placed upon the woolsack, would stand down. It was well known that Loreburn felt increasingly estranged in a Cabinet that had come to be dominated by Liberal Imperialists. But it was not until the morning of June 4, 1912, that he sent for Haldane and entrusted him to convey his letter of resignation to the King. An hour and a half later, Haldane had his royal audience:

"Who is to succeed?" said the King. I replied I did not know, as the Prime Minister was away. "My choice, if the Prime Minister agrees," said the King, "would be a man who was quite capable of combining three offices—ambassador at Berlin, Lord Chancellor, and War Secretary. I know one who would do them all easily!" (This was his joke!)

Haldane took for granted, as did his colleagues, that he would be named. ". . . It would be a pleasure to you," he told his mother. "But I can honestly say that I do not much care whether I am Lord Chancellor of Great Britain or not."[1]

[1] June 5, 1912, HP 5988, ff. 4–6; writing to her on the 16th, he revealed his feeling "that it is the place you have always desired for me." HP 5988, f. 23.

There was a deep ideological gulf between the two Liberal lord chancellors, a fact reflected in the strong words that often passed between them. Loreburn distrusted Haldane, "with his closed mind and passion for intrigue,"[2] as a warmonger; the latter, in turn, regarded Loreburn as a disgruntled Little Englander. The outgoing chancellor took stock of their differences in a letter he wrote his successor: ". . . You have always been an Imperialist 'au fond' and always, in my opinion, it is quite impossible to reconcile Imperialism with the Liberal creed which we professed and on the face of which we received the support of the country."[3] It was on grounds of poor health that Loreburn surrendered the woolsack, but his subsequent career left no doubt that he had fallen out once and for all with his colleagues.

News of Haldane's appointment was well received by lawyers who recognized his capabilities, by friendly politicians who considered it a fitting reward for past service, and not least of all by Opposition journalists who celebrated his departure from the war office. The *Daily Express* admitted that "within his limitations, he [had] worked hard and planned soundly" as war minister, but it respectfully suggested that he would be more in his element upon the woolsack. "Lord Haldane is in his proper place at last," Horatio Bottomley told the readers of *John Bull*: "But won't his judgments be a study! He can never say 'No' to a question under 20 minutes! Still he knows something about law." Leo Maxse in the *National Review* refused to concede Haldane even this: "He was always a prodigious gas-bag, but never a great lawyer, and as he has abandoned the law for nearly seven years in order to play ducks and drakes with the British Army. . . , he is clearly unfitted for the lord chancellorship." But Maxse consoled himself that "for the moment it does not make very much matter who is lord chancellor," and he cited Loreburn for "conspicuous service to his country . . . by bribing Lord Haldane . . . out of the war office and on to the woolsack, where he will be comparatively harmless. . . ."

When the House of Lords assembled on June 11, Haldane sat in "the great Lord Eldon's place." He described the scene to his mother in terms designed to afford her the greatest possible satisfaction: "In long and solemn procession—preceded by macebearer—purse bearer—

[2] C. P. Scott's memorandum of Dec. 2, 1911, Scott Papers, Add. MSS. 50, 901, f. 51.

[3] [June] 1912, HP 5909, ff. 281–82.

and followed by train bearer and others—I passed along the corridors yesterday and took my seat on the Woolsack as Lord Chancellor."[4] To Edmund Gosse he did not hesitate to admit that there were "too many clothes in this office. . . ."[5] Still, he was now "free from the worry of the war office and . . . thankful for the change."[6]

As lord chancellor, Haldane found anything but the tranquility he had anticipated. He was quickly at work upon bureaucratic and judicial reforms ("It reminds me of war office days"[7]). And as the war office had no representative in the Lords, where its foremost critics sat, Haldane was obliged to defend the Government's army policy in arduous debate. Elizabeth Haldane appealed to Sir Kenneth Muir Mackenzie, permanent secretary to the lord chancellor, to keep her brother from over exertion, and he replied with similar fears:

It is preposterous that he should continue to do army work, or to be responsible for such matters as the Insurance Act; nor should he continue chairman of commissions or other interests during his chancellorship—amongst other reasons is this, that the lord chancellor should be so sublime and authoritative as not to take any part in any sublunary things or to be expected to be engaged in controversies where differences of opinion might prevail.[8]

This advice would have been difficult for any lord chancellor to follow, but impossible for Haldane, one of the few Liberals in a strongly antagonistic upper house and the author of several of the policies under heaviest fire. Nor was he disposed to sit back and leave unpleasant tasks to others. He undertook the defense of a wide range of Government measures, including several about which he nursed private doubts. Attacking his speech in the Lords on August 5, 1913, the *Daily Express* recognized him as the Government's "general utility spokesman." These were the years in which he secured his position as scapegoat for Liberalism.

Military matters continued to claim the better part of Haldane's attention, so much so that he was moved upon occasion to regret his transfer from the war office. His successor, Colonel J. E. B. Seely, lacked the stature to defend the policy he had inherited; and as the debate became more heated, contemporaries looked beyond Seely to

<hr />

[4] June 12, 1912, HP 5988, f. 18.   [5] June 12, 1912, Gosse Papers.
[6] Haldane to his mother, July 6, 1912, HP 5988, f. 57.
[7] Haldane to his mother, Aug. 3, 1912, HP 5988, f. 103.
[8] June 24, 1912, HP 6023, ff. 142–43.

the originator of that policy. Haldane's elevation to the woolsack was the signal for Lord Roberts and his National Service League to intensify their campaign. The adoption of any variety of national service had been unlikely while Haldane remained war minister, for he had staked his reputation upon the preservation of the voluntary system. Now, it was hoped, the Government could be more easily pressured. But to understand this new militancy on the part of the conscriptionists, one must examine their earlier relations with Haldane.

Though he was to become their bugbear, Haldane began his ministerial career the darling of the Roberts brigade. Like many Radicals, they refused to believe that he did not have up his sleeve some scheme for universal training. Lord Roberts launched his agitation for national service not to harry but to help Haldane. Lord Esher, who read Roberts's manifesto, assured him that "the whole plan would work in very well with Haldane's ideas."[9] And Roberts confided to Lord Milner, another official of the National Service League, his belief that "in his heart . . . Haldane . . . is very grateful for what we have been doing, and is very pleased that I am to speak a few days before he explains in the House of Commons what he proposes to do."[10] Roberts recognized the differences between himself and the Liberal war minister, but wrote them off as differences of emphasis or detail. In the summer of 1906 he and Lady Roberts paid a brief visit to Cloan to iron them out in friendly discussion. It was not yet apparent how little agreement there was between the two positions.

It was not principle but practical considerations that led Haldane to reject Lord Roberts's proposals. He saw that a large conscript army had its military advantages, but he doubted with good reason whether the British people, capable of great sacrifice in time of war, would tolerate the establishment of such a force in peacetime. Since the seventeenth century they had looked upon a standing army as a menace to their hard-won liberties. "A national habit of mind, such as that of the Swiss, which would lead to universal training, . . . would be a great gain to the public, perhaps quite as much from an educational as from a military point of view. But," he cautioned Lord Rosebery, "to press this now would be, to use a old phrase of your own, to show that the man who did so 'knew not the stomach of his people.' "[11] The British

9 Feb. 5, 1906, Roberts Papers.   10 June 14, 1906, Milner Papers.
11 Dec. 6, 1907, Rosebery Papers.

had an ingrained hatred of compulsion, and to thrust it upon them would create a crisis in public confidence that might in the end prove militarily disastrous. It was far better for the Government to maintain the voluntary system and with it the good will of the people. This was not defeatism, but rather a shrewd diagnosis of the British temperament, with its resistance to regimentation and its abiding faith in individualism. Lord Roberts did not seem to understand, Haldane complained to J. A. Spender in the summer of 1906, that to coerce men to serve overseas was a sure way to eliminate "the chance of getting them to go voluntarily."[12] Exactly a half century later, Reginald Maudling employed the same logic in criticizing the Labour Government's compulsory regulation of prices and incomes: "It will deter voluntary cooperation. If you ask a bloke to volunteer, he may. If you say 'volunteer or else' he will say 'to hell with you.' "[13]

There were strategic reasons too for opposing the Roberts scheme. It would take years, Haldane calculated, to make the transition from one system to another; all the while Britain would be left without adequate defenses. Lord Nicholson and the General Staff were of the opinion that "the moment compulsory service was adopted, the recruiting for the Expeditionary Army and the Overseas garrisons would be affected gravely, and consequently . . . there would be a hiatus during which the German General Staff, which was not in the habit of missing chances, would probably attack."[14] Whether or not Haldane shared this fear of German aggression, he could not afford to leave the country vulnerable while one structure was dismantled and the groundwork laid for another. Consequently he adhered to the system of voluntary service, introducing reforms to improve its efficiency. Looking back, he did not regret the course he had taken. Had he adopted conscription, the risks would have been considerable, the gains conjectural, and it was entirely doubtful that Britain could have been any better prepared by August 1914.[15]

Lord Roberts might sincerely have believed that he was rendering Haldane valuable service, but the latter thought otherwise. The agitation

---

12 Aug. 24, 1906, Add. MSS. 46, 390, f. 150.   13 *The Times*, Aug. 4, 1966.
14 Haldane's wartime memorandum, HP 5919, f. 136.
15 At the end of the war, Sir Auckland Geddes, Director of National Service, expressed "the fully matured opinion that, on balance, the imposition of military conscription added little if anything to the effective sum of our war efforts." Quoted in Lord Simon, *Retrospect* (London, 1952), p. 107.

for national service put off recruits and, at the same time, aroused suspicion among the working classes. Although Roberts had endorsed the idea of a Territorial Force, he and still more his lieutenants weakened it by insisting that without conscription it would prove useless. Arnold-Forster, an ally of the conscriptionists, deduced that professional soldiers went along with Haldane's project "only . . . because they believe it will come to smash, and that Conscription must follow."[16] Leo Maxse predicted that the imminent failure of "the hateful principle of Patriotism by Proxy" would pave the way for compulsion. Colonel Repington, writing in *The Times* on June 6, 1908, implored those "anxious . . . to secure the desirable object of national training" not to condemn the Territorial Force out of hand. But his advice went unheeded. The national service enthusiasts were too impatient to realize their goal to concede the value of any aspect of the voluntary system.

Daggers were drawn as early as July 1908, after Haldane made the offhand remark that he expected to achieve a success at the war office sufficient to bury compulsion. "Mr. Haldane will not bury Compulsion," Maxse assured the readers of the *National Review*. "Compulsion will bury Mr. Haldane, unless he escapes to the Woolsack." In the same issue, Lord Newton, a loyal supporter of Roberts, appealed to the leaders of the Opposition "to abandon the[ir] attitude of benevolent neutrality" toward Haldane and to denounce him for the imposter he was. It was a savage attack, and it reflected at least in part the sentiments of Lord Roberts, who continued to hold back from the fray. ". . . I am delighted that you keep hammering away at the 'German Peril' and the absence of anything like proper Home Defence," Roberts told Maxse on September 2. "It is most unfortunate that not a single man on the Front Opposition Benches seems to care one straw about Home Defence."[17]

Roberts's fellow-conscriptionists were dismayed by his reluctance to spearhead a more vigorous campaign. The *Daily Express* was unable to do more for the cause, its editor, R. D. Blumenfeld, explained to Gwynne of the *Morning Post*, because it lacked a sufficiently authoritative spokesman:

Obviously Lord Roberts is the man to do it but for some reason or other he holds aloof. I am certain that if I had his name and undoubted influence

16 Arnold-Forster to his sister, Sept., 1907, quoted in Mary Arnold-Forster, p. 327.
17 Maxse Papers.

to work with, we could soon rouse public interest to such a pitch that some sort of reasonable general service would be insisted upon in a short time. But Lord Roberts has never given me the slightest hope in that direction; on the contrary he has distinctly discouraged any efforts on my part to go ahead[18]

For the time being, Roberts preferred to allow others to raise their voices and to save his own for private negotiation. He praised Blumenfeld's idea for a feature that would "bring home to the people of this country [the fact] that invasion is a possibility,"[19] but he remained noncommittal when Blumenfeld invited him to put his views in print.

On April 7, 1909, Roberts wrote to Balfour to solicit support for a Bill he proposed to bring before the Lords after Easter recess. It called for a system of "universal military training, with the object of providing Haldane's admirable framework with the required number of adequately trained men," and he implored Balfour "to speak out fearlessly" on its behalf. "I have always hoped that the question of National Defence could be kept free from Party politics," Roberts professed, "but I cannot help thinking that this is no longer possible. . . . Like all other Great Questions, [it] will have to be settled on Party lines, which is greatly to be regretted."[20] Balfour, however, declined to affiliate himself with "Roberts's Rabble,"[21] and stood by unmoved while the Bill went down to defeat. "The Mandarins on both sides played an even more pitiful part than usual," Maxse complained in the August *National Review*. This disappointment was sufficient to disillusion Lord Roberts with fabian techniques. That summer, the National Service League embarked upon a vigorous campaign in the constituencies and in the press.

As criticism grew more vocal, it came from unexpected quarters. Lord Esher distressed Haldane by contributing a curious piece to the September 1910 *National Review*: on the one hand, he praised Haldane as "far the ablest and most successful War Minister this country has ever had"; on the other, he confessed that he could see "no sign" that voluntary enlistment, upon which Haldane relied, was bringing forth sufficient recruits to maintain the Territorial Force at minimum strength. This was the result, he believed, of "the sirocco of democracy

[18] Oct. 6, 1908, Blumenfeld Papers.   [19] Oct. 18, 1908, *Ibid.*
[20] Balfour Papers.
[21] Balfour used this term during "an interesting two hours" of conversation with Fisher. Fisher to Harcourt, n.d., Harcourt Papers.

withering in our people the spirit of sacrifice." The country could be saved only by "imposing by law upon our children the duty to bear arms in its defence."

Lord Esher, who did not think he had spoken the least out of turn, could not understand why he was "getting bullied by the S. of State and others."[22] He assured Haldane that he had intended no "trouble or injur[y] to the splendid work you have done. . . ."[23] Haldane did not doubt this, but he wondered how a man of Esher's experience could be so oblivious to the significance his words would carry. He could easily refute Esher's arguments with statistical evidence, but he could do little to allay the suspicions they engendered. "When the man whose presence—not only on the Defence Committee, but in my inmost counsels—suddenly proclaims his opinion, the world takes him to intend the natural consequence of his action," he stiffly rebuked Esher.[24] His worst fears proved justified. His critics, most of whom took an equally dim view of Esher, noted gleefully that the rats were deserting a sinking ship. R. J. Marker, who had been private secretary to Arnold-Forster, was persuaded that conscription was imminent by the fact that "Esher has jumped round, and he is seldom behind 'the cat.' "[25] A "Unionist Free Trader" writing in the *National Review* the following March, inferred from Esher's article that Haldane's "friend and apologist" had repudiated him.

Haldane retaliated by commissioning Sir Ian Hamilton, recently appointed adjutant-general, to write *Compulsory Service*, to which he contributed an introduction that occupied more than a quarter of its 148 pages. The book appeared in November 1910 and took the form of an open letter to the war minister, pledging continued support against critics of the voluntary principle. Both the text and introduction dwelled upon the fact that Britain's insularity made unnecessary, even burdensome, the large, nonprofessional land force that conscription would provide. For his part, Sir Ian preferred "half a loaf, in the shape of a force created for over-sea purposes, instead of a stone in the shape of a great defensive army, of no earthly use except to hang round our necks whilst we struggle in the slough of insolvency." Both insisted

---

[22] Esher to Kitchener, Sept. 3, 1910, Kitchener Papers.
[23] Sept. 8, 1910, HP 5909, ff. 53–54.
[24] Sept. 7, 1910 [copy] HP 5909, ff. 49–51.
[25] Marker to Blumenfeld, Sept. 2, 1910, Blumenfeld Papers.

that patriotism would turn out sufficient men, and that a voluntary army was better suited to the needs of a far-flung empire on the Roman or British model. "If you wish to maintain the Empire," Sir Ian preached, "you must encourage the voluntary spirit."

Haldane was gratified by the finished product and by the response it evoked. "The little book I sent you on 'Compulsory Service' has rushed through its first edition and is causing grief to Lord Roberts and Co.," he boasted to McKenna on December 23, 1910.[26] The next month a second edition appeared, replete with a memorandum from Sir Arthur Wilson, the first sea lord, that minimized the possibility of invasion. This, Haldane informed his mother, had created "a tremendous sensation. Hundreds of leading and other articles are appearing. . . . The book has done its work in educating the public."[27]

No small measure of the attention *Compulsory Service* received was because its title page carried the name of Sir Ian Hamilton. A close friend of Haldane, he was even a closer friend of Lord Roberts, who had brought him to India as his aide-de-camp in 1882 and had since taken a paternal interest in his career. Hamilton was a man of cultivated intellect, universally admired for his genial personality. To virtually everyone he was "Johnny," and it was with good reason that his nephew and biographer, borrowing a line from Wordsworth, dubbed him "the Happy Warrior."[28] The effect of Hamilton's declaration in favor of voluntary recruiting was comparable to that of Lord Esher's espousal of conscription. Those who surrounded Lord Roberts considered it a treacherous defection, though in truth Hamilton had never deceived them about his views. Lady Hamilton, a guest at the Roberts's house near Ascot at the time the book appeared, recorded in her diary the "unhappy thought that the dear Bobs are nourishing vipers in their bosom." But her host bore no grudge, and the Hamiltons received their usual invitation for the following year's Ascot. Others were not so magnanimous. Haldane defended Sir Ian against critics in the Commons on March 18, 1911, and "gave them back as good as they gave him."[29] And when this "brave and good general" was unjustly relieved of his command at the Dardanelles in the autumn of 1915, Haldane,

26 McKenna Papers.   27 Jan. 19, 1911, HP 5985, ff. 11–12.
28 Ian B. M. Hamilton, *The Happy Warrior* (London, 1966), see pp. 240–43.
29 Haldane to his mother, HP 5985, f. 101.

who had firsthand knowledge of such things, realized that Sir Ian's "stand in the old days against conscription has not helped him."[30]

The conscriptionists might have been caught off guard by the Hamilton-Haldane manifesto, but it did not take them long to reply in kind. In March 1911 there appeared the first edition of *Facts and Fallacies*, a three-part handbook upon which Lord Roberts collaborated with anonymous contributors. The first section, "The Nation's Peril," was written by Roberts with the assistance of J. A. Cramb, professor of modern history at Queen's College, London; the second was "written by a well known writer on problems of imperial defence" who was, in fact, L. S. Amery; and finally, "The Argument from History" was provided by "a writer who has given much time and thought to that subject," Professor Cramb again. The latter is better remembered for his book, *Germany and England,* that appeared in June 1914 and had gone into six editions by the following September, after international events had borne out his prognosis of conflict between the two countries.

Each side came away from the debate confident that it had had the last word. Yet it is doubtful whether either converted anyone who had not been sympathetic all along. Meanwhile, Haldane's position grew more difficult, for he was now involved in a personal duel with Lord Roberts, a patriarch of empire with more than a half century of military experience, who commanded fierce personal loyalties. Many of Roberts's followers never forgave Haldane his impertinence. "All the ministers treated Lord Roberts with contumely," Charles Whibley recalled in the September 1915 *Blackwood's Magazine*. "It was Lord Haldane who, vaunting his own prowess in military matters, dismissed Lord Roberts as no strategist." At the end of March 1911, Haldane joined Roberts in the House of Lords and within days they were trading arguments on the chamber floor.

It was Haldane, who, by taking a peerage, carried the duel into the upper house; it was Lord Roberts who carried it into the columns of the national press. He adopted this course, he explained to Maxse in an open letter dated December 15, 1911, because Parliament's preoccupation with the constitutional crisis left no time for army matters. On the same day, he sent a similar letter to the *Daily Express*, accompanied by private injunctions to its editor:

[30] Haldane to his mother, Oct. 19, 1915, HP 5994, f. 110.

The question is not a Party one but neither Party will deal with it and my hope rests in the press. If you and other editors will kindly do all you can to enlighten the public to the necessity for our having a proper National Army, all will go well; otherwise the country will get into serious trouble. No amount of bolstering up the Territorial Force will do any good.[31]

A day later, he urged Blumenfeld not to allow the *Express* "to drop . . . the question of our unpreparedness . . . particularly as regards the shortcomings of the rifle and gun. We ought to press for an enquiry about both, and see who is to blame."[32] He no longer made even a pretense of support for Haldane or the Haldane reforms. And he was not disappointed by the editors to whom he appealed.

It was not accidental that the campaign against Haldane grew more vindictive at the same time that there occurred a change in the Unionist leadership. A number of the same men were responsible for both. The rebels who had brought down Balfour were confident that anything was within their grasp. By February 1912 the *National Review* had replaced its slogan "B. M. G." (Balfour Must Go) with "H. M. G." (Haldane Must Go). Andrew Bonar Law, the new Unionist leader, courted the conscriptionists by consulting Lord Roberts and Sir Henry Wilson before his January 12 Albert Hall debut; though he stopped short of advocating compulsory service, he offered a welcome indictment of Haldane's record. Walter Long, too, flirted with the National Service enthusiasts, but preferred to keep compulsion a personal rather than a party affair: ". . . It was quite evident" from the Unionist M.P.s he canvassed "that there is a great divergence of opinion on the subject, many of them being afraid that if these questions were to be included in the Party Programme they might bring us some trouble and difficulty."[33] Unlike most Liberal frontbenchers, who rejected conscription out of principle, the leading Unionists—neither Milner nor Curzon belonged to the charmed circle—refused to commit themselves out of expediency; they realized the disastrous effects such a declaration would have upon the precarious unity of their party. Perhaps the best definition of the Unionist position came from F. E. Smith in the April *National Review*: while the party would "endeavour to encourage the movement in every way," it was no more prepared than its opposition to impose the compulsory system upon an unprepared public. As Smith's friend,

[31] Blumenfeld Papers.   [32] *Ibid.*
[33] Long to Blumenfeld, March 11, 1911, *Ibid.*

Winston Churchill, patiently explained to Lord Roberts on February 7, 1913: "The kind of thing you have in mind would require a Government of its own to do, and such a Government will have to be united on many other things besides National Service."[34]

The attacks did not abate with Haldane's departure from the war office in June 1912. If anything, they became more acutely personal. Critics continued to believe that the only way to discredit the system was to impugn the abilities and intentions of its author. On July 10 Lord Percy sent Maxse the manuscript for another article in which he concentrated upon "Haldane's crooked ways rather than his crooked thoughts."[35] And publicly and privately, Lord Roberts worked to undermine Haldane's achievement. "The time has come," he proclaimed to Blumenfeld on September 22, "when the people must be made to understand the weakness of our Army, and the Territorials to feel that they can be of no use until the Force is raised under a system of Compulsory Military Training."[36] In the weeks that followed, Roberts told audiences at Manchester and London that the Territorial Force was "a failure in discipline, a failure in numbers, a failure in equipment, and a failure in energy." His speeches were given prominent attention in the *Daily Express*, the *Morning Post*, the *Daily Mail*, and the *National Review*.

Haldane confessed that Roberts's "campaign against the Territorials" caused him considerable "anxiety": "I am not there to scour the country in reply. He may do a good deal of damage."[37] He reproved his colleagues for their failure to speak out in his defense and for allowing "the Unionist Party . . . to drift unchallenged."[38] He was particularly distressed by the silence or, still worse, the garbled replies of Colonel Seely, his successor at the war ministry. Colonel Repington dismissed Seely as a personable nonentity who "does nothing and carries no guns." It was his belief, he told Haldane on November 27, that "Seely's jealousy of you leads him to accept placidly criticisms of your work, and to this alone can I attribute the headway he has allowed to be given the movement against the T. F." Repington offered the alarming calculation that the "general efficiency of the [war] office" had fallen by half in recent months, and he criticized Seely for giving free rein

[34] Roberts Papers.   [35] Maxse Papers.   [36] Blumenfeld Papers.
[37] Haldane to his mother, Nov. 28 and 29, 1912, HP 5988, ff. 207–209.
[38] Haldane to Spender, Nov. 28, 1912, Spender Papers, Add. MSS. 46, 390, f. 174.

to Sir Henry Wilson, that inveterate intriguer who later inflicted such damage upon Haldane's reputation.[39]

Time and again Haldane came away from debate confident that "we smashed up the proposal for Compulsory Service on scientific grounds."[40] But rational arguments were powerless against the emotional outpourings of his adversaries. The *Daily Mail*, which now counted Lord Percy among its contributors, remained insistent that the "whole military system, based as it is on voluntary service, . . . has broken down hopelessly." The *Daily Express* continued to condemn the Territorial Force as "a dangerous delusion, suicidal to itself and fatal to the country." Haldane found welcome escape in his judicial work, which was at least free of controversy. In September 1913 he took time out to make his only transatlantic visit—he remained only five days—to address a meeting of the American Bar Association at Montreal. His remarks on international conciliation won him applause from his audience, a warm letter from Bethmann Hollweg, praise from the German press, and grumblings from Maxse in the *National Review*.

Back in England, Haldane was embroiled in the Ulster crisis, which reached its climax at Curragh in March 1914 and still smouldered when the nation went to war that August. Unable to prevent the passage of Irish Home Rule by constitutional means—the House of Lords had its powers shorn in the attempt—the Opposition resorted to subterranean methods. This was their last-ditch effort against a Government they were unable to dislodge and parliamentary institutions they had ceased to respect. They gave the Protestants of northern Ireland assurances of undying support and defended the right of Sir Edward Carson's Ulster Volunteers to take arms to preserve the Union. In short, the Tories were playing "the Orange Card" as Lord Randolph Churchill recommended in 1886, when Gladstone had first committed the Liberal Party to Home Rule.

Ideally, the lord chancellor should have remained aloof. But neither his party's weakness in the Lords nor the incompetence of his successor at the war office permitted Haldane that luxury. The security of the army was at stake, and this concerned him intimately. A high proportion of officers were Ulstermen by birth. An even higher proportion professed Ulsterite sympathies and had no desire to place northern Irishmen,

[39] HP 5909, ff. 272-73.
[40] Haldane to his mother, Feb. 11, 1913, HP 5989, f. 56.

Protestant and royalist, at the mercy of southerners, Papist and seditious. Opposition leaders, Bonar Law and Lord Roberts among them, urged them to disobey orders to coerce His Majesty's most loyal subjects, even if such orders were issued in the King's name. The ethic of obedience conflicted with political allegiance and no one could be sure which would prevail.

The situation required self-possession and a strong hand, neither of which Seely revealed. It is the opinion of A. T. Q. Stewart, who has written most recently and persuasively on the subject, that had Haldane remained at the war office, the army crisis would have been averted.[41] Certainly events would not have been permitted to drift toward civil war. Lord Esher, who came to lunch at Cloan, found "Pussy"—his nickname for Haldane—"very bellicose about Ulster" and brimming with ideas. "He wants to send a composite force of picked troops into the province at once," Esher reported to Loulou Harcourt,

and he wants to give [Sir] Arthur Paget, as staff officer, that fellow [Sir Nevil] Macready who did so well in Wales [at the 1910 Tonypandy disturbances]. He is opposed to taking any action against Carson and he would not give way an inch on Home Rule. I have no views about his politics, but I think there is a great deal to be said for his military preparations. If you send an overwhelming force into Ulster for the purpose of maintaining order a good time beforehand, I don't believe for a moment you would have any serious trouble. It would certainly be a mistake to wait until Carson has served out his rifles and ammunition. There has been sufficient provocation already to justify the strengthening of the forces of order. Had it been possible to send a division of troops to S. Africa six months sooner you would have had no S. African war on anything like the same scale.[42]

Yet Haldane shared the Government's inability to follow a clearcut line. Like the Prime Minister, from whom he took his cue, he preached resolution one day and conciliation the next. In a public speech at Birmingham on December 2, he asked to keep the door open to "conference and compromise." And at the start of the new year he was hopeful of "a temporary settlement . . . on the basis of the exclusion of Ulster from the Home Rule Bill."[43] In the House of Lords on February 11 he appealed to "the leaders of the Unionist Party not to fan . . . sentiment in Ulster unduly, but to do their utmost to keep it within

[41] The Ulster Crisis (London, 1967), p. 108.
[42] Oct. 2, 1913, Harcourt Papers.
[43] Esher to the King, Jan. 6, 1914, Journals and Letters, III, 151–52.

bounds." His efforts only added to his unpopularity among his political opponents: "Haldane is an atrocious humbug," Bonar Law wrote to Lord Lansdowne in disgust.[44]

The confrontation came in March. It need never have come if matters had rested in more capable hands. A Cabinet committee recommended on the 17th that steps be taken to safeguard northern Irish arms depots against Carson's vigilante forces. Troops were to be moved in from the southern counties and across St. George's Channel. Churchill, the dominant member of the committee, spoke in menacing tones of putting "grave matters to the proof" and issued orders to bring the Third Battle Squadron within striking distance of Belfast Lough. Bonar Law charged that the Government was planning to convert Ireland into "a new Poland" when he moved a vote of censure in the House on the 19th. But there are no indications that anything more was contemplated than the reinforcement of depots and strategic points in and around Belfast.

Lieutenant-General Sir Arthur Paget, the commander in chief in Ireland, was meanwhile summoned to Whitehall for consultation. He expressed fears to his political superiors that the movement of troops into Ulster would touch off civil disturbances. Moreover, he hesitated to put the loyalty of his officers to the test. Seely pacified him with promises of unstinted support and, more foolishly, with the right to grant special dispensation to those officers who resided in the troubled area: in the event of conflict, they were to be allowed to "disappear" without loss of their commissions. Others who resisted orders were to be removed. These concessions were given orally, and Paget returned to Ireland on the morning of the 20th to convey them as best he could to his senior officers. Unfortunately, he did not seem to understand Seely and they did not seem to understand him. He presented the assignment to his men as a wartime operation rather than a precautionary maneuver. His intemperate language (the country might be "ablaze" within twenty-four hours, he warned them) raised the specter of civil war at the same time that Sir Henry Wilson was divulging war office plans to the Government's enemies.

Seely had intended his concession to apply only to Ulsterite officers of senior rank. Paget failed to make this clear. That afternoon, Brigadier-General Hubert Gough, commander of the Third Cavalry Brigade sta-

---

[44] Dec. 13, 1913 [copy], Bonar Law Papers.

tioned at the Curragh, informed Paget that he and fifty-seven of his seventy officers preferred to accept dismissal sooner than embark upon "active military operations against Ulster." The Liberal press damned this as mutiny, while the Unionist press hailed it as patriotism. In truth, it was the sorry product of mutual misunderstanding and precipitate action.

The Prime Minister was not alarmed when news of the Curragh incident was brought to him at the bridge table that evening. He took the realistic view that this was a "strike," not a mutiny, and expressed confidence that the whole affair "will be cleared up in a few hours." He had no use for those who were attempting to make political capital out of the situation, and told Lord Stamfordham, the King's secretary, "that the main responsibility for all this mutinous talk rested with Lord Roberts, who is in a dangerous condition of senile frenzy."[45] At the same time Asquith took belated steps to restrain Churchill and canceled the order to bring the Third Battle Squadron to Irish waters.

The war office would have been only too glad to let the matter drop. It called Gough to London and advised him on the 23rd that he could resume his command, no questions asked. But Gough, at breakfast that morning with Sir Henry Wilson, had rehearsed questions of his own. He refused to accept reinstatement unless he could return to Ireland with written assurance that the army would not be used "to crush political opposition to the policy or principles of the Home Rule Bill." Seely agreed against his better judgment and without consulting the Prime Minister. Sir Spencer Ewart, adjutant-general, drew up the document. Seely redrafted it with the help of Lord Morley *after* the Cabinet that morning,[46] and Sir John French, chief of the Imperial General Staff, affixed his initials to it. Did any of them realize that they had surrendered the historic principle of civilian authority over military power?

It was not until evening that Asquith saw a copy of the guarantees that Gough had received. By then it was too late to recover the document or to keep its terms from becoming known. The closing portion,

[45] Asquith's letters of March 21 and 22 to Venetia Stanley, quoted in Jenkins, pp. 309–11.

[46] Morley's complicity is difficult to explain. Margot Asquith, writing to Lady Islington, ascribed it to the fact that "J. Morley is quite deaf and *much* too vain poor dear to own up that he did not know what was going on (in the Cabinet)." *Ibid.*, p. 312.

with the phrase "crush political opposition," gave credence to rumors that the Government—or, at any rate, Churchill and Seely—had intended a "pogrom" against Ulster. Churchill, in the House, rebutted this "hellish insinuation," but the impression remained. Finally, on the afternoon of Friday the 27th Asquith publicly disavowed the concordat with Gough by promulgating a new army order, from which the "peccant paragraphs" (as Balfour called them) were omitted. French and Ewart, repudiated by the Government, promptly tendered their resignations. Haldane helped French compose a conciliatory letter to the Prime Minister, who looked upon it incredulously as "a long hazy diplomatic document which Haldane has drawn up, and over-persuaded the wretched 2 Generals to accept, as a *pièce justificative* for not resigning."[47] When he returned from his country weekend on the 30th, Asquith accepted the resignations of French and Ewart, along with that of Colonel Seely, whose position had become untenable. He announced that he would fill the vacancy at the war ministry himself, adding the burdens of that office to those of the premiership.

Haldane was more than a spectator to these muddled events. He worked long hours behind closed doors to devise an "accommodating formula" that would retrieve the Government's authority and, at the same time, allow French and Ewart to save their honor and their offices. "If I could handle the situation alone or were back at the war office for 48 hours, I am sure I could settle matters," he told his mother on the 27th. "But it is now very difficult."[48] His public efforts to smooth things over were no more successful and far more open to misconstruction. In a speech to the House of Lords on the 23rd, he strenuously denied that the Government had issued orders or intended to issue orders "for the coercing of Ulster." He maintained, however, that the Government reserved the right to conduct "warlike operations"— something quite different, he insisted—if the need arose. The speech had a dual purpose: it was intended to make it easier for Ulsterite officers to return to duty; and, he hoped, it would underscore the Government's determination to uphold law and order.

The speech failed on both counts, partly because of its ambiguities, and partly because members of the Cabinet were so hopelessly out of step with one another. Most people failed to appreciate Haldane's subtle

[47] Asquith to Venetia Stanley, March 30, 1914, quoted in *Ibid.*, pp. 313–14.
[48] HP 5991, f. 111.

distinction between "the coercing of Ulster" and "warlike operations"; they wrote it off as another of his legal sophistries. And Radical critics, who thought the time had come for a "democratic army," accused the lord chancellor of going too far in his attempt to appease the enemy. At the same time that he and Morley gave the House of Lords assurances that coercion was never the question, Churchill and Grey took a more belligerent line in the Commons. Not until Asquith spoke on the 27th was it apparent to Haldane that the Government would make no concessions to its political opponents or to recalcitrant army officers.

What was to be done about that March 23rd speech? He considered it an embarrassment to himself and his colleagues. It was delivered, he explained to his mother, "in ignorance of what had really happened" that morning between Seely and Gough.[49] He was not the only minister to be caught red-faced by subsequent disclosures. The *Daily Express* graciously conceded on the 25th that Asquith, Morley, and Haldane had not "deliberately deceived Parliament" about the army situation, but were "themselves fooled and deceived throughout." Others were not nearly so deferential. "I hope we shall see Morley's resignation today," Sir Henry Wilson wrote to Lord Roberts on the 31st. "Then perhaps poor fat Haldane, and after that perhaps the Government."[50]

By a single stroke, Haldane forfeited whatever sympathy he might have received. Before his March 23 speech was printed in *Hansard*, proof was sent to him for verification. In order to "get rid of the ambiguity" (as he put it), and to close ranks with Asquith and Grey, he revised the text to read that the Government had issued no orders, nor intended to issue orders for the "immediate" coercion of Ulster. Did he think that his move would go undetected? Rather he expected others to see it, as he did, as a necessary act of clarification. Lord Midleton, always poised to strike, brought up the matter in the House of Lords on April 1. He compared the transcription of the lord chancellor's speech in the March 24 *Times* with the official version that had just appeared. Haldane replied that he had "corrected" the speech "not for the purpose of giving a different sense . . . [but] to prevent the sentence being used, as it had been mercilessly in the last few days, wrenched from its context and given quite a different sense. . . ." The Opposition was not satisfied. Lord Lansdowne pointed out that any

[49] March 26, 1914, HP 5991, ff. 109–10.   [50] Roberts Papers.

clarification or correction should have been made in a statement to the House, and he disputed Haldane's argument that the meaning of the original speech had not been altered.

There can be no doubt that Haldane had neither intended anything underhanded nor calculated the effects of his action. "I was made the subject of a debate in the H. of Lords yesterday," he told his mother on the 2nd:

The enemy wrenched a sentence of mine from its context and were quoting it falsely to make out that I differed from Sir E. Grey. I put a word into the corrected official report which made it clear that it must not be read apart from the sentences which went before and after, and gave them back as good as they gave me. There was a fine row which did no harm.[51]

Yet he was eventually forced to admit the foolishness of his action. He had given his enemies new ammunition against him and the opportunity to allege a further act of ministerial perfidy. The episode was indicative of his great defect, his mistaken belief that, engaged in political controversy, he could nonetheless stand above politics.

Haldane was ridiculed in verse on the editorial page of the *Morning Post* and in a cartoon on the front page of the *Daily Express*. The latter portrayed him in professorial garb, lecturing his attentive colleagues: "Now, Gentlemen, remember whenever you make an awkward speech you can always alter it in the Hansard reports afterwards." A map of Europe labeled "Greater Germany" and the motto "Gott segne Deutschland" hung behind him, and his platform was built of massive volumes inscribed "Schopenhauer," "Nietzsche," and "Kant Cant." This presaged the direction that the attacks upon him would take.

Arnold White, writing in the *Express,* cited the incident as a sad commentary upon Liberal integrity. Lord Percy and Leo Maxse, both in the May *National Review,* developed this theme: "To deliberately mislead either House of Parliament and the country," Maxse asserted, "is now regarded as the greatest of ministerial gifts, and the surest passport to Party esteem and promotion. Mr. Asquith is a past master in this noble art, but he must now surrender the laurel to his colleague on the Woolsack." Haldane's apologists, who condemn these critics for playing the party game with such venom, have underestimated the detrimental effects of his indiscretion. The Opposition leaders were

[51] HP 5991, f. 119.

genuinely distressed by the absence of agreement, which implied an absence of good faith, on the part of the ministers (Haldane included) with whom they were secretly negotiating a solution to the Ulster problem. J. H. Campbell, Carson's closest colleague, denounced "Haldane's performance in tampering with his speech" to Bonar Law, and he rejected as "ludicrous and false" Reginald McKenna's explanation "that the original conveyed the same thing" as the doctored version:

ludicrous because if true, no change was necessary, false because the reference to the "future" in the original demonstrates that immediate coercion was not in Haldane's mind. It is bad enough that ministers should contradict one another from day to day, but when it comes to a Lord Chancellor tampering with the records of debate we have reached the limit.[52]

The Government's equivocations and its reluctance to make a clean breast of the Curragh episode rebounded in a series of stunning defeats in spring by-elections. The most celebrated victim, C. F. G. Masterman, was a member of the Cabinet who could not obtain another seat until 1923. "The amount of mud that is being thrown at ministers is wonderful," Haldane wrote to his mother on April 23. "But we take these things with equanimity. The P. M. does not turn a hair."[53] A month later Asquith, persevering with Home Rule, was shouted down in the Commons, "a form of protest" that the *Daily Express* considered "proper and justified" in the case of a politician who "deserves neither respect nor a hearing." Public confidence and political propriety were at an ebb.

It was upon such a situation that continental events intruded. But it took time for the danger to become evident. The black borders on the front pages of British journals throughout July were a memorial tribute to Joseph Chamberlain, who died on the 2nd, not the Hapsburg archduke assassinated on the 28th of the previous month. The August *National Review*, sent to press on July 27, contained only a postscript on the Balkan crisis. Early on the 28th, Haldane expressed the belief "that there is no power that really wants war. The next twenty-four hours will decide." He took consolation "that no act of violence has occurred so far, and that the Governments have taken time to reflect."[54] That day, Austria-Hungary declared war on Serbia. Still Haldane refused to lose heart. To John Burns, whom he met at Westminster the next morning, he recommended that "[we] predispose our minds

---

[52] April 3, 1914, Bonar Law Papers.   [53] HP 5991, ff. 141–42.
[54] Haldane to his mother, HP 5991, f. 277.

to peace. Peace may ensue more from that than from any other cause."[55] After the Russians and Germans had mobilized, he admitted that "things look black, but there is hope so long as the frontiers are not actually crossed."[56]

Britain's declaration of war on August 4 came after days of fierce debate within the Cabinet. A number of resignations were threatened, though only two were received: Lord Morley's and John Burns's. *John Bull* regretted the departure of Burns, the first workingman to attain Cabinet rank, but it was glad to be rid of Morley: "Like Lord Haldane, all he knows he has learnt from books . . . and that is not worth a tinker's cuss in the conduct of public affairs." The *National Review* praised Morley and Burns for having "the sense and patriotism to retire" rather than infect the Government with their doubts; it speculated that Masterman, Harcourt, Simon, Lord Beauchamp, and Haldane would follow suit. This was nonsense, particularly in the case of Haldane, who had never wavered in his support of the entente and who was among the few to take a consistently strong line during that fateful weekend. In the years that followed, he remained adamant that the guilt was Germany's and that a lasting peace would not be possible until the German General Staff was forced to concede defeat. How had such misapprehensions about him arisen?

The outbreak of war found Asquith holding down the war office, which he had assumed on a temporary basis the previous March. It had never been a satisfactory arrangement, but in time of national emergency it was an impossible one. The Prime Minister called upon Haldane to put into motion the military machine that he had created and best understood. "I am finishing my judicial work tomorrow," Haldane notified his sister on August 3, "and then I take over the war office—remaining chancellor and Asquith remaining war minister and delegating the work to me."[57] A day later, busily at work in familiar surroundings, he proudly reported that "the organisation of 1908 is turning out admirably so far." At this point he took a dim view of suggestions that the conduct of the war be entrusted to Lord Kitchener, whom the Government had asked to stand by for no specific purpose. "The public would be comforted, but I doubt whether the soldiers

[55] Burns's Diary, July 29, 1914, Add. MSS. 46, 336, f. 126.
[56] Haldane to his mother, July 31, 1914, HP 5991, f. 283.
[57] HP 6012, f. 49.

would. They know what they want and like working with me."[58] On the morning of the 5th, Sir Ian Hamilton received word from Haldane that he had taken the war office expressly to keep Kitchener out of it.[59]

But the events of August 5 convinced Haldane that Kitchener's presence in the Government as secretary of state for war would inspire a "public confidence" that far outweighed any disadvantages. He consequently "pressed the P. M. to resign the war secretaryship and to appoint K., [who] . . . was best for the nation."[60] His critics refused to believe that he had come to this conclusion by his own initiative. Though it was Haldane who proposed Kitchener to the Prime Minister and who, in fact, sounded him out at Asquith's behest, it was rumored that it had been necessary to lift him bodily from behind his old desk. Even Kitchener, Haldane told his sister, had expected hard feelings on his part. On the same day that Haldane was urging Kitchener's appointment, the *Daily Express* deplored what it took to be "the return of Lord Haldane to the War Office: This is no time for elderly doctrinaire lawyers with German sympathies to play at soldiers." Northcliffe took up the cry in the *Evening Standard* and *Daily Mail,* and subsequently claimed he had been solely responsible for forcing Kitchener upon a reluctant Government. L. S. Amery recorded that Milner and Lord Lovat, acting on his information, had forced Asquith's hand by inducing Kitchener to threaten he would leave for Egypt unless he received a definite appointment.[61] Austen Chamberlain, however, insisted it was Balfour who first suggested Kitchener's nomination and Unionist pressure that secured it.[62] Asquith, not to be outdone, later recalled that Kitchener was "the only person whom I had ever thought of as my successor" as war secretary.[63] Thus nearly everyone claimed credit for bringing into office the man whom most of them recognized as a failure within a year's time.

---

[58] HP 6012, f. 51. Haldane did not exaggerate the support he received from the generals. Lord Nicholson urged him "to go back to the War Office" on the 3rd: "I need hardly tell you what a delight it would be to serve under you again" (HP 5910, f. 240). And Douglas Haig expressed the hope on the 4th "that you will, even at great personal inconvenience, return to the W. O. for as long as war lasts and preparations are necessary" (HP 5910, ff. 251–52).

[59] Hamilton, p. 266.

[60] Haldane to his mother, HP 5992, f. 8; to his sister, HP 6012, ff. 52–53.

[61] *My Political Life,* II (London, 1953), 21–23.

[62] Memorandum, August 4, 1914, Chamberlain Papers.

[63] *Memories and Reflections,* II, 81.

Haldane's temptation to linger at the war office was partly nostalgic and partly utilitarian: it was a good feeling to be back among old friends; it was an even better feeling to be performing a service that no one else could do nearly so well. But his enemies imputed a third motive, far less creditable. Haldane had gone to the war office, Maxse proclaimed in the September *National Review*, "for the express purpose of obstructing the despatch of the Expeditionary Force," and had he not been evicted within thirty-six hours, Britain would not have committed troops until it was too late. The idea was preposterous, but it was not the figment of Maxse's imagination. It came, as one might expect, from Sir Henry Wilson,[64] who informed Lord Milner on the 4th "that whilst the Government has at last given the order to mobilise, they had given it in an incomplete form." According to Wilson, instructions should have been given to "mobilise and embark"; instead, the war office called upon the troops only to "mobilise." Wilson inferred that this purposeful omission was intended to delay the dispatch of the Expeditionary Force four days and possibly longer. Milner, "very anxious that the Opposition should put fresh pressure on the Government," came at once to see Chamberlain, and together they visited Lord Lansdowne. Chamberlain went off on his own to see Balfour, who agreed to write a letter of remonstrance to Haldane. "Is it not a fundamental principle of strategy in a crisis of this particular kind," he asked the *de facto* war minister, "either to keep out of the conflict altogether, or to strike quickly and strike with your whole strength?" He implored Haldane to retain no more than two divisions for home defense and to dispatch the other four "immediately for field operation in the North East of France."[65]

Haldane invited Balfour to meet with him that night at eleven o'clock as Britain's ultimatum to Germany expired. "I gathered from him," Balfour informed his colleagues the next morning, "that the Government were still hesitating as to the proper course to be adopted—but on military, not on political grounds." Haldane explained that it might be best to keep the Expeditionary Force at home until it could be built into a "much more formidable army" of greater assistance to the French and more likely to survive the impact of battle. Besides, he pointed out, "if we deprived ourselves of Regular Troops now, the free action

---

[64] The following is based upon Chamberlain's memorandum of August 4, 1914, Chamberlain Papers.

[65] HP 5910, ff. 242 ff.

of the Fleet might be hampered." Balfour left him "rather depressed by a certain woollincss of thought and indecision of purpose, which seemed to mark his conversation—otherwise very interesting." He thought to himself "that if we were to wait until our possible Expeditionary Force grows to be a really formidable army, we should have to wait six months—probably much longer—before we could turn our half-drilled Reserves into a Field Force capable of meeting the Germans."[66]

How can one explain the reservations that Haldane expressed to Balfour? Did the creator of the Expeditionary Force lack sufficient confidence to put it to use? It becomes obvious that Haldane articulated not his own fears, but those of his colleagues. He was too firm a believer in Cabinet solidarity to break rank in such circumstances. And he was too self-conscious about his anomalous position at the war office to speak with any great personal authority. Yet his reticence inspired charges against him. Until the Imperial War Council met for the first time on the 5th, the Opposition had no way to gauge Haldane's true sentiments. At that time, he delivered a strong plea to send the entire Expeditionary Force—all six divisions—abroad. His listeners included Lord Roberts and Sir Henry Wilson. He was overruled by Kitchener, who was fearful of invasion and reluctant to denude the island of troops. The next evening the Council met again—Kitchener was not present—and approved the immediate dispatch of four divisions, along with one cavalry division. This was what Balfour had requested two days earlier, and Haldane privately informed him of the decision. A fifth division followed within two weeks, and a sixth in mid September. Yet the story persisted that Haldane had sought to delay, perhaps even prevent, the embarkation of the Expeditionary Force. As late as March 1917, the *National Review* paid posthumous tribute to Kitchener, without whose "fortuitous presence . . . Lord Haldane would inevitably have remained War Minister, and we should have had abundance of 'clear thinking,' but no Army that could have counted in Continental warfare."

Haldane had foreseen the difficulties of Kitchener's appointment. In previous years he had not considered the Mediterranean command

---

[66] Memorandum of August 5, 1914, Balfour Papers; another copy is to be found among the Bonar Law Papers.

or even the Indian viceroyalty too high a price to pay for keeping the hero of Khartoum at a comfortable distance from Whitehall. Now, however, he recognized the supreme propaganda value at home, in the dominions, and among the allies, of attaching Kitchener's magical name to the war effort. But he knew that Kitchener would require close supervision. Whether in South Africa or India, he had shown little aptitude for organization or tactics. Worse, he refused to take instruction, was slow to admit mistakes, and slower still to rectify them. As Sir Ian Hamilton, his chief-of-staff during Boer War days, had observed, Kitchener "has been for so long on a pinnacle that he is in some ways like a spoilt child for all his greatness."[67]

Haldane complained to Sir Almeric Fitzroy on August 9 that the new war secretary "had some difficulty in recognizing that he has not to begin the organisation of the army *de novo,* but merely takes over a highly perfected system, which he is asked to make the best of."[68] Kitchener never took the trouble to understand that system and, as a result, it was in large part dissipated and destroyed. Lady Hamilton (Sir Ian's wife) wrote in her diary on the 12th that Kitchener was "playing hell at the war office—what the papers call 'standing no nonsense,' but which seems to mean listening to no sense."[69] The idea of a general staff was more than he could grasp, and he never gave life to the embryonic system entrusted to him. Secrets remained locked between his massive brows, and he neither communicated the military position to the civilians nor vice versa. "If I had had my way," Haldane lamented to Haig on January 4, 1917, "you would have taken the place at the head of a real great Headquarters Staff in London on the 4th August 1914. But with Kitchener, who knew nothing of these things, this was impossible."[70]

Kitchener's attitude was evident from the first morning, when he was briefed by Sir Charles Harris, permanent head of the finance department:

His knowledge of home Army affairs was so out of date that he thought the Special Reserve was the same as the National Reserve—"those old gentlemen I have seen parading with umbrellas in Hyde Park"—while, as to the Territorials, he then and there declared that he could take no account of

[67] Hamilton to his wife, Dec. 25, 1901, quoted in Hamilton, p. 184.
[68] *Memoirs,* II, 564.   [69] Quoted in Hamilton, p. 267.
[70] Blake (ed.), *Private Letters of Douglas Haig* (London, 1952), p. 188.

anything but Regular soldiers and was going to issue at once an appeal for 100,000 recruits.[71]

Harris, French, Haig, and others attempted to reason with him, but to no avail. His prejudice against the Territorials prevented them from developing into the force that Haldane had envisaged. Lloyd George recalled his first "lengthy and intimate conversation" with Kitchener one evening in early August: "he spent nearly the whole of the time in deriding the Territorial Army. He was full of jest and merriment at its expense."[72] Nearly two years later, Lord Esher wrote to Asquith in exasperation of his inability "to get K. to understand that for recruiting purposes Haldane had devised the plan of Local Authorities in the shape of the County Associations."[73] The new armies that Kitchener raised competed with the Territorials not only for recruits but also for supplies, driving up prices and creating havoc. That the Territorials never realized their potential reflected no discredit upon their creator, who importuned Kitchener to recognize their worth. When given the chance, they fully justified Haldane's hopes. "How well the Territorials have done!" Haig wrote to him on March 11, 1915. "I only wish the organization of the Territorial Army had been taken as the basis of the New Army and built upon instead of starting de novo. We would now have another 12 or more divisions in France."[74] At war's end, Churchill gave Haldane great satisfaction by paying public tribute to the "great work" of the Territorials and by saying that they "would have done still more for the war if Lord Kitchener had not over-ruled me."[75]

Haldane's relations with Kitchener, usually cordial, were strained by the latter's slighting remarks about the Territorial Force. Sir Maurice Hankey's minutes of War Council meetings—Haldane joined on January 7, 1915—are punctuated with sharp exchanges on the subject. One can hardly blame Haldane for his reluctance to see the product of six years of labor discarded and abused. Nor is it difficult to appreciate his chagrin at being relegated to the sidelines. "I am seeing much of K.,

---

[71] Letter to The Times by Sir Charles Harris, August 28, 1928; Harris left among his papers a letter from Sir Evelyn Wood, dated August 31, 1928, on which he noted that Kitchener was "colossally ignorant at the start." Haig, too, was "struck" by the secretary of state's "ignorance of the progress made by the Territorial Army towards efficiency." Blake (ed.), Haig, p. 69.

[72] War Memoirs, I, 232.   [73] April 10, 1916, Asquith Papers.

[74] HP 5911, f. 21.

[75] Haldane to his mother, April 3, 1919, HP 6001, f. 124.

and am doing miscellaneous things," he wrote pathetically to his sister on September 26, 1914, "but they are all small compared with what one would like to be doing."[76] Most of all, Haldane pitied his former war office comrades, whose advice was spurned and whose duties were pre-empted. He "begged" Balfour to "smooth down" Sir Stanley von Donop, master-general of the ordinance, whom Kitchener had thrust aside.[77] The press attacks to which Haldane was subjected made it impossible for him to intervene more openly. Kitchener "has not been a great success in administering the war office," he told his mother on November 6, 1915. "I wish I could go back there, for I think I know what is required and how to accomplish it. But, thanks to certain newspapers, that cannot be."[78]

Kitchener, who resisted any attempt to pry information from him, was permitted a free hand of which Haldane hardly approved. He in turn looked with suspicion upon the keen interest that Haldane, virtually alone among their colleagues, took in war office affairs, and upon Haldane's continued intimacy with his generals, particularly Sir John French. A Cabinet memorandum that Haldane circulated on April 8, 1915 on "The Future Relations of the Great Powers"—it was a prescient appeal to extend the entente into a peacekeeping agency after victory—brought a counter-memorandum on the 21st from Kitchener, who advocated an eventual return to splendid isolation. He was the only minister to take written exception to Haldane's remarks and, judging from the infrequency of his intrusions into matters of foreign policy, personal antagonism was responsible.

Haldane began the war firm in the belief that "Lord K. and Lord Roberts and I are like brothers over this grim business."[79] As usual, he overestimated the reasonableness of those with whom he dealt. Roberts revealed to Sir Henry Wilson that he had far from forgiven the Government that had stubbornly refused to countenance his proposals: "The unaccountable disbelief of the Authorities as to the possibility of our ever being engaged in war, and their determination to shut their eyes and their ears to the preparations being made in Germany are facts that posterity will never be able to understand."[80] The movement

[76] HP 6012, f. 68.
[77] Balfour to Lord Robert Cecil, April 16, 1915, Cecil Papers.
[78] HP 5994, ff. 147–48.
[79] Haldane to his mother, Aug. 6, 1914, HP 5992, f. 11.
[80] Aug. 7, 1914 [copy], Roberts Papers.

for national service now took new urgency, and within weeks Lord Fisher acknowledged that he was "getting most damnable letters about conscription and . . . even high persons in the Cabinet are ratting because of Courtly influence."[81] Wrathful indignation was provoked by the Government's decision in September to proceed with Irish Home Rule, deferring its implementation until the war was won. Haldane attempted to allay opposition in the House of Lords, where he prophesied on the 15th, two days before the Bill received royal assent, that "six months of this common struggle" would remove prewar suspicions and impart "a common patriotism." Sir Henry Wilson was not convinced. "So you have passed Home Rule," he wrote to Leo Maxse from the front. "All right; when this war is over a lot of us with some knowledge of war will be at Carson's disposal."[82]

It was precisely this bitter feeling, of which Haldane was only dimly aware, that gave rise to the press agitation against him and others. It began cautiously, even respectfully, and did not gather momentum until the year's end. *John Bull* had unkind things to say about Haldane's war secretaryship, but its editor, Horatio Bottomley, did not yet deny that Haldane's "proper place [was] on the woolsack." While it demanded the resignation of Prince Louis of Battenburg, it merely called upon Haldane to "lie low" and to confine himself to judicial affairs. The *Daily Express* brought up his name only in retaliation, after the Liberal *Daily News* alluded to Sir Edward Carson as a friend of the Kaiser. And the *National Review*, for all its disparaging remarks, had yet to entertain ambitions for his removal.

The change came in the autumn, and it was presaged by a growing distemper on the part of Lord Roberts. On October 20 he expressed the wish to see every German on British soil deported to Holland, and complained to Maxse of his countrymen's complacency: "I am not sure if it would not be a good thing if a limited number of Germans did land and sack a few towns!"[83] In the last weeks of his life, he was convinced that a German invasion was imminent. "Their plans are carefully thought out," he told Lord Milner on November 7. "They have spies all over the country."[84] Eight days later he was dead. The war office, which remained impervious to his conscriptionist arguments, placarded London with portraits of the old warrior bearing the inscription: "He

[81] Fisher to Spender, Aug. 29, 1914, Spender Papers, Add. MSS. 46, 390, f. 129.
[82] Sept. 21, 1914, Maxse Papers.   [83] *Ibid.*   [84] Milner Papers.

did *his* duty. Will you do *yours?*" The *Daily Express* dedicated its issue on the 16th to "the man whose warning the nation did not heed." The *Daily Mirror* presented a "special Lord Roberts Memorial Number." The obituary in the *Daily Mail* included a short tribute from Haldane, coupled with an oblique attack upon him: "Unlike others who might be mentioned, Lord Roberts, though honoured by the Kaiser, was never hypnotised by him." The *National Review* was more explicit. Its December number appeared two weeks later, draped in black and consisting of a sustained diatribe against Haldane.

Within weeks of Lord Roberts's funeral, his self-proclaimed lieutenants unleashed a full-scale offensive against Haldane. How much longer Roberts might have restrained them remains open to question. Nor is it at all certain that, had he lived, he would have withheld his own waspish voice from the anti-Haldane clatter. But his death removed all restraints, including that of good taste, from the agitation against the man who had once vowed his determination to help bury conscription and had now helped bury its foremost advocate. Lord Roberts proved in death a far more formidable adversary than he had ever been in the House of Lords, for it was no longer possible to reply to charges leveled in his name. Moreover, that name was now put to purposes which he would have been far too much a gentleman to condone.

CHAPTER V

THE WINTER OF DISCONTENTS

. . . I need not say that at a time of public excitement like the present fiction and truth are very liberally mixed.

—HALDANE*

State funerals at St. Paul's have always been occasions for national catharsis. Lord Roberts's, which came at a critical juncture, was no exception. By this time, with the opposing armies embedded in trenches that stretched from the Channel coast to the foot of the Alps, even the military experts were confounded: "I don't know what is to be done," Lord Kitchener confessed to Sir Edward Grey; "this isn't *war*."[1] It was no longer possible to ignore the fact that Great Britain was engaged in a long and desperate struggle for survival; the Cabinet belatedly admitted as much within days of Roberts's death. Nor could one continue to believe in the overwhelming superiority of allied forces on land or the effectiveness of the British Navy at sea. A good many British illusions accompanied the old warrior to the grave, and it was impossible not to reflect that he had warned, for various reasons, against many of them. The scaremonger became in retrospect an oracle. By the late autumn of 1914, British optimism had given way to profound disillusionment, creating an atmosphere conducive to hysteria.

The Great War confronted British society with situations unlike those of any other military experience in British history, before or since. This was the first war that Britain fought as a nation-in-arms, the first to summon forth not only her impressive reserves of courage and self-sacrifice but also, less happily, her truculence. The Boer War, the only

---

* House of Lords, Nov. 18, 1914.
1 Grey, *Twenty-Five Years* (New York, 1925), II, 72.

other military venture within living memory, had been an isolated enterprise against South African farmers capable of inflicting considerable embarrassment but never defeat. The war of 1914–1918 was a mortal combat against a far more formidable foe. At the same time that it posed far greater challenges to the nation's military capacity, it also subjected her social fabric to untold strains. Britain had entered the war a divided society. Prewar passions continued to boil beneath the lid of national solidarity, and such self-imposed restraints as the party truce made them all the more intense. "Although all hatchets are for the moment buried," Lord Derby told Grey in January 1915, "one cannot entirely forget all that went before this war broke out."[2] Uncertain of its resources and unsure of its leadership, the British democracy was put on trial for its life. It would eventually come through the ordeal with the self-confidence that sustained it through its finest hour in 1940.

Comparisons between British behavior during the two world wars are inescapable.[3] In the second, public opinion was more mature and the issues were more clearly drawn. Many people were chastened by recollections of their fanaticism during the previous war. And the presence within Britain of large numbers of German refugees—not necessarily Jews—who had fled Hitler's tyranny made it difficult to generalize about the enemy. But in the First World War there were no such restraints. British fears of Germany and German influences approached the level of paranoia. Anyone with German ancestry, a German name, or, still worse, a German accent, was immediately suspect. Had the British Government yielded to popular clamor, subjects of British descent, let alone resident aliens, would undoubtedly have been treated as shamefully as the United States treated her citizens of Japanese extraction after the attack upon Pearl Harbor. Matters never went that far, but often far enough to betray the ideals for which Englishmen professed to fight.

British society under the impact of the First World War also bears an unflattering resemblance to America gripped by McCarthyism. Vicious campaigns were waged against public figures whose backgrounds or sympathies were brought into question. Lord Haldane, not the only victim, was probably the most abused. He was called a spy and it was

<hr>

[2] Trevelyan, p. 314.
[3] Anti-Semitism in England during the Second World War is quite another matter, no less disgraceful and certainly less justified than anti-Germanism during the first.

said that he was an illegitimate half-brother of the Kaiser and that he kept a secret wife in Germany. Sir Ernest Cassel, despite his friendship with Edward VII (and possibly because of his friendship with Haldane), was openly accused of treason. Sir Alfred Mond, Sir John Brunner, and Sir Edgar Speyer, all prominent in Liberal and financial circles, were suspected of German birth or affinities; in Speyer's case, the attacks grew sufficiently violent for him to return to his birthplace—New York—after renouncing his baronetcy and resigning his privy councilorship, the chairmanship of the London Underground Electric Railways Company, the presidency of the Poplar Hospital, the trusteeship of the Whitechapel Art Gallery, and his duties as councilor for the King Edward Hospital Fund. To be sure, many of these individuals had had connections with Germany before the war, but this was a commentary upon their commercial successes and in no way upon their patriotism. Insinuations were also made about Lord Milner's family background: was his father's name Charles or Karl? The editor of the *Daily Express*, R. D. Blumenfeld, whose father had left Nuremberg in the aftermath of the 1848 revolutions, was occasionally embarrassed when the anti-German furor (to which the *Express* contributed) rebounded: he protested to Horatio Bottomley that "it was low down" for *John Bull* to "attack people with German names who had commissions in the Army."[4] Many were impelled to change or anglicize their names; Bottomley kept a running list. The novelist, Ford Maddox Hueffer, made himself sound more English (and more symmetrical) by repeating his first name as his last. And the kingdom's most prominent family changed its name in 1917 from Saxe-Coburg to Windsor.

Cultural contamination, as great a fear as military infiltration, often attained ludicrous proportions. *John Bull*, always vigilant in the nation's interest, uncovered evidence that in one regimental canteen British soldiers were served rations of pickled beans on tin plates shamelessly stamped "Made in Germany"; its editor indignantly demanded "patriotic pickles" for His Majesty's fighting men. London shops ran advertisements to assure customers that they employed no German sales help. These appeared in newspapers which in turn offered similar assurances to their readers:

[4] Note by Blumenfeld on an undated letter of apology from Bottomley, Blumenfeld Papers.

cr. Radio Times Hulton Picture Library

Horatio Bottomley Plumps for Recruits

The Chairman and Editor of the *Daily Express* is not and never has been a German.

The paper on which the *Daily Express* is printed is not and to our certain knowledge has never been made in Germany.

There is not one German on the staff of the *Daily Express*.

At the same time British companies vied with one another to reap the profits of xenophobia. Lever Brothers urged loyal Britons to support home industry ("The clean, chivalrous fighting instincts of our gallant soldiers reflect the ideals of our business life") and particularly to buy Sunlight Soap, so "typically British." Bovril boasted that it was "British to the Backbone," and an enterprising chemist in the Strand insisted that there was nothing German about his eau de Cologne except its unfortunate name. Hundreds of products followed suit, and the Christmastime newspapers were filled with advertisements imploring the British consumer to avoid Bavarian greeting cards, Austrian tree decorations, and sweets in unfamiliar wrappers. Companies accused one another in print of having enemy—or at least foreign—ingredients or investors; the Royal Worcester Kidfitting Corset Company proudly proclaimed that it had

No German Capital	No German Busks
No German Partners	No German Steels
No German Hands	No German Trimming
No German Coutil	Nothing that is German

until its leading competitor, the J. B. Side-Spring Corset Company, pointed out that Royal Worcester was an American concern.

"DO NOT BELIEVE RUMOURS," cautioned the front page of the *Daily Express*, at the same time that its inside pages frightened readers with the serialized adventures of "The Beautiful Spy." As the war entered its first winter, with no end in sight, British society took refuge from an unwelcome reality in flights of fantasy. Stories circulated through September and October (in *The Times*, among other places) of the countless Russian soldiers, arctic snow still upon their boots, who traveled the length of Britain to take their place along the Western Front. Lord Northcliffe provided photographs in the *Daily Mail* of the trains that sped these mythical cossacks through the night. Englishmen quieted their doubts about the morality of their cause by believing blood-curdling accounts of enemy outrages upon the women, children, and art treasures of little Belgium. Only the latter proved to any extent true. This receptiveness to rumor deprived wartime society of its perspective on men and events; it became capable of believing anything and, at the same time, of respecting nothing.

Cosmo Gordon Lang, the archbishop of York, cited the "foolish attacks" against his friend, Lord Haldane, as "an instance of the way any war wrecks the ordinary instincts of humanity."[5] He might have cited as another the torrent of abuse that greeted his own speech that autumn condemning "the gross and vulgar way in which the German Emperor" was depicted in the British press. Lang, as befitting a man of his station, was unduly generous; it was not, as he asserted, simply the normal passions of war that undermined Britain's tolerance and devastated her sense of moderation. The hysteria was not nearly as spontaneous as most of its victims, he and Haldane included, tended to presume. To a shocking extent it was fomented by opportunistic journalists and conniving politicians who sought to wield power and to take their revenge for earlier slights and injuries.

[5] Lockhart, pp. 250–51.

Lord Northcliffe

cr. Radio Times Hulton Picture Library

With few exceptions, those who were pilloried were Liberals in attitude or political affiliation. This was not because the Liberals themselves were above this sort of thing—their journals made irresponsible remarks about Sir Edward Carson and, especially, Lord Milner—but, being the party in power, they were more vulnerable to attack. And they had the misfortunte to have an Opposition better versed than they in the arts of vilification. They could be accused of having failed to prepare the nation for war and of incompetent leadership during recent months. In addition, their private lives often lent themselves to caricature and innuendo. While they by no means monopolized the supply of taste and intellect within public life, the Liberals were more readily identified as esthetes, incapable of the ruthless response that the war required. Haldane, for example, was pained to hear of an Edinburgh resident whose contribution to the war effort was a bonfire of Goethe's works. His attitude, however admirable, played directly into the hands of his enemies. Typical was his decision, a week before the armistice, to receive in his home two Germans who came to London to confer on famine relief. Lord Morley considered his friend "bold, and had abstained from asking them himself, for he was told that they were watched by detectives. But," Haldane wrote his sister, "I said I did not care a straw."[6]

Lord Haldane was not the only minister whose fidelity to friend-ships and principles made him suspect. The Asquiths' intimacy with Robert ("Robbie") Ross, Oscar Wilde's friend and literary executor, elicited slanders that would later reverberate in the 1918 Pemberton Billing case. Margot related in her *Autobiography* how:

The D.......ss of W...... and others continue spreading amazing lies about me and mine: they would be grotesque if they were not so vile. Elizabeth [her daughter] is in turn engaged to a German Admiral or a German General; Henry has shares in Krupps; I "feed Prussian prisoners with every dainty and comestible," and play lawn tennis with them at Donnington Hall—a place whose very whereabouts is unknown to me.[7]

Both during his premiership and after, Asquith was publicly accused of keeping German maids and governesses at Downing Street. But German chauffeurs were even more frequent a charge. Lewis Harcourt, the colonial secretary, offered the defense that his chauffeur, who had been with him for years, was naturalized. A reader volunteered private infor-mation to the editor of the *National Review* that Haldane was "con-stantly" driven by his chauffeur, "a full-blooded German," to the prisoner-of-war camp at Olympia, where he would "hob-nob with the *German prisoners,* and [bring] them cigarettes and all sorts of luxu-ries. . . ." The informant had learned "on good authority" that the commandant at Olympia resented such visits and that "the sentries who guard the prisoners are hardly to be restrained from hissing Lord Haldane." The story was too ludicrous even for the *National Review,* though the *Morning Post* published two letters to the same effect on May 14. But if the sentries at Olympia were denied an opportunity to hiss the lord chancellor, others had better luck. Toward the close of 1914, an audience at a West End theater broke into catcalls when Haldane took his seat for a performance. Two years later, presiding over a discussion at the Sociological Society on the legal aspects of international relations, a woman interrupted him with shouts: "Shame on you, Haldane! What do you know about international law or politics?

[6] Nov. 10, 1919, HP 6013, f. 71.   [7] II, 221–22.

You are a pro-German." She and a companion were removed, but a third woman rose a few minutes later to protest Haldane's presence and call him a traitor.[8]

Those who insulted Haldane to his face or to his friends were generally articulate people (who could find their way to a meeting of the Sociological Society), often female, and more often titled. Christopher Addison recounted with disbelief the "rubbish" that one Tory matron had told his wife about Haldane. Lady Hamilton confided to a friend that she and Sir Ian never issued an invitation without taking the precaution to ask "Do you object to meeting Lord Haldane?" More often than not, she reported, guests answered in the affirmative. The Duchess of Wellington (Margot's "D. . . . . . ss of W. . . . . ."?) heard from Lady Mansfield Clarke that the lord chancellor's brother, the Oxford physiologist, was secretly experimenting with bombs to blow up the kingdom; she conveyed this information to Leo Maxse. Lady Primrose (Rosebery's daughter-in-law!) learned from her sister-in-law, a friend of Grey's sister, that Haldane literally held Grey "under a *hypnotic influence*"; she promptly alerted Bonar Law. The Duke of Argyle forwarded to Maxse information he had obtained from his solicitor about alleged financial irregularities on the part of Haldane and his youngest brother, William, Crown agent for Scotland. Sir S. K. MacDonnell, formerly private secretary to the third Marquess of Salisbury, helped the editor of the *Daily Express* keep an eye on Haldane's servants at Queen Anne's Gate. And years later Lady Milner (Maxse's sister) refused to travel aboard the same train as "that scoundrel Haldane."

By far the most preposterous example of wartime gullibility was the infamous Pemberton Billing case that broke in the spring of 1918. The defendant was a journalist-politician on the Horatio Bottomley model who was in fact Bottomley's protege. He professed the existence in Berlin of a black book that contained the names of 47,000 British public figures who had been sexually corrupted by German agents; among the few names to be divulged were those of Henry and Margot Asquith, Robert Ross, Haldane, and the judge who presided at the trial. Billing's charges, made in his own journal, the *Vigilante*, were echoed by Bottomley in *John Bull*: "How can any decent man boast of finding a 'spiritual home' in this land [Germany] of male perverts and female

8 "Lord Haldane," *Fortnightly Review*, Sept., 1928, p. 301.

decadents?" Bottomley asked, with obvious reference to Haldane, in his June 8 survey of "vice in high places." Margot Asquith, who considered the whole affair a further attempt by Lloyd George and Lord Beaverbrook to blacken the Asquith name, was incensed: "Truth *used* to 'prevail sooner or later' but now it *never prevails*. It is as out of fashion as Christ's teachings."[9] Haldane, for whom the Black Book case had the depressing air of *déjà vu*, was resolved to "take no notice. Some people may believe Billing, but not many. Other people worry about their names being used, but I do not bother."[10] He never ceased to marvel that journalists could fabricate such nonsense. But even more incredible was the fact that a vast number of Englishmen found such stories not only fascinating but plausible. "For the first time for generations," the *Daily Express* professed in its New Year's Day editorial for 1913, "men . . . have begun to believe that there is widespread corruption in public affairs." The experience of war made that belief more prevalent and more twisted. If the Pemberton Billing case had any significance, it, like the press agitation three years earlier, attested to the fact that the British public not only had a taste for sensationalism but also that it considered members of the old political order capable of any deviation, public or personal.

Particularly during the winter of 1914–1915, when national confidence was at an ebb, British society took out its fears and disappointments upon scapegoats. Public opinion was as fearful of dissent as it was of the enemy, and it had an exceedingly difficult time distinguishing between the two. In a number of cases, no genuine effort was made. The extremist journals were unable to decide whether to send Ramsay MacDonald, perhaps the most prominent pacifist, to the Tower or the gallows. It was seriously argued that anyone who criticized the war, if not the Government, was rendering the nation a disservice by giving comfort to the enemy: Blumenfeld lectured Edward Lyttelton, the outspoken headmaster of Eton, that "this is no time to dismay public opinion by making speeches criticising national policy."[11] This, of course, is a traditional argument, but rarely in British history has it achieved effects comparable to those during the First World War. "There is not a place in Great Britain today," Lord Morley wrote

---

[9] Margot Asquith to Haldane, June 26, 1918, HP 5913, ff. 182–85.

[10] Haldane to his sister, June [3], 1918, HP 6013, f. 35.

[11] Note by Blumenfeld on Lyttelton's letter of August 18, 1915, Blumenfeld Papers. Lyttelton was soon pressured to resign the headmastership of Eton.

Andrew Carnegie on November 30, 1914, "where you could hold an open meeting to criticize the war—either its origins, its circumstances, or its consequences. The president of the Peace Society," he complained, "is a member of the Cabinet!!"[12]

Even the editors of anti-ministerial journals, themselves largely responsible for whipping up this intolerance, hesitated to appear as vehement in print as in private. Their criticism of the Asquith Government was usually backhanded and oblique, neither as explicit nor as constructive as that which the *Manchester Guardian* had offered during the Boer War or journalists like William Connor (Cassandra) would offer during World War II. When the Northcliffe papers came out too openly against Lord Kitchener's war office performance, copies were burned in protest at the London Stock Exchange. It was rare, however, that anti-Government journals were so plainspeaking. Like the members of the Long Parliament, to whom they often compared themselves for other reasons, these editors and columnists professed loyalty to the men and institutions that they assiduously worked against. This was a subterfuge that allowed them to pursue their designs without incurring public censure. They assured their readers that they had no desire to turn the Prime Minister and his party out of office, only to stimulate a more vigorous and efficient war effort. They congratulated themselves for helping Asquith marshal the resources of the nation. Yet at the same time they waged relentless campaigns against certain ministers through whom they hoped to discredit the Government as a whole. Because the political truce made it impossible to launch a frontal assault, they resorted instead to flank attacks. Yet it was obvious to all concerned that their object was not the removal of certain members— Haldane, Simon, McKenna, or Masterman—so much as the destruction of the ministry itself. When Asquith and Kitchener continued in office after May 1915 without Haldane, most of Haldane's critics conceded that they had been angling for bigger fish all the while.

Why, then, had they concentrated upon Haldane in the first place? For one thing, he was among the least popular of ministers whose work, if it was known to the public, tended not to be appreciated. For another, he was known to be an old friend of Asquith, and it was thought that the premier would sooner sacrifice office than a friendship: by attacking Haldane it was therefore possible to attack Asquith's honor

[12] Morley-Carnegie Correspondence.

if not his name. It was also possible to attack through Haldane the Liberal Government's military program for the past decade, its prewar relations with Germany, and its attitude toward the conduct of the war. In several respects, it was even possible to cast aspersions upon the Government's naval policy and certain welfare programs. Often as suspicious of one another as they were of him, these journals did not necessarily have much in common beyond the fact that each recognized the convenience of Haldane as a scapegoat. To be sure, Haldane was only one of several ministerial targets (particularly at the outset of the campaign), but his name appeared with sufficient regularity to assure him an overall prominence. Like Arnold White, who contributed scathing columns to the *Daily Express,* each came to consider "the downfall of Haldane" a matter of "life or death to the Unionist Party." This was the supreme test case, a means to circumvent the political truce: "If we do not destroy him there is no reason why the Radical boches should not go on for thirty years."[13]

Two questions are crucial to an understanding of the press agitation against Lord Haldane. First, could his assailants have possibly taken seriously the assorted charges that they leveled against him? Second, to what extent, if any, was there a link between these journalists and his parliamentary opponents? Before either can be answered, one must identify the participants in the anti-Haldane agitation. This was not, as many accounts suggest, a single-handed villainy perpetrated by Lord Northcliffe; nor was it a national outcry. The handful of offending journals, all London-oriented and, with one exception, London-based, were either among the highest of the high Tory or the most scurilous of the gutter press; they were the *National Review, John Bull, Blackwood's Magazine, The Times,* the *Daily Mail,* the *Daily Express,* and the *Morning Post.* Other publications, Liberal as well as Unionist, often called Haldane's policies into question, but their criticism differed in quantity, quality, and intent. "I . . . was of course critical about certain points," John St. Loe Strachey, editor of *Spectator,* admitted to Elizabeth Haldane, "as I should have been if the Archangel Gabriel had been Secretary of State for War, but to attack him in the way in which he was attacked was outrageous."[14]

To an extent that is often not realized, Haldane's enemies knew

13 White to Maxse, Feb. 4, 1915, Maxse Papers.
14 June 15, 1915, HP 6025, ff. 120–21.

cr. London *Daily Express*, January 12, 1915

"THE THREE SACKS"

"Two are shown above, the third everyone is patiently awaiting"

their victim personally. Leo Maxse had dined with him regularly earlier in the century as a fellow-member of the Webbs' Coefficient society, as had W. A. S. Hewins and F. S. Oliver. Blumenfeld had known him since 1900. And Haldane had come into frequent contact with Geoffrey Robinson and Lord Northcliffe regarding war office work and educational proposals. Even Horatio Bottomley, a member of the 1906 Parliament, had brushed past Haldane in the lobbies. It appears quite obvious that these individuals persecuted him not out of ignorance but out of a first-hand appreciation of his vulnerability.

So astute an observer as Beatrice Webb was inclined to exonerate the "better class Conservatives" from "hunts" of this type, which she saw as the work of "such minor M. P.s as Hewins, [Sir Richard] Cooper and [Lord Charles] Beresford."[15] She might have added to her list William Joynson-Hicks, Ronald McNeill, and Jesse Collings, among others. These backbenchers were undeniably in collusion with Haldane's enemies in Fleet Street—Beresford planted material in the correspondence columns of the *Morning Post*—but at the same time the agitation received at least the tacit approval of certain Opposition leaders who might easily have muzzled their supporters. Lord Milner remained the sphinx of British politics, though his word would have carried great weight with Maxse, Gwynne of the *Morning Post*, and Robinson. F. E.

15 Unpublished diary, May 3, 1915, XXXII, f. 107, Passfield Papers.

Smith, who later praised Haldane as "a sturdy patriot surrounded by mealy-mouthed traitors,"[16] said nothing. Austen Chamberlain kept in close touch with Maxse, an old friend, whose denunciations of "Haldane and Haldaneism" he read with lively interest.[17] And Arnold White, columnist for the *Express*, sent word to Maxse that he had "talked at length with Bonar Law, Carson and Long," who indicated "no desire to abandon the campaign against Haldane just as the scent is burning"; to the contrary, he found each of these Unionist leaders "in one way . . . [or] another . . . anxious to be present in Whitehall or St. James' Street when the plump body of the Member for Germany swings in the wind between two lamp posts."[18]

A. J. Balfour, the Opposition leader best qualified to speak in Haldane's defense, proved as usual a fair weather friend. Besides, Balfour was so suspect within his own party that his support would have been a mixed blessing; still, he might have induced other members of the Unionist hierarchy to speak out. Lord Robert Cecil, who later admitted that "no one knew better than he how loyal [Haldane] had been," rejoined that "he . . . had behaved no worse than A. J. B."; but Edmund Gosse reminded him "how badly A. J. B. had behaved."[19] Lord Lansdowne, whom Haldane considered "a very good but not a very strong man,"[20] remained silent. So did Lords Salisbury, Selborne, and Derby, each of whom surely knew better. On March 15, 1916, Haldane informed his mother of an encounter with Lord Derby, who "was very friendly" and who paid tribute to "my labours at the War Office, with which he was in entire agreement. But they are all nervous about speaking out," he complained.[21] Did these Unionists behave any more shamefully than Asquith or Grey, who either preserved an official silence or replied with insufficient evidence and effort? Lord Knutsford was fully justified when he told Haldane that had "Grey and Asquith . . . stuck more to you in *public*," Salisbury and Balfour, among others, would have felt obliged to do the same.[22]

Haldane's antagonists were encouraged not only by the active support they received from one section of the Opposition front bench, but also

16 *Britannia*, March 1, 1929.
17 Chamberlain to Maxse, Feb. 1, 1915, Maxse Papers.
18 Feb. 4, 1915, Maxse Papers.
19 Gosse to Haldane, Aug. 23 [1917], HP 5913, ff. 186–89.
20 Haldane to his mother, March 14, 1918, HP 5999, f. 107.
21 HP 5995, f. 86.   22 June 21 [1916], HP 5913, f. 99.

cr. London *Daily Express*, January 16, 1915

"WOODMAN, SPARE THAT TREE"

"Sturdy looking tree this! Wonder if I dare have a cut at it,
or perhaps I could graft on an olive branch or two"

by the timidity of other parliamentarians, Unionist and Liberal. In this
sense, Bonar Law, Balfour, and Asquith were equally culpable. Strachey
was unfortunately mistaken in his presumption that "to have leading
articles in [Haldane's] defence was paying too much a compliment to
idiotic and muddle-headed people who attacked him so ungenerously
and so stupidly."[23] The longer responsible journalists and politicians
hesitated to offer a public contradiction, the more it appeared that the

[23] Strachey to Elizabeth Haldane, June 15, 1915, HP 6025, ff. 120–21.

charges against Haldane, however absurd, were well grounded. The attacks grew more vehement as resistance failed to materialize. With the collusion of less scrupulous Unionist politicians, certain anti-ministerial journals had found a way to settle old scores against a Government unassailable during wartime by more creditable means.

The anti-Haldane brigade was led by the *National Review*, a monthly owned and edited by Leo Maxse (it rhymes with taxi, he told his readers), who, under one name or another, contributed the bulk of its contents. That Maxse had a way with a phrase was undeniable— even Asquith found his style "very diverting"[24]—and his contacts were sufficiently high placed to provide him with considerable inside information; he was largely responsible for exposing the Marconi scandal in 1913. Each issue of the *Review* began with the editor's intensely personal review of the "Episodes of the Month," so personal in fact that it did not appear when he was "laid up . . . with the prevalent chill" or otherwise indisposed. The articles that followed were variations on the same themes; they were written either by Maxse (often under a nom de plume) or by one of his steady contributors, most of whom at one point or another were critics of Haldane: H. O. Arnold-Forster, Rudyard Kipling, Arnold White, F. S. Oliver, Lovat Fraser, Leverton Harris, William Joynson-Hicks, Lord Willoughby de Broke, Sir Henry Wilson, or the Duke of Bedford. Padding out each issue were mundane features on recreation ("The Financial Aspects of Foxhunting"), travel, family life ("The Eternal Servant Problem"), or the gardens of England. In the March 1915 number, Maxse took time out from his attacks upon Haldane to investigate the effects of war upon wildlife.

The *National Review* was passionate in its devotion to certain causes and rabid in its opposition to others; there was never a middle ground. In either case, it bestowed its praise or abuse directly upon the individual who, in its opinion, personified that cause. Maxse was a zealot for Tariff Reform (Joseph Chamberlain), National Service (Lord Roberts), the British Empire (Lord Milner), a pro-French foreign policy (Sir Edward Grey), and a big navy (Lord Charles Beresford). He denounced egalitarian legislation (David Lloyd George), Irish Home Rule (John Redmond), the Blue Water naval school (Lord Fisher), Tory

---

[24] Asquith to Harcourt, July 4, 1919, Harcourt Papers.

defeatism (A. J. Balfour), the City of London (financiers with "English hearts and German pockets" or vice versa), and, especially, any attempts to accommodate Germany (Lord Haldane).

As early as the 1890s, Maxse was convinced of the inevitability of a war with Germany. And no sooner had the ink dried on the Versailles Treaty than he began to warn against another. In neither case was this as much a tribute to his powers of prophesy as a testimony to the potency of the hatreds he and others like him disseminated. In 1910 he offered fifty pounds to John Dillon's favorite charity if Dillon could prove, as he had told the House of Commons, that the *National Review* advocated preventive war. Nonetheless, Maxse's journal hammered away month after month at the German menace and preached that it was only a matter of time before Berlin would attempt to destroy Britain. In the first few years of the century, Maxse had been mildly critical of the steps that the Unionist Government was taking to prepare for the coming struggle. But after the Liberals came into office in December 1905, his fears and condemnations knew no bounds. Britain's fate had fallen into the hands of politicians (not statesmen) more concerned with party advantage than imperial destiny. The Liberals, or Radicals as he preferred to call them, would give away the British Empire "with a pound of tea"; they were too small-minded and self-seeking to defend the nation's interests, let alone its honor. England, under Liberal rule, had been reduced to "an island in the German Ocean, governed by Scotsmen, kicked by Irishmen, and plundered by Welshmen."

The vitriol that flowed from Leo Maxse's pen seemed like eyewash held alongside the columns of Horatio Bottomley's *John Bull*, a weekly lower in tone and higher in sales. Its editor was neither as socially respectable nor as politically responsible as Maxse, whom he somehow managed to surpass in self-publicity. In early May 1915, after hearing of official plans to remove the banners of the eight "enemy garter knights" from St. George's Chapel, Windsor, he announced his intention to tear them personally from the chapel rafters; he then boasted that his threats had been responsible for their removal. Bottomley, who spent his early years in an orphanage, conducted an exhaustive search for his father's grave with the view to mark the site with a monument to the editor of *John Bull*. With his taste for chorus girls and Pommery Nature (1906 vintage), he found himself in the bankruptcy courts nearly as often as he was prosecuted for libel. From 1906 to 1912 he sat in the Commons, but found the pages of *John Bull* a more convenient forum. His experiences at Westminster convinced him that parliamentary institutions—as he told a Trafalgar Square rally of transport strikers on May 26, 1912—were "played out." The alternative that he proposed was what he called a Business Government, conducted by nonpartisan professionals; and he did not hesitate to promote himself for the leading assignment.

The Great War provided Bottomley with his golden opportunity. After years of warning against the German peril, he could advertise himself as "the voice in the wilderness that was heard at last." He profited handsomely by pandering to his countrymen's passions and prejudices. He sold insurance against zeppelin raids and shares in a John Bull cooperative bank; he solicited donations for a John Bull charity fund; and he lectured, at hefty fees, to capacity audiences around the country. The proceeds were not accounted for, nor did they keep him solvent for long.

Bottomley was no doubt hurt by the disdain he received from party politicians. When war came the Government not only refused his services as a recruiting agent but also neglected to provide *John Bull* with the Press Bureau releases that were sent even to the provincial journals. But Bottomley took pride in *John Bull's* reputation as "a negligible journalistic quantity," and in his own as "an unfashionable, irresponsible and discredited politician": these, he knew, provided each of them with considerable popular appeal. ". . . *John Bull* is read by a million people every week," he boasted in his issue of August 3, 1912,

and that million not the least thoughtful and intelligent section of the community, and somehow or other, they believe in their Editor. They believe in his cry for the abolition of the musty, rusty, idiotic and corrupt system of Party, and the substitution of a Business Government for a Business Nation; they even believe that it may be his destiny to take an active part, some day, in bringing that great change about.

In addition to pleas for money and confidence, Bottomley printed columns in Cockney dialect ("In the Barber's Chair"), occasional blue cartoons, and incessant denunciations of Germany. Unlike Maxse, he was explicit in his demands for a preventive war, and chastised the Government for failing to seize the Agadir Crisis of 1911 as a favorable opportunity. Bottomley's other targets included Irish Home Rule, the

Salvation Army, Bernard Shaw, and officials of the Church of England. Like Maxse, he deplored the pacifism of Ramsay MacDonald and Keir ("Kur") Hardie, yet he refused to condemn the entire Labour Party; and although he ridiculed the suffragettes, he did not oppose votes for women. Undoubtedly the greatest difference between Bottomley and Haldane's other enemies was the fact that *John Bull* would have no truck with Lord Roberts's National Service scheme, which it regarded as an attempt on the part of the military authorities to extend their influence within British society. In his first three issues for 1912, Bottomley examined the nation's defenses and advised "How to Fight Germany". He found that the Territorial Force was "going to the dogs" because the "military bureaucrats," wanting nothing less than Conscription, were "driving away youths . . . by their idiotic rules and regulations." Bottomley, for altogether perverse reasons, therefore found no fault with Haldane as an army reformer. Instead, he attacked the lord chancellor as a "bookworm" whose head was turned by Goethe and Schiller and who, in turn, turned the heads of his Cabinet colleagues. Bottomley was so incensed by the fact that Haldane took long walks through the Perthshire hills with a canine companion named Kaiser (what better indication could there be of the sympathies of a self-confessed dog lover?), that one trembles to think what he would have said had he known that, a half century later, the kennel at Cloan would be occupied by a dachshund.

The third of the anti-Haldane journals was the most dissimilar. This was *Blackwood's Magazine*, a monthly founded at Edinburgh in 1817 as an antidote to the whiggish *Edinburgh Review*. Unlike the others, it was not stamped with the personality of its editor, who did not even identify himself on the title page; he was, however, George Blackwood, a member of the family that has provided the magazine with its editors since its inception. *Blackwood's* contributors, who were listed, tended with few exceptions to be little known during this period. Aside from a regular column on current events, inappropriately titled "Musings without Method," *Blackwood's* was exclusively literary. Its columns, which had previously introduced the works of George Eliot and Anthony Trollope, now serialized features that ranged in quality from the lesser novels of John Buchan to the fictional diary of an Indian subaltern. The "Musings" revealed the same dedication to empire as the stories they accompanied. They were written during the first twenty-nine years of this century by Charles Whibley, whose authorship was a poorly kept secret. The column, as was fitting, was discontinued after his death. Whibley also contributed, again anonymously, "Letters of an Englishman" to his friend Lord Northcliffe's *Daily Mail*. He was staunchly Unionist, ardently imperialist, and devoted to Lord Roberts. Not so much anti-Liberal as anti-democratic (he praised Lord Kitchener for having "never once in his life stooped to the making of a popular speech"), his prime targets included Woodrow Wilson, mass literacy, trade unionism, the Parliament Act, Home Rule, and, above all that "noisy futile abstraction called the People."

Until others led the way, Whibley was relatively kind to Haldane, whom he regarded as a more sober Radical than Lloyd George, Churchill, or McKenna. Although he occasionally derided his style as "austere" or "unctuous," he was inclined, as late as March 1914, to ascribe any deficiencies in Haldane's military reforms to the "strenuous opposition" the war minister encountered from the parliamentary left. And the following month he paid tribute to Haldane the Philosopher for the "commendable lucidity" (!) of his Creighton Lecture at the University of London. But at the close of 1914 Whibley was quick to jump aboard the anti-Haldane bandwagon, and he continued to beat his drum for nearly a year.

Aside from the incidental fact that they were all London dailies, the remaining participants in the anti-Haldane agitation had relatively little in common. The *Morning Post* was edited by H. A. Gwynne, who had served his journalistic apprenticeship as a Boer War correspondent and who, from 1911 to 1937, led a crusade for imperial preference and the empire. R. D. Blumenfeld's tenure at the *Daily Express* was no less impressive (1904 to 1932), though in this period his rule was less absolute; he had worked on the *New York Herald* before settling in England at the turn of the century. Both *The Times* and the *Daily Mail* were the property of the mercurial Alfred Harmsworth, Lord Northcliffe, who had acquired *The Times* in 1908 as a monument to his self-esteem while he maintained the *Daily Mail* as a platform for his views. Like all proprietors of *The Times*, Northcliffe took pride in performing a service to the nation by preserving the traditions of this "entirely independent and impersonal organ." Yet although he respected *The Times*, he did not venerate it as others have. He found it neither as financially nor journalistically gratifying as the *Mail*, which he founded in 1896 and continued to edit himself. Both Northcliffe papers participated in the wartime agitation against Haldane, but Northcliffe spoke through the *Mail*, while *The Times* was, as always, the voice of Printing House Square.

The Times was the most trenchant of Haldane's critics, though its contributions to the campaigns against him were neither generous nor dependable. Yet a sentence in its columns was more telling than paragraphs from Maxse and, to be sure, pages from Bottomley. The Liberal newspapers would retaliate on Haldane's behalf by recalling pro-German (and bitterly anti-French) statements that Lord Northcliffe had made before the war; it was to no avail, for he had the authority of *The Times* behind him. Lady Horner, Haldane's long-time friend, had previously voiced fears of *The Times's* excessive influence and wished that the Liberal press "were stronger and that someone read it!"[25] The *Manchester Guardian* might have been more consistently righteous, the *Westminster Gazette* more incisive, and the *Daily News* and *Daily Chronicle* more judicious in their editorial comment; this hardly mattered, for *The Times* remained *The Times*.

In 1912 Lord Northcliffe replaced G. E. Buckle, the editor he had inherited when he bought *The Times* four years earlier, with the younger and more spirited Geoffrey Robinson. Until he clashed with Northcliffe in 1919, Robinson, who took the name Dawson in 1917, remained in charge of *The Times*; and after Northcliffe's death in 1922, the new owner, J. J. Astor, restored him for a further tenure of eighteen years. Robinson came to *The Times* with a distinguished background in scholarship and imperial affairs. He had served his apprenticeship in South Africa as a member of the Milner "Kindergarten," from which he graduated into journalism. Ironically, Leo Maxse, the life-long enemy of Germany, had hailed the appointment of Robinson who, under his later name, would achieve an infamous reputation as an appeaser: "Although a Fellow of All Souls," Maxse wrote in the *National Review*, "there is no touch of the prig about a man who has seen too much of the world to imagine himself omniscient and infallible, or to regard Balliol as the hub of the universe." Northcliffe, more farsighted in this case, soon found fault with his editor's German sympathies. The last person who could have denounced Haldane as pro-German, Robinson instead condemned Haldane for being complacent and ineffectual. In a circular letter that he prepared on August 3, 1916, for friends removed from the political scene, he explained:

25 Lady Horner to Elizabeth Haldane, Jan. [13], 1910, HP 6022, f. 15.

Personally, I have never underrated Haldane's work at the War Office. He did try to make it efficient, so far as he could obtain efficiency without incurring [un]popularity. But he never made a fight for anything, and nearly every step of progress was made at the price of some concession. Moreover all this good work, which is unquestionable in the Privy Council as well as at the War Office, does not get over the simple fact that Haldane stood to the public as the great expert on German intentions, and that he was either hoodwinked or concealed his fears. The whole Liberal Government must share the blame, but Haldane has brought special condemnation on himself by allowing his vanity to push him to the front.[26]

While *The Times*'s attitude toward Haldane reflected its editor's Milnerite affiliations, the *Daily Mail*'s reflected Lord Northcliffe's own concerns. Northcliffe had for years taken a keen interest in air power and had offered, publicly and privately, suggestions to the Government. He deplored the fact that the British were not paying as much attention to the Wright brothers' recent experiments as either the French or the Germans, and he attempted to remedy the situation by hiring a French aviator to demonstrate his daredevil skills over England's seaside resorts. Haldane, whom Northcliffe first approached in 1909, did not lack an interest in the subject: the following year, combating vertigo by recalling Goethe's climb to the tower of Strasbourg cathedral, he braved a five-hundred-foot ascent in an airship. Lord Hankey, who served as secretary to the Air Committee, a permanent subcommittee of the Committee of Imperial Defence, described the opposition that Haldane's schemes for aerial warfare encountered from the admiralty, the war office, and private industry. Haldane later helped the Lloyd George Government set up a ministry for air. Yet Lord Northcliffe came away with the distinct impression that Haldane "showed but a sympathetic, scientific interest in the matter—no more," and he recalled that "the only person who took an intelligent interest . . . was Lord Roberts. Lord Haldane was suave and obviously bored."[27] Others, including Joynson-Hicks and the Marquis of Tullibardine, shared that impression. The latter related Haldane's "memorable" pronouncement in 1907 "that aeroplanes would never fly."[28]

Northcliffe was not a man to forgive an official rebuff, real or imagined. In the wartime issues of the *Daily Mail* ("the paper that

26 [Copy], Dawson Papers.
27 Northcliffe to Fisher, Feb. 5, 1915 and Northcliffe to Repington, Jan. 25, 1915 [copies], Northcliffe Papers.
28 Tullibardine to Bonar Law, March 2, 1912, Bonar Law Papers.

persistently forewarned the public about the war"), he reproached Haldane for refusing to heed his advice. Not only had Haldane neglected to provide an adequate air force, but the "late Minister of War was busily cutting down the British artillery" at the same time that "the Germans were steadily increasing theirs and providing heavy howitzers. . . ." These charges were repeated not only in editorials, but by Lovat Fraser in the regular column he contributed to the *Mail*. Fraser, who also wrote for the *National Review* and *The Times*, criticized Haldane in each capacity; but the content and intensity of his criticisms differed from one publication to another. The contrast between one of Fraser's anti-Haldane columns in the *Daily Mail* and an anti-Haldane leader in *The Times* provides striking proof that the Northcliffe sister papers were only stepsisters under the skin.

By far the most obvious contrast at this time between *The Times* and the *Mail* was mirrored not in editorial policy but in circulation figures: *The Times* sold an average of 145,000 copies (at its wartime penny rate) while the *Mail* boasted a daily sale of more than one-and-a-quarter million copies. The *Mail* was equally successful out-distancing its halfpenny rivals, including the *Daily Express* (with a net circulation of under 250,000) that would soon link its name with the fortunes of Sir Max Aitken, later Lord Beaverbrook. In the early war years, the *Express* was in a state of transition, a fact reflected in falling sales and editorial indecision. It was not until the close of 1916 that Aitken acquired control of the paper with which, according to his own account, he had had "a considerable connection . . . of an indefinite character . . . for a number of years." This "considerable connection" was financial rather than editorial. Aitken disapproved of the attacks upon Haldane, to whom he wrote a warm and sincere letter of sympathy at the time of the 1915 Cabinet crisis.

The editorship of R. D. Blumenfeld survived the change of management at the *Express* and, in fact, was strengthened by it. But his earlier participation in the anti-Haldane agitation reflected the uncertainties of his position and those of his paper's future. H. A. Gwynne of the *Morning Post*, distressed by the long silences that punctuated Blumenfeld's campaign against Haldane, attributed them to the fact "that just now the *Express* has got more masters than one"[29] (does this imply that Aitken was a restraining influence?); and Arnold White,

[29] Gwynne to Maxse, March 4, 1915, Maxse Papers.

who wrote a weekly column for the *Express,* assured Maxse that "Blumenfeld understands as well as anybody alive what the situation is, but he has his paper to think of and after all that to an Editor must be the dominant factor in political controversy."[30]

Not only were the *Express*'s attacks upon Haldane more sporadic if not less vituperative, but they also tended to take a different form from those in other papers. Rarely was Haldane attacked directly in an *Express* editorial. For the most part such assaults were limited to front-page fillers and signed political columns. There was little room for political reporting among the social features that crowded the *Express* before Beaverbrook taught the lesson that news made (and sold) newspapers; instead there were elaborate accounts of aristocratic theatricals and masquerades, the weddings and particularly the divorces of the socially prominent, and attempts to solve the servant problem by awarding prizes to those who had served longest the same employer. The *Express* was less constructive in its approach to other, more pressing social problems. "Send the Suffragettes to St. Helena!" it thundered in 1913 in the same spirit that it would treat the resident alien problem a year later.

Beginning on May 13, 1913, and on every subsequent Monday, the *Express* featured a column ("Looking Round") by Arnold White, who had previously written for the *National Review* and, under various pseudonyms, for other right-wing journals. White initiated his column with a diatribe against Joseph Pease, president of the Board of Education, who had twice defeated him in parliamentary elections and who was identified as a practitioner of "passivism—a creed that is incompatible with our national existence" but which was endemic among Liberal politicians. As an antidote to passivism, White championed the monarchy and the empire, and he denounced the Prime Minister for declining to make Empire Day a British holiday, on the grounds that observing the King's birthday was sufficient. Like Maxse, with whom he was in close communication, White believed that the Liberals had retained power since 1906 by negating the influence of the monarchy, and "by sowing hate between class and class" and between the component populations of the British Isles. Free Trade, so far as he was concerned, was a system that fostered "the immigration of leprous

---

[30] White to Maxse, Feb. 4, 1915, *Ibid.*

persons or the importation of leper-tainted garments." Back in March 1909, when his column was carried in the *Manchester Daily Dispatch*, White had hailed Haldane as a war minister whose "achievement stamps him as one of the masterminds of our era"; needless to say, his opinion changed in the interim. The most violent political writing in the *Express* invariably carried White's by-line, and one suspects that on those occasional Mondays when "Looking Round" was "unavoidably held over," it was because the author had gone too far in his denunciations.

Completing the list of the anti-Haldane journals was the *Morning Post*, which claimed to be the oldest of the London dailies, and which was still waging a valiant campaign against the 1867 Reform Act, let alone the repeal of the Corn Laws in 1846. It remained faithful to lost causes so long that it eventually saw many of them come back into fashion. In 1924 the *Morning Post* sent shivers down aristocratic spines by raising the specter of the guillotine when the first Labour Government—in which Haldane sat as Lord Chancellor—took office. And two years later it distinguished itself for its bellicose attitude toward the General Strike (it loaned its presses to the Government's *British Gazette*). Like the ideals it professed, it was on the wane through the whole of this period. In 1937 it was absorbed by the *Daily Telegraph*, which retains several of its features. Like most men of progressive views, Haldane disdained this newspaper, though he could not resist an occasional perusal. "Contrary to my habit, I asked for a *Morning Post* today," he began a gracious letter to Lady Randolph Churchill on July 16, 1898, congratulating her upon one of the first of her son's many public speeches.[31]

H. A. ("Taffy") Gwynne, editor of the *Morning Post*, was an ebullient Welshman with a shock of red hair, enviable political contacts, and a devotion to Rudyard Kipling; in later years his most treasured keepsake was a pencil presented to him by the poet's widow. He made it a lifelong practice to send lengthy memoranda to successive prime ministers, whose private secretaries replied, at best, with curt notes of acknowledgment. The consistency of *Morning Post* policy was due in large part to the longevity (1911 to 1937) and sureness of his command. Unlike Blumenfeld or Robinson, he received the unstinted

[31] Randolph Churchill, *Winston S. Churchill* (London, 1966), I, 396.

support of his proprietor, Lady Bathurst, whose outlook matched his. Under his control, the *Morning Post* was the semiofficial organ of the armed services, the apostle of tariff reform, the patron of high society, and a dependable guide to international finance. It was steadfastly pro-monarchy and pro-Church. Except when it dealt with the socialist peril, it observed a propriety that bordered upon tedium. In this respect, its campaign against Lord Haldane was typical: it was ardent without becoming vulgar and shrill. But as was so often the case in these years, Gwynne was more effective an agitator behind the scenes—in his dealings with Carson, Long, Bonar Law, and others—than he was in print.

By far the most eloquent of Haldane's critics, and among the most insidious, was affiliated with no publication, though he contributed on an informal basis to several. This was F. S. Oliver, one of the most devoted of the Milnerites and one of the few who made politics and political journalism a hobby, not a career. A successful financier, Oliver occupied his spare moments writing an incessant stream of letters to nearly every Unionist leader and editor. But it was essentially between hard covers that his writing appeared. In addition to a biography of Alexander Hamilton and an anti-Home Rule tract, Oliver wrote a fiery indictment of the political order, *Ordeal By Battle*; it was published in June 1915, weeks after the political events it had been designed to precipitate, but it was timely nonetheless. Like all Oliver's writings, published and private, this was an unremitting attack upon democracy and its leaders: inefficient, disloyal, cowardly, and insincere. Its style captured the imagination of Ronald Munro Ferguson, among others, who commended it to Lord Rosebery: "Oliver is severe on the late [Liberal] Government, indeed on all Government! and I think you will enjoy, as I did, his character sketches of some of our friends."[32] F. S. Oliver occupies a special place on the roster of Haldane's critics. Neither an editor nor a publisher, he was a free-lance gadfly who provided a link between them and the anti-Haldane soldiers and politicians; and he expressed in cogent if extreme philosophical terms the case against Haldane and Liberalism.

Despite the great diversity among Haldane's critics, certain similarities emerge. Anti-intellectualism contributed in varying measures to

[32] August 2, 1915, Rosebery Papers.

each of the campaigns. It was most blatant in the case of Bottomley, who considered membership in the "World-Republic of Letters" incompatible with loyalty to King and Country. The *Daily Express* invariably portrayed Haldane in front-page cartoons as a bulbous academic, dressed in cap and gown, and often perched atop thick volumes labeled "Schopenhauer" and "Cant." Like Kipling, whom so many of them lionized, Haldane's assailants disdained "the brittle intellectual who cracks beneath the strain." Northcliffe, who left school at the age of sixteen, advised aspiring journalists that: "University and public school education are often of benefit but in the practical affairs of life they as often require living down."[33] The careers of Maxse, Oliver, and Whibley backed up Northcliffe's observation; all Cambridge graduates, they struggled to redeem themselves in the rough and tumble world of Fleet Street and the City. The most militant misprisers of intellect have invariably been disenchanted intellectuals. Only Robinson, an Oxford man, made no effort to "live down" his university background, a fact that did not endear him to his chief. The others, of course, had nothing to "live down." Yet regardless of the quality of their respective educations, these men found little to admire in the attainments of Haldane, Morley, Asquith, or Balfour. They were far more impressed with Lloyd George or Bonar Law, with whom they could readily identify. This was not necessarily philistinism so much as an awareness, vague in most cases, that the time had come for a new politics, less mindful of tradition and more vigorous in its response to twentieth-century problems.

Anti-semitism was another common denominator, closer to the surface in some cases than in others. This sentiment was as always particularly prevalent among those who aspired to social station; it was usually purposeless and sometimes sportive, as when his colleagues referred to Edwin Montagu as "the Assyrian." Geoffrey Robinson made clear his feelings during the 1930s. Lord Northcliffe, despite his insistence that he was "a very keen friend and student of Israel," encountered frequent difficulty with members of the "Ancient Race," a fact that his biographers ascribe to his susceptibility, "like many Englishmen, to the ancient fear of Jewish willpower with its enormous unconcern for other people's ideals."[34] Leo Maxse's disclaimers were equally

---

[33] Pound and Harmsworth, p. 42.   [34] *Ibid.*, p. 447.

profuse and even less convincing; he saw the Radical Party disseminating "Hebrew influences" through Parliament, the press, financial and social circles. Maxse did his best to "distinguish between the National Jew, who is a patriot, and the International Jew, who is a cosmopolitan and usually an enemy of England and a more or less avowed agent of Germany." It was the latter variety that he found rampant among the Liberals, along with such other pro-Germans as "Quakers, sentimentalists and cranks," all attracted by the party's adherence to Free Trade, from which they might profit at the nation's expense. Arnold White, in an unsolicited defense of R. D. Blumenfeld ("he always reminds me of Disraeli, a name by which I call him in our correspondence"), cited two "classes" of Jews: "those who are as loyal to this country as were the Huguenots after the Revocation of the Edict of Nantes, and those who remain cosmopolitan, indifferent or hostile, secretly, towards England."[35] Horatio Bottomley was not nearly so theatrical: unable to decide whether Jews deserved a national home in Palestine, he was convinced it was "high time Brighton was relieved!"[36]

Although each prosecutor found Haldane guilty on different counts, to each he typified what was worse in Liberalism. A Scotsman by birth ("I'm sure you must be a Jew," Northcliffe liked to tease, "you've got such a Scotch name"), he was cosmopolitan in his upbringing, aloof in manner, and a lawyer by profession. Since Tudor times there had been jests that the House of Commons was no more than a fifth Inn of Court. Now, in the early twentieth century, it could be said that the Cabinet was a sixth. Lawyers, who had always been attracted to the Liberal standard, came to dominate that party largely as a result of the late-Victorian Whig exodus. In the wartime Liberal Government, lawyer-statesmen monopolized the highest offices, including the premiership: they included Haldane, Sir Rufus Isaacs, Sir John Simon, Reginald McKenna, Augustine Birrell, and, a solicitor by training, David Lloyd George.

Sir Edward Clarke, president of the Bar Association and a former solicitor-general, celebrated the prominence of lawyers in official places. But the majority of Haldane's critics were less impressed. Maxse replied to Clarke in the August 1908 National Review: "Does the training of men, however learned and able, who have passed half

35 White to Blumenfeld, Dec. 2, 1915, Blumenfeld Papers.
36 H. J. Houston, The Real Horatio Bottomley (London, 1923?), p. 123.

their lives in chambers and courts, and who are wont to rely on 'instructions', fit them to deal with national and Imperial affairs . . . ? Government is a very different thing." Four months later, he castigated lawyers for deifying The Law and for taking refuge in abstraction; when Haldane and Lord Crewe dismissed Lord Roberts's defense proposals in the Lords, Maxse drew a sardonic picture of "Lord Crewe . . . deprecating the landing of the German army corps, while his friend Mr. Haldane applies to the Court of Chancery for an injunction to restrain the invader." How could one entrust the affairs of state, he asked, to men who had prostituted public service by voting salaries for members of Parliament? And after August 1914, he doubted whether lawyers, accustomed to collecting a fee whether or not they saved their client's neck, could understand that should they lose this case they would accompany the defendant to the gallows.

Others shared Maxse's suspicions of the "Gentlemen of the Long Robe." R. D. Blumenfeld, at first glance, put down Haldane as a dry-as-dust lawyer. An *Express* editorial on June 28, 1913, urged Asquith to take the lord chief justiceship himself rather than to appoint Sir Rufus Isaacs: "Unionists believe him [Asquith] to be a better lawyer than statesman." Arnold White, in his column for November 30, 1914, found the wartime Government "infected with political lawyers" who drew exorbitant salaries for performing dubious services. And F. S. Oliver summed up the case against the lawyer-politician, of whom he considered Asquith the "supreme type." He deprecated lawyers as fast-talking professionals whose "errors for the most part are visited on others . . . [and whose] success is largely a matter of words and pose." Oliver mentioned Abraham Lincoln and Alexander Hamilton as possible exceptions, but cautioned that "Englishmen should have to go back to the 'Glorious Revolution' of 1688 before we could find a parallel to either of these two in our own history."[37]

Members of the legal profession have been disparaged on two counts; critics of the Liberal order used them both. The first was the traditional complaint that lawyers were casuists, prepared to defend any cause for a fee. The second derided lawyers as carping pedants—"maggots of the law"—too entangled in red tape to defend national interests and security. Liberal lawyers were considered, not without justification, to

[37] *Ordeal By Battle*, pp. 203 ff.

be greater sticklers for legality than those of the Unionist variety; they were opposed on principle to schemes for compulsion and committed, even in wartime, to theories of industrial and commercial laissez-faire. Leo Maxse, forced to concede that Sir Edward Carson was "a lawyer by profession," strenuously maintained that Carson was nonetheless "a patriot from the crown of his head to the sole of his feet." Maxse would be loath to say the same about Simon, Isaacs, McKenna, or the Government's most eminent jurist, Lord Haldane.

Even before the coming of war, the Liberals, with their devotion to Cobdenite principles, were accused of weakening the bonds of empire, the defenses of the nation, and the morale of British society. "Don't Care is carrying this country toward catastrophe," Maxse warned in his July 1914 number; "either this country must destroy the Asquith Government or the Asquith Government will destroy this country." The *Daily Express* ascribed the ills of the nation—industrial strife and the women's suffrage agitation—to the prevalent system of "Government by Jellyfish." The war intensified pre-existing fears (and multiplied underwater metaphors): The *Daily Mail*, denouncing the members of the Cabinet as "limpets," proclaimed its belief "that this Government, which did not see the war coming, does not now understand the terrific nature of the struggle before it." Reginald McKenna eventually came to see the situation clearly: "The Liberals," he told A. G. Gardiner of the *Daily News*, "are not thought as a party to be sufficiently venomous. . . ."[38] Critics of the Liberal administration considered it incapable not only of venom but also of resolution. The cleavage of opinion that had existed within the Cabinet in the early days of August 1914 seemed to confirm apprehensions about Liberal incapacity. Only two ministers had made good their threats to resign, but an air of defeatism clung to many of those who remained, engendering false suspicions. On August 6 the *Daily Express* pointed out that: "One prominent member . . . who declared that England would 'only go to war over his dead body' is still alive and still a member of the Cabinet." This was assuredly not Haldane, who had stood by Sir Edward Grey all along; but he was nonetheless compromised by the company he kept.

British opinion, inflamed by propaganda and disheartened by the military stalemate, hungered to strike out somehow against the enemy.

[38] Dec. 29, 1918, Gardiner Papers.

The *Morning Post* recalled with glowing admiration (and dubious historical justification) how Queen Elizabeth, "when she found the Hanseatic League were secret enemies of England, turned every German out of the country." The *National Review* described how Germany was abusing British captives, poisoning the water along the Western Front, spreading typhus and cholera among prisoners, and perpetrating other "diabolical horrors which only Germans can devise." At the same time, it alleged, "German prisoners of war in this country live like fighting cocks. Hague Conventions are strained in their favour." Furthermore, enemy aliens were free to roam about, spying upon military installations. According to Walter Long, the Government disregarded the information volunteered by vigilant citizens about "suspicious characters in important places, such as Harrow . . ., which commands four Railway Lines and London. Apparently nothing is being done. . . ."[39] Like Long, many Englishmen were baffled by what seemed a double standard of warfare. Germany, which had invaded Belgium in defiance of an international treaty and would soon wage unrestricted submarine warfare, seemed to stop at nothing to achieve her goal, while Britain seemed to strait-jacket herself by a vainglorious adherence to outmoded principles of international morality. Various Liberals attempted to explain that for Britain to adopt German methods would constitute an indirect victory for the forces of Prussianism. Few people were convinced. As the months dragged on, it mattered less how Britain fought so long as she got on with it.

As head of the judiciary, Lord Haldane bore the brunt of the blame for the regulations concerning commercial and individual liberties that allegedly hamstrung the military authorities. "Without the written consent of the Lord Chancellor, the Attorney-General, and possibly the Lord Chief Justice," Maxse professed, "a British Naval Officer may hardly look at the enemy." To many the British Government seemed overpunctilious in its efforts to respect the navigational and trading rights of neutrals. Undoubtedly some deliveries were allowed to reach Germany through neutral, particularly Dutch ports. But it remains doubtful whether these shipments were as substantial or as vital to the enemy as critics argued. Yet orthodox Free Trade, whatever its value as a peacetime ethic, was often demoralizing as a wartime policy. No less disturbing in its effects upon the public mind was the Government's

---

[39] Nov. 19, 1914, Gwynne Papers.

reluctance to restrict or even to supervise German and Austrian citizens resident in Great Britain. The home office saw no reason to punish the innocent many for the sake of the guilty few. The arch-protectionist *Morning Post* disagreed, on the grounds that "the vitality of a nation may be measured by its attitude toward the alien." It laid the blame at the feet of its historical villain, Sir Robert Peel, that "convert to penny-in-the-slot politics." Haldane, it explained on April 21, 1915, was the last in a line of Peelites (others included Lord Palmerston and W. E. Gladstone) who betrayed the national interest to accommodate foreign profiteers.

There was one area in which wartime controls were indisputably effective, but it was hardly one that would appeal to the Government's critics. Under the provisions of the Defence of the Realm Act, a statute of virtually unlimited scope, an Official Press Bureau was set up under the direction of the solicitor-general, Sir Stanley Buckmaster. (Maxse retaliated by setting up an "Unofficial Press Bureau" that supplied releases the official one had supposedly forgotten, including Haldane's eulogies on German culture.) Liberal and Unionist journals alike chafed at this system of censorship and regulation. The *Nation*, while "willing to make allowances for the Government," complained bitterly against this "unnecessarily strong measure." The *Daily Express*, in a banner headline, protested this system of "martial law for journalists, but not for German spies." Arnold White, in this case a champion of liberty, uttered grave warnings that should "we emerge successfully from this war, but under the yoke of a vigorous censorship of opinion . . ., we shall only have exchanged the haunting menace of Potsdam for the very tyranny against which Milton protested in 1644." The *Daily Mail* asked in indignation whether "Cabinet Ministers [are] to be above criticism," and deplored the Government's heavy-handed attempt in September 1914 to suppress material in the *Globe* critical of the home office. Northcliffe, writing in the *Mail*, noted the irony that "Ministers, whose motto is or used to be 'Trust the People,' are maintaining a very curious attitude in this war." Privately, he expressed the opinion that "in certain instances . . . treatment has been meted out with particular severity" by Sir John French or the Government "to newspapers that took a prominent part in the anti-Home Rule agitation."[40]

---

[40] Northcliffe to Bonar Law, Feb. 4, 1915 [copy], Northcliffe Papers.

The Press Bureau functioned not as Lord Northcliffe implied, as a weapon of party, nor as he wrote in the *Mail*, as an agency for suppressing "unduly depressing news." Nor was it designed, as Lord Robert Cecil wrote to him, to permit "the concealment of the audacious."[41] Yet this agency incurred resentment that rubbed off on Haldane, who was often called upon to defend it in the House of Lords. The lord chancellor was perfectly sincere when he professed on August 31, 1914, that national security would be the sole criterion whether information was released or withheld. He affirmed this view to Edmund Gosse on November 8, after Gosse had written to say that Lord Charles Beresford was privately insinuating that statistics of naval losses were being doctored: "Do not feel uneasy," Haldane replied. "The policy of the Admiralty is to disclose anything that happens—good or evil—excepting where to prevent information reaching Germany it is important to delay announcements." He closed by admonishing his friend to "avoid pestilential men like Beresford,"[42] whose opinions were of no account.

What Haldane, like many contemporaries, failed to perceive was the extent to which "pestilential men" like Beresford had come to reflect more widespread suspicions and discontents. Liberalism had failed to adapt its policies and their presentation to the twin conditions of a mass electorate and an aggressive popular press. These were forces that Liberalism had itself called into existence, but which nevertheless had taken it unawares. Most Liberals had only contempt for men like Northcliffe, whom they disdained as upstarts and feared as demagogues. Sir John Simon, lamenting the destruction of German bake-shops in London and Liverpool, cited it as "the sort of thing which is published by Harmsworth, and which he and his like have instigated. It must be a great satisfaction to him to feel that he has sold his country for 1/2d."[43] What Simon and most Liberals failed to recognize was the fact that Northcliffe's chest was inflated to fill a vacuum created in public life by Liberal reticence and propriety. He and other press lords might very well have publicized attacks upon German shops to sell papers, but they had the added incentive of pressuring the Government into action which they and many others deemed imperative. There were members of the Cabinet who understood this and who conspired behind the backs of their colleagues with Northcliffe or other Fleet

[41] Dec. 4, 1914, Cecil Papers. [42] Gosse Papers.
[43] Simon to C. P. Scott, May 14, 1915, Scott Papers.

Street magnates. The fourth Earl Grey was willing to "admit" that the Northcliffe press "has sometimes given a wrong impression abroad, but Asquith's Government has never acted except in response to public opinion, and I am most grateful to *The Times* and *Daily Mail* for kicking it into action on many occasions."[44] After the Cabinet crisis of May 1915, Asquith imposed further restrictions upon the publication of war news and criticism. Such measures could not save his coalition ministry any more than they could have saved the Liberal ministry in which Lord Haldane had sat. What was needed was nothing less than a renegotiation of the covenant between the Government and the people. And this, as Haldane came to realize, was a task that Asquith and Liberalism were not equipped to undertake.

[44] Grey to Munro Ferguson, Dec. 1, 1915, Novar Papers, National Library of Australia; copy courtesy of G. C. L. Hazelhurst.

CHAPTER VI

THE OTHER WAR OF ATTRITION

One thing I have learnt very clearly, and that is that private representations, even of the most useful kind, are absolutely ineffective, while an article in The Times *runs the risk of achieving rather more than it intended.*

—GEOFFREY ROBINSON*

Like the vast majority of press crusades, that against Lord Haldane derived its force not from the logic of its case but from the urgency with which it was put. It was an outcry of many voices, raised in a din that deceptively suggested a unison among them. Contemporaries tried in vain to discern a leader: Asquith assumed it was the *Morning Post*,[1] his daughter that it was the *Daily Express*,[2] while most others, including Sir Ian Hamilton, considered it the work of "that reptile Harmsworth."[3] To the extent that anyone provided a sense of coordination, it was Leo Maxse of the *National Review*, but even he performed in his own key. The campaign against Haldane was that rare phenomenon, a chorus composed exclusively of prima donnas.

One cannot comprehend the intentions and strategies of Haldane's assailants, nor conceive of their invective, without examining, day by day, their activities against him. Although the agitation extended from the death of Lord Roberts in mid-November 1914 until the resignation of the Liberal Government six months later, the task is not nearly so laborious as it appears. The attacks ran in fits and starts, often dis-

---

* Letter to Lord Milner, Nov. 3, 1914, Milner Papers.
  [1] Asquith, *Memories and Reflections*, II, 49.
  [2] Violet Bonham Carter, *Winston Churchill As I Knew Him* (London, 1965, p. 395.
  [3] Hamilton to Haldane, Sept. 22, 1915 [copy], Hamilton Papers.

appearing from public sight for several weeks, only to be revived by specific events and disclosures. While such a survey cannot account for the reasons for Haldane's eventual removal, from it one can see in detail the situations for which he was the scapegoat.

Long before Lord Roberts's funeral, each of the contributors to the anti-Haldane agitation had revealed an antipathy, if not an outright hostility, toward Haldane. But for the most part their earlier criticism had differed little from occasional pieces that appeared in other anti-ministerial publications (the *Daily Telegraph* or *Spectator*) or even in several Liberal ones (the *Manchester Guardian* or the *Nation*). At this point, the attacks upon Haldane in these half-dozen journals took on a new intensity: they became more personal in nature, more strident in tone, and, at once, less responsible and more deliberate. These journals not only surpassed other critics of Haldane, but even their own previous performances.

Lord Roberts during his final weeks had grown more impatient with officials and less temperate in his criticism of them. Others went further and deduced that some person of authority was subverting the British war effort. *The Times* had reproduced a letter on October 17 that Professor Quidde, a Munich academic, had written to a colleague at Florence, praising Haldane, whom he did not know, for remaining within the Cabinet as a pro-German influence. It did not comment upon the letter, nor did the *National Review* which reported these "observations of a German admirer of Lord Haldane" in its November number. It was not until the next issue, in which he reported Lord Roberts's funeral, that Leo Maxse produced the letter in full, launching his offensive against its subject.

On November 9 Arnold White ventured the first of his wartime outbursts against Haldane in the *Daily Express*. It consisted of a reiteration of charges that he had made many times before, though not within recent months, that Haldane had "reduced the British Army by 40,000 men, cut down the field artillery, and extinguished the Militia." White, who did not yet call for Haldane's resignation, was no more vehement (nor more logical) than he had been in the past. "The Militia must have had something that answered to our national military needs," he insisted. "It lasted a thousand years." This was, in effect, the same argument with which he had resisted the Parliament Act and virtually every piece of Liberal reform legislation.

cr. London *Daily Express*, March 26, 1914

"LET'S HAVE SPRING CLEANING"

The *Express*, at the same time, was outraged by what it believed to be the Government's reluctance to clamp down on enemy aliens. It described mysterious signals transmitted by lantern from English coastal towns and the suspicious movements of men with Wilhelmine mustaches and heavy accents. Reginald McKenna, the home secretary, explained that neither his liberal principles nor the resources at his disposal permitted him to take the precautions that his critics demanded. The *Express* countered with a proposal, endorsed by William Joynson-Hicks and other Unionist M. P.s, to set up a committee of public safety, independent of Cabinet control, to combat the spy peril. This was symptomatic of a widespread disaffection with established institutions that extended to those who operated them.

For the moment McKenna was the minister under heaviest fire. Haldane, in no way implicated, was rarely mentioned in the initial denunciations of Liberal inertia. But on November 18, in a statement to the House of Lords, Haldane implicated himself. In a reply to the Earl of Crawford and Balcarres, who had raised the issue of enemy infiltration along the coast of Fife, he cited the legal and moral difficulties that confronted the Government for which he was spokesman in the upper house: it was "as inhuman as it was inefficacious," he explained, "to arrest aliens wholesale, irrespective of their guilt or innocence, irrespective of whether or not they had wives and families dependent upon them, in such a way that you might be subjecting absolutely innocent people to the greatest hardship. . . ." In debate on the 25th, the lord chancellor again came to the defense of the home office, but he was less fortunate in his choice of argument. Conceding that there existed within Britain surreptitious "sources of communication with the enemy," he emphasized the need "to go about the search in a scientific way and to cast suspicion where it is most likely to be founded." He acknowledged parenthetically that the Germans, because of "the extraordinary intelligence system which [they] organised in this country long before the war," possessed "certain advantages which they ought not to have. . . ."

As so often occurred during these months, Haldane deflected criticism of other Liberals to himself and, at the same time, seemed to give it justification. What more conclusive proof could there have been of the Government's ineptitude than his casual disclosure that Germany had been permitted to organize and maintain "an extraordinary intelligence system" on British soil? Because the Liberals were notorious for understating the case, it was immediately presumed that the situation was far more dangerous than Haldane implied; if this was so, why did the Government hesitate to take drastic steps? Haldane's remarks in the House of Lords exacerbated fears that they were meant to allay, and, in the process, made him the target of bitter attack. The *Daily Express* and the *Daily Mail* in their respective reports of the debate stressed the peril of the situation. The December *National Review*, published a week later, reviewed Lord Haldane's "very latest performance, which cannot be but encouraging to Professor Quidde." Maxse endorsed the suggestions that had been made by Lord Crawford, a friend and contributor, and denounced Haldane for brushing them aside: "This 'snake in the grass' could not dispute the facts recited, admitting 'that there had been a most systematic arrangement for obtaining secret information . . . which had existed for years. . . .' But as 'an enormous amount of injustice was done' in efforts to supress espionage, Lord Haldane rejected Lord Crawford's sensible proposal." Charles Whibley, writing in *Blackwood's Magazine* the same month, confessed that he too had been irritated by Haldane's manner ("he is as tiresome about his tenure of the War Office as was Cicero about his consulate") and confused by his logic. "Where could you surpass the levity of that pronouncement?" Whibley asked, after presenting a hopelessly distorted précis of the lord chancellor's speech: "in saving England from devastation, we might be guilty of injustice to Germany, therefore let England take her chance. How shall you argue with nonchalance such as that?"

The Government's critics took Haldane's statement not only as further proof of Liberal apathy but also as an alarming indication that the Government was resigned to the likelihood of national humiliation. Those who did not share Haldane's Millite principles tended to confuse his concern for individual liberties with a desire to accommodate the enemy. The misgivings with which many Liberals had entered the war were well known, though precisely who the "pacifists" had been remained in many cases a matter for conjecture. The Liberal press had not by any means been alone in its appeals for nonintervention—"To Hell with Serbia!" Bottomley had first bellowed—but unlike others it had since failed to redeem itself with sufficient bloodthirstiness. It was feared in many quarters that the Liberals, who had hoped to keep the nation out of war, were now stealthily promoting a peace with Germany at the expense of the allies.

Haldane was considered capable of greater mischief than most of his colleagues because of the ulterior influences he was believed to exert upon Sir Edward Grey. For essentially negative reasons, the political right looked upon Grey as the single upright member of the Cabinet: he had rarely spoken on domestic policies and was known to have qualms about democracy; no one could accuse him of political opportunism and his opposition to Germany was beyond question. But prewar experience, particularly the Parliament Bill crisis, had shown him to be susceptible to radical pressures. During the early winter of 1914–1915, it was feared that the well-intentioned foreign secretary lacked the physical powers, let alone the cunning, to withstand the blandishments of less trustworthy Liberals. His health and eyesight were poor, and he took extended weekends, during which his place at the foreign office was filled by his friend, Lord Haldane. There were even members of the Cabinet who found the arrangement unsatisfactory, if only for its effects upon public opinion. Lloyd George proposed "Balfour and not Haldane to act for Grey" should the latter go abroad for a projected allied conference in the early spring.[4] Minds were eventually

[4] March 6, 1915, Hankey, I, 289.

set at rest when Asquith reshuffled his ministry, omitting Haldane and adding, among other Unionists, Lord Lansdowne as minister without portfolio. The *Daily Mail* welcomed the appointment of Lansdowne, a former foreign secretary, as a guarantee "that we shall have no longer those paragraphs, so profoundly depressing to the public, to the effect that 'in the absence of Sir Edward Grey, Lord Haldane is working at the Foreign Office.'"

On December 3, 1914, the front page of the *Daily Express* carried a letter to the editor that was signed "M" and dated "Carlton Club, December 2." Its style removed any doubt that its author was Leo Maxse, who had written to the same effect in the current number of his own journal. "There is a very grave danger," he warned the readers of the *Express*, "of the pacifist and pro-German party in this country yielding to any suggestions of a disgraceful, inconclusive and disastrous peace. In this connection," he went on, "it is disquieting to know that Lord Haldane is 'assisting' Sir Edward Grey at the Foreign Office. In view of this gentleman's past utterances, what is Lord Haldane doing at the Foreign Office? We have just escaped having him again as War Minister! What, indeed, is Lord Haldane's excuse for remaining in public life?" The letter was followed by quotations from prewar speeches in which Haldane had praised the Kaiser and the latter had reciprocated with warm words for "my friend, Lord Haldane."

Maxse, hiding behind his initial, had issued the first of many demands for Haldane's removal from office. Significantly, he had done so as a reader of the *Daily Express* and not as the editor of the *National Review*. In the latter, he hesitated for the time being to go so far, though he dwelled upon the dangers of Haldane's intimacy with Grey: "They are understood to share the same roof." His letter of December 2 was a trial balloon and, as such, was entirely successful; the response gave him the confidence to persevere under his full signature. On the 4th the *Express* endorsed "M's" letter of the previous day and applauded the anti-Haldane articles that appeared in the current issue of the *National Review*: "The sooner Mr. Asquith realizes the unpopularity of the Haldane fetish, the better." Other letters, bearing single initials and the names of the best London clubs, expressed unanimous approval of the attacks upon Haldane. *John Bull* joined the fray on the 12th: "It is a matter of common knowledge that Lord Haldane is giving a hand to Sir Edward Grey at the Foreign Office. Now Lord Haldane loves the

Kaiser, and loves Germany and everything connected with her. . . . Lord Haldane's place is on the woolsack—and nowhere else." Arnold White concluded, like Maxse, that even the woolsack was too close to the center of power; in his column for December 21, he prophesied that if Haldane "remains in office, the next result may be a shameful peace."

By the closing weeks of the year, it was impossible to ignore the fact that a full-scale agitation had been launched against Lord Haldane. His opponents, at least those who trespassed into the open, were few; but they compensated in audacity for what they lacked in numbers. The *National Review* for December deplored the aspersions that had been cast upon the loyalty of Prince Louis of Battenberg, the retiring first sea lord, by "malicious and ignorant people—of whom there are no lack. . . ." Yet in the same issue, and to a far greater extent in those that followed, it attacked Haldane in much the same spirit. The lord chancellor was criticized for having been so "demonstrably and hopelessly astray on every single point on which he professed to be an authority." He had deluded his colleagues about German intentions, reduced national defenses, ridiculed national service, attempted to hold back the Expeditionary Force and, most recently, impeded the war effort by insisting upon the niceties of laissez-faire. Maxse concluded his tirade for January by citing Haldane's retention of office as "simply another symptom of the deterioration of British public life during the past decade" of Liberal rule.

Other publications had equally long lists of grievances against Haldane. The *Daily Express* could never forgive "the man who knew Germany best" for doing "the least to protect Britain." Easier to caricature than other offenders, he was held up as the personification of ministerial sloth. Its parliamentary correspondent, reporting a debate in the Lords on the issue of naturalized subjects, described how "Lord Haldane sat on the woolsack, his silver buckled shoes peeping out from beneath the black robe that goes with the ten-thousand-a-year and the woolsack, his face, set deep in his full-bottomed wig, wore an air verging on boredom, and now and then he yawned." *John Bull* portrayed him on the same occasion, sitting "back in his chair with closed eyes, as though his thoughts were far from the immediate scene. His roving fancy may perhaps have revisited Potsdam, where he and his Imperial friend were wont to walk to and fro in earnest converse. . . ." Arnold

White's columns for December 21 and January 4, 11, and 18 each presented "The Case Against Lord Haldane," and each reiterated charges that Haldane had "deceived the public about the Army, about Germany, and about spies." In reply to one reader's defense of the lord chancellor, the *Express* defined its position:

No one accuses Lord Haldane of having acted in any sense traitorously. . . . [But] if Lord Haldane had not had the wool pulled over his ears by the astute Kaiser, he would probably have listened to Lord Roberts,
AND
Then we should have had a million men under arms on August 4, 1914,
AND
THERE WOULD NOT HAVE BEEN A WAR!

The Earl of Rosslyn also wrote to the *Express* on Haldane's behalf, though he probably accomplished more harm than good by conceding his friend's "strategic error in reducing our guns." But the overwhelming majority of those who wrote letters to the editor agreed with the Duke of Somerset: "This country ought to know what to do with Lord Haldane and at any rate one other minister."

Ever since the middle of November, when Haldane had replied to Lord Crawford in the House of Lords, he was identified with the twin policies of leniency toward resident aliens and neutral shippers. It was at the turn of the year that he was attacked most furiously on this score. The British navy had seized and impounded stores of "neutral copper," primarily American in origin, that had been earmarked for enemy markets. Rumors were rife that Haldane, filling in for Grey at the foreign office, had ordered the release of one such shipment that had thereupon proceeded to a German port. The *Daily Express*, on the last day of 1914, gave full credence to these allegations in a prominent front page article; twenty-four hours later, in the more sober light of the new year, it tempered its accusations and cautiously requested the Government to "declare in unmistakable terms what is, and was, Lord Haldane's attitude. . . ." It took nearly a month for the Government to comply. Lord Derby eventually mentioned the story to Margot Asquith, who repeated it to Sir Edward Grey. The foreign secretary, in a letter of January 25, denied to Derby that there was "one word of truth in the story," and the latter volunteered "to contradict" further reports.[5]

[5] This interchange appears in Trevelyan, pp. 311 ff.

But rumors had been circulating too long to be scotched by a single private admonition to one of the most reasonable of Haldane's critics. For as long as he remained in office, and as late as the following summer, Haldane was suspected by Arnold White and innumerable others of "stand[ing] behind the policy of letting vital supplies and foodstuffs reach the Germans." It had also come to be believed that Haldane was the guardian of enemies within the kingdom. To a considerable extent, his replies to questions, official and unofficial, were to blame. Lord Crawford was no more satisfied by what he heard from Haldane privately than what he had been told from the woolsack. "It was interesting last night," he wrote Leo Maxse on January 7,

when Haldane admitted to me that the police had suggested that the Government should have powers to revoke the naturalization certificates of ex-Germans. Haldane was very unsympathetic, speaking of 'complications of international law.' I should be better pleased if he would think less about international law, and rather more about national safety.

From what Crawford could gather, there existed "a strong section in the Cabinet anxious to take a vigorous line," but these patriots were stymied "by the weaklings on the one side, and Haldane's casuistry on the other."[6]

Without a doubt, the enemies of Liberalism distorted Haldane's words for preconceived purposes. Yet it is equally obvious that, more often than not, he made it uncommonly easy for them to do so. Like the Lord High Chancellor in Dickens's *Bleak House*, he appeared upon the woolsack "with a foggy glory round his head." His vague, diffuse utterances left him open to misinterpretation even by the American ambassador, a neutral in every sense. The *Dacia*, a German-owned ship, had taken to flying the American flag to avoid capture by the British navy. The Cabinet met to consider the matter on January 12, and Grey reported its deliberations on the 21st to the ambassador who had already spoken to Lord Haldane. He had "understood" Haldane "to say that, if German ships were purchased and engaged in purely neutral trade between South America and the United States, there would be no objection on the part of the British Government." Grey refused to concede nearly so much without first consulting the Cabinet.[7] Had

[6] Maxse Papers.
[7] Memorandum for the Cabinet from Sir Edward Grey, Jan. 21, 1915, CAB 37/123/44; see also Prime Minister's report to the Sovereign, Jan. 13, 1915, CAB 37/123/23.

Haldane spoken out of turn, or had his remarks been misconstrued? In either event, his performance caused embarrassment to his colleagues.

Many of the same Opposition journalists and backbenchers who campaigned to intern aliens (and even naturalized Britons) and to assert more stringent controls over international commerce sought to declare certain nonstrategic commodities contraband. American cotton was most often mentioned; not only the German but also the British textile industries were heavily dependent upon it. Repeated attempts were made during February and March, 1915, to enlist Lord Milner's assistance for a campaign for cotton controls, but he appears to have held aloof. The Government's refusal to submit to popular pressures elicited further charges against Lord Haldane which, by this time, were force of habit; they continued even after his departure from the Cabinet in May. On July 20 the *Daily Mail* examined the link between "Cotton and Death," and Rutherfoord Harris, a right-wing Unionist, sent a cutting to Leo Maxse with the notation: "The trail of the beast Schopenhauer."[8] Both Harris and Maxse assumed that Haldane stood behind the continued reluctance of Liberal politicians to take effective steps. Doing his best to "coach my memory," Harris recounted to Maxse a conversation with Lord Sydenham, who declared himself "*convinced* that at the beginning of the War the late Government put the Cotton matter entirely into Lord Haldane's hands," judging him "an expert upon such matters." The lord chancellor had supposedly advised his colleagues that "there was no practical point to be gained in stopping Cotton as far as German military activities were concerned." The enemy could make due with synthetics, but Britain would forfeit American sympathy. Harris recalled that Lord Sydenham's verdict was that "had it not been for Lord Haldane, the late Cabinet would not have gone so hopelessly wrong over the question."[9] Leverton Harris, a Unionist—and a Harris—of another stripe, presented Maxse with a wholly different account of Haldane's earlier activities: his work with the Government to regulate the flow of American copper had left him "no doubt" that Haldane "shares with certain other Cabinet ministers the John Stuart Mill idea regarding freedom of trade, especially of such trade as involves the payment of gold by our enemies"; but he nonetheless remained

[8] Maxse Papers.   [9] Aug. 19, 1915, *Ibid.*

"strongly under the impression that Haldane had very little to do with the decision" regarding cotton.[10]

Neither Haldane nor those closest to him were able to gauge the strength and diversity of the attacks upon him. Edmund Gosse wrote late in December to report "a great deal of gossip" among his "many friends in Unionist circles."

> There is growing up and thriving by ignorant repetition a thoroughly twisted and false legend about your negotiations in Berlin in 1912. I know your indifference to such chatter, and your determination to go straight on and take no notice. But I do seriously think, in the interests of the nation and of public opinion, that things are going too far, and that you must consent to let the facts be known.

Gosse urged Haldane to allow him to send a letter to *The Times*. He did not expect that it would in itself change people's minds, but he calculated that it would coerce the foreign office to publish "a definite, historic account" that would.[11] The lord chancellor hardly required his friend to acquaint him with the situation. Although he had "not seen the *National Review* or *Blackwood*," he was receiving a "stream of anonymous letters," all of a highly defamatory nature. "It would not matter if it were not wartime," he assured Gosse. "But it is wartime and that is an awkward thing." He had consulted Grey, but found him "averse to publishing any more about the earlier negotiations with Germany"; and Haldane was reluctant "to press him at this moment." The *Daily Chronicle* came to his defense with a series of articles that began on January 5, but Haldane was sadly aware that it "counts little."[12]

It was far easier to dispose of the foolish letters he received than of the insidious campaign that elicited them. Haldane was at a loss where to begin. Each time he presumed that the storm had passed, it hit with renewed ferocity. Word reached Gosse that Haldane, in desperation, had offered his resignation to the Prime Minister on January 4, "when the attacks were at their worst."[13] This would not have been the first time that Haldane lost heart: a flurry of press attacks the previous September had prompted the same move. Elizabeth Haldane admitted that her brother "really felt these attacks even more than he should."[14]

---

[10] Aug. 18, 1915, *Ibid.*   [11] Dec. [n.d.], 1914, HP 5910, ff. 305–307.
[12] Haldane to Gosse, Jan. 4 and 6, 1915, Gosse Papers.
[13] Gosse to Elizabeth Haldane, Jan. 14, 1915, HP 6025, ff. 3–4.
[14] Elizabeth Haldane to Gosse, Jan. 11, 1915, Gosse Papers.

Gosse, always on the lookout for an opportunity to prove his devotion, reprimanded Sir Edward Grey for failing to come to the rescue of their mutual friend. At the same time he wrote well-meaning but rather silly letters to the editors of *The Times* and *Morning Post*; in the latter he stated that a portrait of Haldane that hung at Göttingen was now "draped in crepe," and desecrated with the inscription "Dead to Germany." Haldane, touched by the gesture, thanked Gosse for rendering him a "great service" that he expected "to do much good."[15]

Haldane was not indolent in his own defense. He delivered two public addresses in early January. The first, on New Year's Day, was at Auchterarder at a benefit concert to aid Belgian refugees. William Haldane, who had been invited to introduce the program, was indisposed, and the audience heard instead his oldest brother, who was spending the holiday weekend at Cloan. It was apparent that the lord chancellor neither considered the occasion worthy of an original effort, nor did he expect national coverage for remarks made in his own backyard. Yet his speech, reported in the Scottish press, evoked widespread criticism by coming uncomfortably close to something that his enemies would have attributed to him. Again he boasted that "few people . . . had known Germany as he had known her," and he offered the lame excuse that "lately she had gone mad." He told the story of a favorite dog which had disappeared overnight and "worried eleven sheep. That was a sudden outbreak in an otherwise blameless career. And what was true of him was true of Germany." Even the sympathetic *Scotsman*, which reported the speech on January 2, deplored Haldane's "homely and dangerous allegory" in an editorial a day later: "There has been no sudden seizure of madness in Germany. The German people cannot, like the peccant sheepdog, plead . . . an antecedent innocence." Horatio Bottomley, who would not deny poetic license to any man, wondered facetiously whether the "perverse animal" in question was none other than Kaiser, "who, as far as we know, remains a source of joy and comfort to his right honourable and learned master."

On January 8 Haldane delivered a speech in the House of Lords that was better conceived, but, in many respects, equally damaging. Making no explicit reference to the attacks that had been made upon him, he attempted to clarify his position regarding prewar military and

15 Haldane to Gosse, Jan. 9, 1915, *Ibid.*

cr. London *Daily Express*, April 3, 1914

"THE NEW PHILOSOPHY"

"Now, Gentlemen, remember, whenever you make an awkward speech you can always alter it in the Hansard reports afterwards. 'What I have said I have said' is merely a silly formula" (Lord Haldane has been caught altering one of his speeches)

diplomatic decisions, and particularly the vexing issue of conscription. His personal correspondence makes clear that he intended this as a reply to personal critics, but what came across was more a reply to critics of voluntary service. Although he saw "no reason to anticipate the breakdown" of the present system of recruiting, he wanted it to be understood that, in the event of "a great national emergency," he would consider it the Government's "duty" to resort to compulsion. He did not regard this as "foreign to the Constitution of this country," for under the Common Law it was "the duty of every subject of the realm to assist the Sovereign in repelling the invasion of its shores. . . ." Haldane noted with satisfaction that his remarks "had moved the House, . . . as much on the Opposition side as my own."[16] Two days later he described to his sister how he had "let myself go . . . and was cheered by both

[16] Haldane to Gosse, Jan. 9, 1915, Gosse Papers.

sides warmly." He perceived "a great reaction" in his favor among the newspapers; it had come none too soon, "for there might have been danger of 28, Queen Anne's Gate being mobbed if anything had gone wrong."[17]

The Liberal press made a concerted effort to back up Haldane in his attempts to clear his name. Within days of his speech the *Westminster Gazette* and *Daily Chronicle* featured panegyrics to his war office work; the *Nation* chimed in a week later, and the *Daily News* and *Manchester Guardian* contributed in lesser quantity. Nor was the initial response among Opposition journals unfavorable. *The Times,* which had turned down Edmund Gosse's letter in defense of the lord chancellor, now went so far as to accept another deploring censorship of the mails. Haldane was encouraged to think that this might be "a straw which shows how the current is tending to flow."[18] According to the *Daily Mail,* "the importance of Lord Haldane's statement . . . cannot be exaggerated." But the *Pall Mall Gazette* pleased him most by labeling his speech "admirably reasoned and tempered," and by citing it as proof of "how deeply he has thought upon all the questions connected with preparation for war." For a few happy days, he was convinced that in a single afternoon he had dispelled suspicions that had accumulated over a decade. Others knew better. Gosse had no doubt that "the L. C.'s . . . really stirring and noble speech . . . [had] moved even Unionist opinion very favourably," but he did not permit himself to forget that "there are some enemies who are implacable and who do not shrink from subterranean methods."[19]

As a rule, those who approved of Haldane's January 8 speech were predisposed in his favor. It did not silence the most vociferous of his critics and, at the same time, it disconcerted a number of his friends. The *Daily Express,* as was to be expected, found his personal defense "inadequate," though it hailed his reference to conscription as an indication of "the steady, if still slow, awakening of the Ministerial mind." The *Morning Post* asserted that it would accept conscription as nothing less than a permanent principle. Leo Maxse, prepared to cut off his country's nose to save its face, proclaimed that he would sooner "postpone Compulsory Service . . . than receive it as the price of whitewashing Lord Haldane. . . ." J. S. Sandars, who had been Balfour's

<hr />

[17] HP 6012, ff. 86–87.   [18] Haldane to Gosse, Jan. 11, 1915, Gosse Papers.
[19] Gosse to Elizabeth Haldane, Jan. 14, 1915, HP 6025, ff. 3–4.

cr. London *Daily Express*, December 12, 1914

"LORD HALDANE'S DREAM"

"Dear me! How things have changed since I wrote that Germany was my
spiritual home"

private secretary, felt much the same way; he told Maxse that Sir
John Brunner, who had opposed high naval estimates before the war,
had recently confessed that his opinion had changed: "But isn't that
just an instance of what you so happily designate 'patriotism overnight'
—Haldane talking blandly of compulsory service after his anti-Roberts
record. But they are all alike."[20]

The parliamentary correspondent for the *Scotsman*, among the most
astute observers of that confused scene, noted on January 11 that Haldane's "allusion to the possibility of . . . compulsory service has had
a mixed reception among his fellow-Radicals." Had the lord chancellor
stated no more than a "mere truism, . . . that every subject is bound
by duty, as well as by common law, to prevent or repel invasion," or
had he paved the way for the introduction of conscription? Like many
Liberals, the editor of the *Nation* preferred to think that Haldane had
affirmed his earlier stand against compulsion, though he had conceded
its possibility in the unlikely event that "there were not enough volunteers." The *Glasgow Herald*, reporting "widespread interest" in Haldane's speech of the 14th, recalled "an earlier pronouncement . . . on

[20] Jan. 31, 1915, Maxse Papers.

the subject" which lent credence to the view that conscription was in the offing; six years earlier he had predicted to an interviewer that in a "time of need, . . . not improbably . . . a short and sharp Act of Parliament [would be] passed" that would "impose an obligation on all to serve for home defence." Had the appropriate moment arrived? Was "home defence" all that he had meant when he cited "the duty of every subject of the realm to assist . . . in repelling the invasion of its shores"? The confusion generated among Liberals by Haldane's speech was reflected most clearly in a letter that A. F. Pollard, professor of constitutional history at the University of London, sent to the editor of *The Times*; the author was unable to decide whether Haldane's *"obiter dictum"* was either a "simple truism" (if so, why the fuss?) or an "unconstitutional paradox" designed to deprive the nation of its historic liberties in the name of its historic liberties. By creating further uncertainty, Haldane had brought his past policies and his present attitudes into question among those whose support he depended upon. He had made clear the need for a definitive statement without providing one. The fault, in the deeper sense, was not his, for Liberalism lacked the answers that he was called upon to deliver.

Despite Haldane's self-defense in the House of Lords, the press agitation continued spasmodically during the remaining weeks of January and picked up when the monthlies appeared in early February. Augustine Birrell, who regarded the attacks upon Haldane as *"intolerable,"* seethed with indignation at reports that Lord Selborne ("that poor result of intercourse between a half-worn-out Chancery barrister and a middle-aged Lady of Quality") was openly professing that the lord chancellor was a traitor. "Amongst the lower ranks of the Tory ex-Ministers," Birrell told Sir Matthew Nathan, under-secretary for Ireland, "temper is rising. It is a pity that their abilities are as low as their tempers are high."[21] Winston Churchill took the trouble to write Haldane a note on January 18, counseling him "not [to] allow this trash to worry you even for one hour, and [to] go your own way paying no attention to it. . . ."[22] But unlike Churchill, Haldane had no public face behind which to take refuge. He was genuinely distressed not only by the things that were written but also by the seeming indifference of certain colleagues. He had encouraged Sir Robert Donald, editor of

[21] Jan. 13, 1915, Nathan Papers.   [22] Jan. 18, 1915, HP 5911, f. 1.

the *Daily Chronicle*, to publish as a pamphlet a series of articles in his defense, only to have Lord Kitchener veto the publication as an invitation to further controversy. Kitchener and the Prime Minister also thought it best to expunge from Sir John French's dispatch of February 2 lengthy passages bestowing praise upon Haldane and his war office reforms.

John Bull brought the month of January to a close with a denunciation of the "Three 'Duds': Haldane! McKenna!! Masterman!!!" *Blackwood's Magazine* ushered in the next with another installment in the romance between Haldane and the Kaiser. The *National Review*, not to be outdone, devoted over thirty pages to merciless reiteration of familiar charges: Haldane had tried to ruin the nation's defenses, to sell out British interests at Berlin, to insinuate himself into the war office at the outbreak of war, and to bar the way to national service. Arnold White, returning from a visit to the Conservative Club at Liverpool, assured Maxse: "You have sown good seed and I found the attack on Haldane well supported by sober and serious men."[23] Jesse Collings, Unionist M. P. for Bordesley, Birmingham, could not wait long enough to finish the February *Review* before he wrote to congratulate its editor for "dealing with Lord Haldane in a manner that ought to carry conviction to readers of the shameful scandal of his presence in the British Government." Collings took consolation in "the fact that when he was in the House of Commons, I never trusted him. I regarded him as a fat conceited man . . . who regarded nothing but his own interests."[24]

Not all of the responses to the February number of the *National Review* were as favorable. At long last there was a reaction from Downing Street, though unfortunately it came from the member of the Asquith family whose words were most abundant and least effective. Margot, with lavish excuses for her "British candour" and warm regards for members of the Maxse family, wrote a typically Margot-like letter, frank and discursive, that tended to be not so much illogical as irrelevant. "Dear Mr. Leo," she began:

I don't want to hamper you in any way from attacking Haldane or Henry. In times of war people who make personal attacks to discredit the Ministry are so rare that I can't criticize or get vexed when I read you & *Daily Xpress*,

[23] Feb. 1, 1915, Maxse Papers.   [24] Feb. 8, 1915, *Ibid.*

but there are some *facts* that you should know. On page 875 of your review you write that Haldane was appointed War Minister in lieu of Lord K. *Haldane was never appointed War Minister.* He was never even *thought* of. Henry had decided on K. to succeed him & *asked* him long before the press mentioned it or anyone knew. In the "Bloody Week" as you call it or in any other week the Gov't. *never* sat on the fence. Everything was fixed long before the press had any idea. (Of course, if you mean we should have declared war on Germany several months before the Germans declared war on Russia, or made war several years ago, then, of course, I plead guilty.)

You were educated in France and despise German education. (This is poor Haldane's crime; he can speak and read German!) But a great many remarkable men have not been educated in England only and I think every man should know French and German. You think it was terrible for Haldane to strive for Peace because you always wanted war with Germany, and I must say you were *most frank* about it; but I daresay if Haldane *hadn't* striven for Peace you would have denounced him with the same bitterness for having been able to go to Germany and *not* tried to make peace. I can't think when you *wanted* war so *genuinely*, why you are so frightened now, and think all men are spies. I see you quote the *Daily Xpress* on page 886. Do you think the *Daily Xpress* worth quoting on the Kaiser's bon mots.?! . . . However that's a trifle! On page 894 you say Haldane provoked civil war in Ireland. Do you know—though I know you won't believe me (*I am absolutely truthful*) the German people quite believed in the old parrot cry of "Civil War in Ireland". I know this for a fact because Kuhlmann told me himself that he thought there would be "Civil War" in Ireland. I of course thought he was pulling my leg, but he *sincerely* believed Lord Londonderry and Co. and 100,000 men were going to fight led by Lord Aberdeen.

Why do you hate Henry and Haldane? I can understand your hating Henry, but why Haldane? You should have one talk to Sir John French or any of our Generals at the front or any of our Tommies and ask them if we had gone to war when you were in office whether the British public would have been satisfied with the Army perfection then—? or whether at any time in your administration you could have sent out the huge number of men Haldane's Army has sent out? They would laugh. Conscriptionists out there (when I went to look for my nephew's . . . tomb) were angry with Lord Roberts for only starting his National Service when it became fashionable and he became old. Even the strongest Tories think it amazing to try and discredit our Army. . . .

Well, dear Mr. Leo, I am only writing good-naturedly. I could never be angry with my beloved Admiral Maxse's son or Violet's [Lady Edward Cecil's] brother, but you have got *hundreds* of your facts wrong: . . . McK[enna] fictions, Haldane fictions, etc., are past belief. But I think you are *quite* right to attack Henry. Go on calling him a lazy man. The only men you must not attack are our Generals. Promise me you'll never attack Sir John French. Do tell me how poor poor Violet is and where Henry Bentinck is. Tom Bridles has just left us. He is one of our best soldiers; but if I say this, you will hate him, I fear. He is a great friend of mine. Remember me to your most delightful wife.

Maxse apparently tried to justify his various arguments, for five days later Margot wrote him a second letter, somewhat shorter and a good deal less cordial. *"It is an absolute lie,"* she proclaimed in her opening sentence. "Haldane was *never* [thrice underscored] made War Minister on August 3rd or any other day in 1914, nor even thought of for the place! How can you be so silly!" With assiduous monotony, she proceeded to demolish each of his *"wonderful* Fabrications."[25]

Maxse had considerably more to occupy his time than his correspondence with the irrepressible Margot. The agitation against Haldane had begun to flag, its participants weary and disheartened, and Maxse attempted to stimulate a renewed interest. The *National Review*, after all, appeared only monthly and could not sustain the struggle singlehandedly. *Blackwood's Magazine* had neither the frequency nor readership to render material assistance. True, the *Morning Post* remained constant, but its circulation was limited and its tone restrained. *John Bull* was in a league of its own, too incorrigible even for Maxse. *The Times* and *Daily Mail*, subject to the whim of Lord Northcliffe, were undependable allies, silent as of late. The *Daily Express* had abruptly halted fire in mid-January, and even Arnold White seemed to have exhausted himself.

The defection of the *Daily Express* pained Maxse most of all. It had apparently forgotten that Haldane was the first order of business and had begun to dissipate its energies upon Reginald McKenna ("Mr. McKenna Must Go"), who refused to impound potential spies at the same time that he ordered the release of detained suffragettes. H. A. Gwynne of the *Morning Post* confessed that he was equally unable to explain why R. D. Blumenfeld, editor of the *Express*, had "stopped over the Haldane business."[26] On March 3 Maxse wrote directly to Blumenfeld, ostensibly to congratulate him for "returning to the charge

---

[25] Letters of Feb. 1 and 5, 1915, *Ibid*. It is, of course, impossible to capture the unique flavor of a "Margot Letter" in print; in the above, punctuation has been changed or inserted where required for intelligibility.

[26] Gwynne to Maxse, March 4, 1915, *Ibid*.

re: Haldane"; but it was obvious from his letter that this was an hyperbole calculated to lure Blumenfeld from his premature retirement:

In the general moral cowardice of the age in which we live, any newspaper which would devote itself in season and out of season to the exposure and expulsion of this most dangerous charlatan would not only perform a conspicuous service, but would gain undying kudos, which even the business end of the newspaper would ultimately appreciate. We do most sorely stand in need at the present time of a patriotic organ which will push things through right to the end regardless of any of the innumerable forms of pressure which are invariably brought to bear on any Editor who tries to do his duty. . . . The *Daily Express* has a very great opportunity, if it chooses to use it. On the other hand, if it does not push this business through, I am quite sure—if you will not mind my saying so—its reputation is bound to suffer.[27]

Blumenfeld immediately replied with assurances that he "agree[d] with everything you say in your letter, and I have not in any sense retired from my position of 'keeping at it.' "[28]

The *Daily Express* did not resume its campaign with anything like the militancy that would have satisfied Maxse. Its thrusts came at odd intervals and, by and large, carried little conviction. After February, even Charles Whibley, writing in *Blackwood's Magazine*, began to muse without method about other subjects, forgetting Haldane until the following autumn. Once again Haldane presumed that the agitation had expired, when, in truth, his enemies had only paused to catch their breath.

The time had come, Haldane believed, to make another effort to rehabilitate himself. He would not rest until he had read a vindication of himself in *The Times*. But neither Lord Northcliffe nor Geoffrey Robinson showed the least intention to accommodate him. They printed nothing explicitly critical, but at the same time avoided anything complimentary. Haldane attempted to apply indirect pressures to break this conspiracy of silence. Friends wrote letters to the editor that *The Times* declined to print and books that it neglected to review. In addition, Haldane granted interviews to French and American journalists, hoping that Printing House Square would take notice of his disclosures.

The most significant of these interviews came on March 7, when Haldane discussed the origins of the war with the London correspond-

27 Blumenfeld Papers.   28 March 4, 1915, Maxse Papers.

ent of the *Chicago Daily News*. His statements reflected sensitivity, insight (aside from the fact that he saw no chance of American intervention in the war), and an impeccable patriotism; yet the results were disappointing. Only the Liberal press paid any attention, while Maxse took the opportunity to complain that the lord chancellor divulged information to neutrals that he apparently lacked the courage to share with his countrymen. Sir George Prothero, editor of the *Quarterly Review*, was convinced that his friend's reputation would have been saved had his remarks received the coverage they deserved: the maneuver had failed "partly because it *was* an 'interview,' partly because English newspapers, perhaps resenting its publication in a foreign paper, to a large extent boycotted it."[29] But most of all it had failed because Haldane's critics were waiting for the appropriate moment not to repent but to renew their transgressions.

That opportunity came on April 23, when *The Times* released information that hours before the declaration of war, Haldane had received a letter of an undisclosed nature from Albert Ballin, one of the architects of his 1912 Berlin mission. On July 23, 1914, Ballin—during a visit to London—had dined at Queen Anne's Gate along with Grey and Morley. He had written a week later to thank his host and to express the "hope that at the last hour it will be possible to find a peaceful way out of this terrible chaos."[30] Haldane was annoyed at *The Times* for "raising a new hare." He had indeed received such a letter, he told his mother, but "did not answer it. There is nothing in the matter. But I wish they would let things alone." Three days later, he assured her of his determination to ignore the controversy: he had the letter in safekeeping, and there it would remain.[31]

Others, less eager to bury the matter, must have appreciated Haldane's reticence which made an innocuous incident appear ominous. "What did Herr Ballin write to Lord Haldane?" asked the *Daily Express* in a banner headline on the 24th; this was the first time in three months that the lord chancellor was accorded such prominence. Two days later, Arnold White denounced each minister, with Haldane heading the list. Maxse, writing in the May *National Review*, found it "no surprise" that

[29] Prothero to Haldane, May 24, 1915, HP 5911, ff. 58–63.
[30] The complete text of Ballin's letter appears in Haldane's *Autobiography*, pp. 271–73.
[31] April 23 and 26, 1915, HP 5993, ff. 157–59.

Haldane would engage in last minute correspondence with the enemy. Convinced that incriminating evidence was being suppressed, Maxse appealed to "some peer" to demand the text of Ballin's letter "if it is not spontaneously volunteered from the Woolsack."

It was Lord Hylton who acted upon Maxse's suggestion during a question period in the House of Lords on May 5. After describing at length the immense power that Ballin wielded "behind the Throne," he cited Ballin's recent statements to the effect that the British foreign office had "brought about" the war by failing to make clear its commitments to the states of Europe. In this connection, Hylton introduced the subject of the Haldane-Ballin correspondence and invited the lord chancellor to reconcile, if he could, Ballin's contradictory declarations.

Haldane rose from the woolsack to assure his fellow-peers that "no State document, nothing of importance, is in my possession which could be disclosed that would interest the public." (Why did he insert "which could be disclosed"?) Nor had he carried on a private correspondence with Ballin or any other German. Herr Ballin had written, he explained, "a private note," and he professed "great objection to publishing private correspondence." There were certain courtesies due even "an alien enemy," particularly one who had written in time of peace. "All one can say is that Herr Ballin has been very unfortunate," he concluded, confessing that he found "it difficult to bring myself to believe that there has not been some lapse of memory" on the part of this "remarkable man" which would explain his recent "divergence of view."

"The Ballin business went off peacefully this afternoon," Haldane notified Gosse. "I dealt with it myself, but would not present the letter."[32] Could he seriously have thought that he had heard the last of the matter? *The Times* the next morning expressed disbelief that Haldane had "found nothing stronger to say than that Herr Ballin had been 'very unfortunate.'" The *Daily Mail* reported Haldane's full statement without comment, allowing it to stand as its own indictment. Horatio Bottomley cited this as another example of the Government's fanatical desire to give the enemy the benefit of every doubt ("I believe that if the Kaiser visited us today, they would give him a state reception"): "Look at Haldane's *apologia* . . . for Herr Ballin," he fumed,

[32] May 5, 1915 [copy], Gosse Papers.

"attributing to him 'treachery of recollection' rather than damned lying."

There remained those who refused to take Haldane's word for the contents of the Ballin letter. Arnold White, writing on the 10th, was convinced that it contained additional material embarrassing to the recipient who, on the eve of battle, had "entertained at dinner the deadliest enemy this country possesses." No mention was made of the fact that two evenings later Ballin had been the guest of Winston Churchill. The *Daily Express* sprinkled among its columns pro-German quotations from its Haldane anthology, and repeated its front page query: "What *Did* Herr Ballin write to Lord Haldane?" On the 7th it offered a reward of a hundred pounds to any reader who could relate what "Bal" had written to "Hal" in August 1914 from the latter's "spiritual home."

The early days of May saw a recrudescence of press attacks comparable in scale to those that had ushered in the year. And these were far more potent, for they capitalized upon the comparatively kind words Haldane had expressed in time of war for German statecraft and German morality. Again there were widespread appeals for Haldane's resignation: "No man not endowed with the skin of a rhinoceros," wrote Lovat Fraser in the May 11 *Daily Mail*, "would, in his place, have clung to office for a single day after the purpose of Germany was revealed." Again there were assertions that Haldane's continued presence in the Cabinet was an impediment to conscription, to an effective naval blockade of Germany, and, in Arnold White's opinion, to a "betterment in the treatment of British prisoners" in German camps. Unmistakably a storm was building up. But before it could burst German submarines had torpedoed the passenger liner *Lusitania*, crowding the anti-Haldane agitation off the front pages.

The sinking of the *Lusitania* unleashed anti-German riots across England. In the Camden Town and Kentish Town sections of London, over one-hundred-fifty German-owned shops were either pillaged or destroyed. The situation was even worse in the East End. Troops were brought into Liverpool to quell disturbances that had raged for three days and nights, and into Southend, where a zeppelin raid added to hysteria. The loss of so many innocent lives at sea seemed to confirm the countless rumors about German barbarities: the story that some forty British soldiers had been cremated alive in a Belgian airplane shed, and another that Canadian officers had been crucified by their Hunnish captors. Certain journalists, including Bottomley and White, could not resist linking the outrage upon the *Lusitania* with the name of Herr Ballin, the lord chancellor's friend, who was alleged to be Germany's arch-proponent of unrestricted submarine warfare.[33]

In the wake of the *Lusitania* disaster British opinion demanded vigorous reprisals against an enemy that would apparently stop at nothing to realize its goals. Horatio Bottomley, at his most extreme, called for "a vendetta against every German in Britain, whether 'naturalised' or not. . . . You cannot naturalise an unnatural Beast—a human abortion—a hellish freak. But you *can* exterminate it." Others were more reasonable but no less adamant. "The People Demand a Lead from their Leaders," proclaimed the *Daily Express*, and so far as it was concerned the "only way" was "conscription." The Northcliffe papers preached the same sermon, reviving plaintive tributes to old Lord Roberts. The outcry was too loud to ignore and, once again, it fell to Lord Haldane to offer a reply on the Government's behalf.

The occasion was a debate in the House of Lords on May 13 on a Bill to amend the Army Act to facilitate the compilation of a register of men available for military service. Haldane advised his listeners that the measure had not been introduced out of necessity ("It may hardly be wanted at all"), but merely "in order that the Secretary of State [for War] may be delivered from an uncertainty which ought not to be allowed to hamper him any longer. . . ." Acknowledging that the Bill, "in many respects," constituted "an approach to the principle of applying compulsion," he insisted that the country was not "face to face with that problem at present." If and when an emergency arose, the Government was prepared "to reconsider . . . the voluntary system . . . in the light of the tremendous necessity with which the nation is faced."

Lord Lansdowne, leader of the Opposition forces in the upper house, greeted Haldane's speech as "an indication that this very grave problem is engaging the attention of himself and his colleagues." J. L. Garvin, writing in the *Pall Mall Gazette*, was equally receptive. Even the *Daily Express* took heart that the "Government listens to the Voice of the

---

[33] There was a letter to the editor of *The Times* to this effect on May 11 from Sir Valentine Chirol, formerly Berlin correspondent for that paper and the man considered by many to be the most knowledgeable authority on foreign affairs.

Nation." Yet not all Unionist opinion was satisfied. In a letter to the *Morning Post,* Lord Portsmouth took exception to Lansdowne's remark that this was a "momentous announcement." And Lord Milner, another official of the National Service League, put down as "wicked nonsense" Haldane's view that "National Service may become necessary, but not yet, not yet. If we are ever to fight with our whole manhood," Milner told Austen Chamberlain, "surely we are past the eleventh hour in the possibility of making use of it. What are we waiting for? The nation is ready if it ever will be."[34]

But it was within Liberal circles that Haldane's remarks touched off the greatest furor. Had the lord chancellor, in a throwback to his Liberal Imperialist days, gone too far in his efforts to court the other party? Was his speech a portent of the Cabinet's decision to embrace this most illiberal of causes? The *Manchester Guardian* emphatically denied on the following day that Haldane's statement in any way "foreshadowed the ultimate intention of the Government to adopt conscription." Had he not "said much the same in much the same words four months earlier?" it asked, pointing to the fact that the voluntary system remained in effect. The *Guardian* preferred to regard as the "important part" of Haldane's speech his assertion that "the War Office have as many men as they can handle from the present methods of recruiting." The *Nation* attached much the same significance to Haldane's remarks, though it went further in lamenting the "doubtful speech" as a blunder that would "increase the disquiet which is already felt" by unwittingly providing "the conscriptionists" with "a text and a forecast."

Haldane, engaged for years in the conscription controversy, was embroiled still further. It is doubtful that he had meant to attract attention to himself. His speech, without endearing him to his enemies, had weakened his position among his friends. No one doubted for a moment that the issue at stake transcended that of army recruiting: it was a headlong conflict between the forces of Freedom and those of Control. Military compulsion, its critics feared, was the concession of a principle that would be applied to every realm of society. Was this the assertion of state direction over industry and labor? Would it stifle political dissent and outlaw collective bargaining? General Wolseley,

[34] May 17, 1915, Chamberlain Papers.

advised by a French authority that conscription was less useful "for procuring men, . . . [than] for the purpose of control," was notably impressed with the information that French "agitators, strike leaders and so on were sent into the trenches long ago."[35] And Chamberlain acknowledged that Opposition leaders had been preparing a manifesto "on the subject of the immediate preparation for calling forth the whole resources of the nation in one form or another (*i.e.*, as soldiers or workers)," when Asquith took the initiative from them.[36]

It was in this emotion-charged atmosphere that *The Times* published shocking evidence of a munitions shortage and the Prime Minister exchanged his Liberal ministry for a coalition. It was inviting for contemporaries to see a cause and effect relationship between the two events. Lord Loreburn was "not surprised to hear this change of Government is a Press intrigue. Nor am I surprised," he told Lord Bryce, "that for the first time in our history a Press intrigue had succeeded."[37] Bryce agreed that "there is an intrigue worked through the Harmsworth press," and though he was hard put to explain it, he considered its success "a thing of evil omen."[38] But the view taken by these Liberal elder-statesmen was justified only in a more narrow sense than either realized. Asquith's hand was indeed forced by a conspiracy in which *The Times* had played a vital part, but Northcliffe could not have succeeded on his own. And however much it might appear to the contrary, the intrigue that brought down the last Liberal Government was not an outgrowth of the agitation against Haldane and other ministers. Yet neither side was capable of perceiving where one left off and the other began. It appeared that Haldane was sacrificed to public ignorance and journalistic opportunism. "After the war," Sir Frederick Pollock, the eminent jurist, wrote to Haldane, "we must deport Northcliffe and Co. to Berlin, making it one of the terms of peace that it will be considered an act of war if we ever hear of them again."[39] Margot Asquith vowed to take vengeance upon the *Morning Post* and *The Times* ("and I can do a great deal") for what they had done to Haldane.[40] "What a 'jolly' you must be having," Sir Henry Wilson

---

[35] Memorandum by Wolseley, May 20, 1915, Kitchener Papers.
[36] Chamberlain to Milner, May 20, 1915, Milner Papers.
[37] May 24, 1915, Bryce Papers.
[38] Bryce to Scott, May 26, 1915, Scott Papers, Add. MSS. 50, 908, ff. 95–96.
[39] [May 26], 1915, HP 5911, f. 129.
[40] Margot Asquith to Mrs. Haldane, May 24, 1915, HP 6082, f. 8.

wrote in jubilation to Leo Maxse, "with Squiff [Asquith] to bow you in and Haldane to bow you out."[41] And Horatio Bottomley, eager to share the glory, took pains to deny "rumours" that he had accepted a post in the new Government.

Although Haldane's assailants were eager to take credit for driving him from office, and although politicians of both parties were glad to allow them to do so, personal factors had been vastly more important. As the *Manchester Guardian* was quick to perceive, Haldane's "old colleagues should have" and could have resisted the "newspaper clamour." Instead they tended to display a lack of courage that justified the worst that had been said about them. The fierce press attacks that are invariably cited as the reason for Haldane's downfall had pretty much run their course by mid-May, though the announcement of his departure prompted a revival that flared through the summer months. Haldane was quite right when he told friends that these calumnies had undermined his public position and lessened his effectiveness upon the woolsack. Yet even at this date an emphatic statement on his behalf, accompanied by the publication of official documents, would have counteracted any mischief. Liberal and Unionist leaders alike accepted Haldane's resignation with the silent composure with which they had previously abided the press attacks. In the explanation lies a key to the political events of May 1915.

41 May 21, 1915, Maxse Papers.

CHAPTER VII

THE MAY CRISIS

Rumours of all sorts, resignations and recriminations galore, suspicion abroad, mischief afoot, and surrender to what should be resisted in high places. I am afraid the P[rime] M[inister] and Government are faltering in their duty, faltering with the people and surrendering to . . . [the] Opposition. If this be so, we are pilloried for the first time as a divided . . . [and] diminished party. . . . If this is proved, [the] P[rime] M[inister] will and should suffer for this weakness.

—JOHN BURNS*

Before one can evaluate the significance of the 1915 Cabinet crisis that deprived Haldane of office, one must determine the chronology of decisions and events, the mechanics of destruction, so to speak. That in itself is no easy matter. A. J. P. Taylor, who has written with shrewd insight on the subject, has cited it as "one of the few political episodes in the first world war on which solid evidence is lacking."[1] To a certain extent the paucity of material can be explained by the fact that politicians consulted one another so frequently and so informally during these weeks that they rarely found it necessary to commit their thoughts to writing. Yet it becomes obvious that the few individuals who were privy to the secrets of May 1915—Haldane was most certainly not among them—made a conscientious effort to leave behind as little evidence as possible of their motives and actions. They knew that disclosures would shake public confidence, disrupt political alliances, and, not least of all, belie the noble principles they professed.

One must begin by discarding the platitudes that have long shrouded

---

* Diary, May 20, 1915. Add. MSS. 36, 337, f. 96.
1 *English History, 1914-1945* (Oxford, 1965), p. 30n.

the episode, precluding an analysis of the issues at stake. Of these, the most recurrent has been that it was Lord Fisher's resignation from the admiralty that precipitated the crisis: it posits that the Prime Minister, presented with Fisher's ultimatum, had no choice but to seek support from the Opposition if he was to avert the full-scale parliamentary debate that would expose his administration to embarrassment and probably to defeat. This view has been propagated by such disparate authorities as Asquith's daughter, Lady Violet Bonham Carter (now Lady Asquith of Yarnbury) and Lord Beaverbrook. It has been seconded by Robert Blake, who wrote his biography of Andrew Bonar Law from manuscripts in the Beaverbrook archives, and by Roy Jenkins, who received special manuscript material from the Asquith family for his life of Asquith. For this reason, any discussion of the Cabinet crisis of May 1915 must begin with a review of the situation at the admiralty.

On the morning of Saturday, May 15, Lord Fisher, the first sea lord, announced in hasty communications to Asquith and to the first lord of the admiralty, Winston S. Churchill, his intention to resign and to depart for Scotland "so as not to be embarrassed or embarrass you by any explanations with anyone."[2] In both letters, strewn with his characteristic exclamation points and multiple under-scorings, he reiterated his opposition to the Dardanelles project and his inability to cooperate any longer with Churchill, the leading proponent of that project. His misgivings on both scores had been frequently expressed, but, as Churchill later explained, Asquith had always "overruled" them, "almost with a gesture."[3] It is significant that when Fisher had threatened to resign earlier that week, he was restrained not by the Prime Minister, but by "the earnest words spoken to me by Kitchener," the secretary of state for war.[4]

Asquith's daughter has written that Fisher "behaved in a lower, meaner and more unworthy way than any Englishman since war began." For obvious reasons, she has preferred to ascribe the events that followed to Fisher's perfidy rather than to deficiencies in the Liberal leadership. Fisher, she recorded in her diary, "had simply *run away* from the Admiralty, deserting his post and work, had pulled down all the blinds in his own house and left a red-herring trail in the direction

[2] Fisher to Asquith, [May 15, 1915], Asquith Papers.
[3] *Great Contemporaries* (London, 1937), p. 123.
[4] Fisher to Asquith, May 12, 1915, Asquith Papers.

of Scotland." Asquith, she tells us, dispatched various lieutenants, including David Lloyd George, to "[scour] the Continental railway stations" (why?) until the truant had been "found, caught, carried in a retriever's mouth and dropped—bloodshot and panting—at the door of the Cabinet Room."[5] To say the very least, this was not the way the situation appeared to the reporter from the *Manchester Guardian* who was patrolling the sidewalks of Downing Street. When Fisher arrived at Number Ten that afternoon, he found Asquith comfortably settled in the rear of his motor car, ready to leave London for The Wharf, his country retreat. Journalists observed nothing unusual in Fisher's appearance, save the obvious fact of its timing. Asquith discharged his chauffeur and returned indoors, where he remained closeted with his guest for nearly an hour. Then, instead of leaving for the country, he sent for Lord Kitchener, with whom he spent the remainder of the afternoon. The stage was set for the upheaval that took place two days later on the 17th.

But one must not mistake the trappings of the crisis for the crisis itself. "Jacky" Fisher, however erratic his penmanship and behavior, was an unlikely individual to resign unconditionally, particularly if he realized that he might topple a Government in the process. He had thrived for years on the heady scent of political controversy, vowing to friends that if ever he was forced to "go under, . . . it will be with guns firing and colours flying! I won't flee—I'll be kicked out!"[6] This, despite accounts to the contrary, was pretty much what happened in May 1915. Although it remained possible either to retain Fisher's services or to replace him without reconstructing the ministry, Asquith instead seized Fisher's fortuitous resignation as a pretext for changes which were in any event forthcoming.

As Fisher told C. F. G. Masterman, whom he met by chance soon afterward, it defied the wits of man to provide a logical explanation for what had occurred: "Kitchener, who can't get a thing right, gets the Order of the Garter and I get the order of the boot."[7] The Prime Minister informed Lord Stamfordham, the King's secretary, that he had found "Fisher's mind . . . somewhat unhinged" during their May 15 interview and that he had suggested that Fisher "should see Mr. McKenna—with whom he is on the most intimate relations"—but

[5] Diary for May 15, 1915, quoted in *Winston Churchill*, p. 389.
[6] Fisher to J. A. Spender, July 10, 1909, Spender Papers, Add. MSS. 46, 390, f. 61.
[7] Lucy Masterman, *C. F. G. Masterman* (London, 1935), p. 289.

the latter reported to Asquith the next day "that Lord Fisher's decision was evidently irrevocable."[8] Fisher, however, provided an entirely different version of events: he had found Asquith full of "kind I might even say affectionate words," and two days later he received "a secret letter" from the Prime Minister revealing plans for an overhaul of the Government and strongly implying "that Winston would not be in the Cabinet." At this point, Fisher recounted to Pamela McKenna, wife of the outgoing home secretary,

I was in the ascendant and had I left it all there I should presumably have prospered, but in the innocence of my heart I wrote out conditions that in my view made for success in the conduct of the war and the abolition of the submarine menace. . . . Up to 2 P.M. on Saturday, May 22, the Prime Minister did not give me any idea of his hostility thereto and approved of my coming to Scotland, but the same afternoon he sent a curt dismissal so I rather suppose something sudden occurred. . . .[9]

Before he left for Scotland, Fisher advertized his forwarding address—care of the Duke of Hamilton—should Asquith want him back, and he went so far as to offer to withdraw his demands and "work with Balfour."[10] It was widely known that he wanted desperately to return, and his hostess, the Duchess of Hamilton, wrote to Lord Rosebery in bitter indignation when politicians declared that Fisher had "deserted his post": she protested that Fisher "had no idea of leaving London till an hour before he started and had no idea he was to be curtly dismissed."[11] Fisher described the situation in precisely these terms in a "strictly private and personal" letter to the King on June 7.[12] It is clear that he was as surprised as anyone not only that his resignation was accepted with alacrity, but also that it became Asquith's excuse for the shakeup that followed. Prominent Liberals, at a loss to explain what was going on, found it impossible to reconcile the admiralty crisis with the ensuing cataclysm: "Why the fact that Winston quarrelled with Fisher should mean your giving up the L[ocal] G[overnment] B[oard]," Masterman wrote to Herbert Samuel, "is a *non sequitur* which today and tomorrow will find difficult to understand."[13]

[8] Lord Stamfordham's memorandum, May 19, 1915, Royal Archives, G.V., K770/3.
[9] Fisher to Pamela McKenna, May 16 and 29, McKenna Papers.
[10] Lord Stamfordham's memorandum, May 20, 1915, Royal Archives, G.V., K770/8.
[11] June 11, 1915, Rosebery Papers.   [12] Royal Archives, G.V., G775/10.
[13] May 26, 1915, Samuel Papers.

If one discounts the significance of the admiralty crisis, what does one substitute in its place? Unfortunately historians have tended to fasten upon other "immediate" causes to explain these complex events. It is often stated, without taking chronology into account, that Asquith created a "national" administration to convince the Italians of Britain's resolve and thereby to hasten Italy's entry into the war; this explanation ignores the fact that, by this time, the Italians had already specified a mobilization date and, in any event, the fall of a British Government, particularly over a Mediterranean issue, seems a doubtful way to impress Rome with British reliability. It has also been alleged that Asquith and Churchill, anticipating disaster at the Dardanelles, wanted to share the blame with the Unionists; this, too, is mistaken, for as late as May 21, Churchill remained sufficiently optimistic about the Dardanelles venture to offer to "stand or fall" by its outcome.[14] As late as June 5, in a speech to constituents at Dundee, he confidently predicted that British troops at the Dardanelles were "separated only by a few miles from a victory such as this war has not yet seen."

Finally, and with infinitely greater justification, historians have identified the so-called shells scandal as either a complement or an alternative to the admiralty crisis in bringing down the Liberal Government. The day before Fisher paid his unexpected call upon Asquith, *The Times* carried a dispatch from Colonel Charles à Court Repington, its military correspondent, who ascribed the failure of British troops to make headway along the front to "the want of unlimited supply of high explosive." This theme was further developed in a leader, "Shells and the Great Battle," which quoted extensively from Repington's report. There had been rumors of a munitions shortage since early spring which Asquith, with Kitchener's assurances, took pains to deny in a speech at Newcastle on April 20. "Before Mr. Asquith made his Newcastle speech," Lord Stamfordham recorded in a May 19 memorandum,

he asked Lord Kitchener what he might say: Lord K. replied that [Sir John] French, who had been to England a few days previous, assured him that he was perfectly satisfied about ammunition and Lord K. told the P. M. that there were 1,000 rounds per gun. Now he hears that the greater amount of these was shrapnel which is more or less useless.[15]

[14] Churchill to Asquith, May 21, 1915, Asquith Papers.
[15] Royal Archives, G.V., K770/3.

Repington's dramatic exposé on May 14, followed as it was by well-documented accounts of inefficiency in the Glasgow munitions industry, brought into question not only Lord Kitchener's ability as an administrator, but also Asquith's ability to supervise and to coordinate the performances of his ministers. It raised doubts about the Prime Minister's integrity, his grasp of the military situation, and, among those who knew him well enough, about a carelessness that had crept into his once fastidious personal demeanor. Excessive drinking and a frivolous social life seemed a reflection if not a cause of his political distress. Captain George Lloyd (later Baron Lloyd), who interrupted his parliamentary career to serve at the Dardanelles, wrote to Austen Chamberlain that Asquith—who had come to be referred to mockingly as "Squiff"—had, by categorically denying the existence of a munitions shortage, provided "another proof of the inaccuracy of the 'in vino veritas' proverb."[16]

As J. A. Spender, editor of the Liberal *Westminster Gazette*, told Lord Esher on the 17th, "Repington has put the Government very neatly between devil and deep sea. . . ."[17] But what Spender undoubtedly did not yet realize was the fact that Repington's revelations were not nearly so politically important as the uses to which they were put. The May 14 dispatch was the product of an elaborate intrigue to bring about a new and more energetic wartime leadership. By reconstructing the ministry, Asquith was not capitulating to pressures from outside, for which he was well prepared, so much as reacting to pressures from within the Government that had taken him completely by surprise.

It is futile to search for pertinent information among the private papers of the leading contenders in the struggle, particularly those of Liberal persuasion, for these individuals were determined to hide the facts of the matter not only from posterity, but also often from their own colleagues and supporters. It is equally unrewarding to examine the private papers of those politicians who spent the weeks of late May in London, for they transacted much of their business in spur-of-the-moment meetings or by telephone. There was, however, at least one political figure sufficiently far removed from the precincts of Westminster and Whitehall to receive written reports, sufficiently prominent in party affairs to be kept informed by colleagues, and suf-

---

[16] May 22, 1915, Chamberlain Papers.   [17] Esher Papers.

ficiently detached from the proceedings to feel no obligation to destroy the communications he received. This was Sydney, Viscount Buxton, a member of the Campbell-Bannerman and Asquith Cabinets who, early in 1914, had been raised to the peerage and sent to South Africa as governor-general. From several fellow Liberals, particularly Charles Hobhouse, the postmater-general, Lord Buxton received encyclopedic accounts of political developments at home. These reports, like any historical testimony, must be weighed carefully: Hobhouse's prejudices against certain colleagues are obvious and these were, no doubt, exacerbated by the fact that the formation of the first coalition cost him his place in the Cabinet. Yet even after allowances have been made for Hobhouse's personal feelings, the account he presented to Buxton of the Cabinet crisis remains more complete, more dramatic, and more far-reaching in significance than any other first-hand account that has come to light.

Like many Liberals, particularly those who sat upon the backbenches, Hobhouse was keenly distrustful of Winston Churchill, whom he described to Buxton as a spendthrift, a headline-seeker, and a perpetrator of "rash adventures."[18] On the last day of April, he reported a "good deal of 'inside' trouble caused as you can guess by Winston . . . [who] has been at his old game of intriguing all round." Churchill, according to this account, had combined with A. J. Balfour and David Lloyd George—the first a former premier and the second a premier in the making—and with J. L. Garvin, editor of the *Observer* and the *Pall Mall Gazette*; their intention was no less than to overthrow Asquith along with Sir Edward Grey, the foreign secretary. They had invited Lord Kitchener to join them, but the war minister refused "partly from loyalty, partly from prudence and partly from distrust." At that point, Hobhouse continued, the rebels turned against Kitchener, presumably hoping to bring down Asquith and Grey by discrediting an equally prominent and far more vulnerable member of the Government. To this end, they enlisted the assistance of Sir John French, commander of the British Expeditionary Force, whose enmity toward Kitchener could be traced to Boer War days. The intrigue elicited "a violent attack on Ll[oyd] G[eorge] by K[itchener] in Cabinet" that left most of their colleagues mystified. Hobhouse, who had yet to obtain

[18] Dec. 4, 1914, Buxton Papers.

"the key" to what was going on, had mixed feelings; though he remained a steadfast supporter of Asquith, he was profoundly disturbed by repeated evidence of Kitchener's ineptitude:

As K. . . . has been deceiving his colleagues as to the numbers in France, I felt the less pity for him. For some reason he wanted us to think there were 500,000 men there. Why, I can't imagine. . . . What could be the object of falsification? . . . I gather that the P. M is alive to what has been going on, but not to the actual details—and is, for him, dissatisfied.[19]

By this time, others too were dissatisfied with Kitchener's performance at the war office. Never particularly popular among his Liberal associates, upon whom he had been thrust when war was declared, Kitchener came under increasing fire from his former enthusiasts— particularly the Northcliffe press—for his failure to prove the zealous advocate of compulsion that they had anticipated. Much to their distress, he not only added to the Government's ineffectuality, but also provided the Liberals, as L. S. Amery put it, with a "splendid Kitchener umbrella" beneath which they could take sanctuary from the winds and rains of justified criticism. Asquith could easily have dispensed with Kitchener's services, but he had come to rely increasingly upon the measure of public confidence which Kitchener, virtually alone among his ministers, inspired.

Yet, however much popularity the presence of Lord Kitchener—the hero of Omdurman, Khartoum, and Fashoda—conferred upon the Government, it could hardly be denied that in practical matters he was very much a liability, who could neither understand the military organization that Haldane had bequeathed to him nor cope with details of departmental administration. Time and again he proved true Margot Asquith's prophesy that he "would be a terrible muddler."[20] The shocking state of affairs at the war office was sufficiently well known to provide the subject for a memorandum by the fourth Marquess of Salisbury, a leader of the old-guard Unionists, who concluded that while it might be useful to retain Kitchener for publicity purposes, it would be more sensible to transfer the duties of the secretaryship of state for war to a more versatile under-secretary.[21] Salisbury's scheme, outlined

[19] April 30, 1915, Buxton Papers.
[20] Margot Asquith to Haldane, May 18, 1915, HP 5911, ff. 39 ff.
[21] Memorandum of April 10, 1915, Lord Robert Cecil Papers; Salisbury, not at all unreasonably, favored a more dynamic under-secretary than H. J. Tennant, who was Asquith's brother-in-law.

on April 10, was stillborn, but shortly thereafter steps were taken within the Government to end the confusion that Kitchener personified and Asquith's idle leadership seemed to invite.

Charles Hobhouse, writing to Lord Buxton, left no doubt that such steps were initiated by Churchill, and that Balfour, French, and Lloyd George were eager accomplices. Churchill and Lloyd George launched "a joint attack on K[itchener] and Grey" at a Cabinet during the first week in May, "and then W. S. C. went to France. . . ."[22] Churchill's Channel-crossing was, for obvious reasons, kept secret until his return. According to the Prime Minister, Churchill had conferred in Paris "on important Admiralty business," which is likely to have included Allied naval support for Italy in the Adriatic. On his return, Churchill broke journey at headquarters, where he spent the weekend of May 8–9 as the guest of Sir John French. It was this aspect of his travels that aroused the greatest interest and speculation. During a question period in the House of Commons on May 12, Lord Robert Cecil asked the Prime Minister to reveal the nature of the first lord's business at headquarters, and Asquith, in a terse statement, denied that Churchill had "discharg[ed] any duties on behalf of the Government. . . ." Members of the House who broke into gleeful shouts of "joyride" obviously failed to realize how well Winston Churchill could combine the pursuits of business and pleasure.

Churchill had extended his stay on the Continent not to pay a social call upon French, with whom he was in close communication, but to confer with another of French's guests, Colonel Repington of *The Times*. Following the example set by his father three decades earlier, Winston sought to wield the editorial columns of *The Times* as a weapon against his political superiors. Repington, Geoffrey Robinson, his editor, and Lord Northcliffe, his publisher, accorded Winston a more cordial reception than their predecessors had accorded Lord Randolph in 1886, when the latter had solicited *The Times*'s support in his attempt to pressure Lord Salisbury. The Northcliffe press, to the consternation of the proprietors of other anti-ministerial journals, had always displayed a certain partiality for Churchill, possibly because he and his friends were a source of information. At this point, Northcliffe and his editor were not only eager for information with which they might discredit

[22] June 19, 1915, Buxton Papers.

Kitchener, and through him the Asquith Government, but they were also anxious to coordinate their campaign with moves within the Cabinet. For nearly six months they had made unsuccessful assaults upon Lord Haldane and other ministers. It was time for a new strategy.

On Friday, May 14, *The Times* gave prominent attention to Repington's dispatch on the munitions shortage which, Hobhouse insisted, Churchill "unquestionably inspired"[23] when he, French, and Repington had met the previous weekend. Other sources corroborated Hobhouse's information. Arnold Bennett recorded in his journal (though he remained silent in his column in the *Daily News*) that he had been told by Reginald McKenna that: "Crisis made by Repington's article in *The Times*. Churchill with French at same time as Repington. Rep's article 'arranged.' "[24] The King, writing to the Queen from his railway carriage on the 19th, expressed relief that Churchill ("the real danger") would be ejected from the admiralty for "intriguing with French against K."[25] French acknowledged in his diary on the 15th that "there was trouble about Repington's presence at my headquarters," and three days later that he had received a sharp rebuke from Kitchener.[26] And Douglas Haig heard of "an organised conspiracy . . . against Kitchener . . . [in which] Sir J. French's personal staff are mixed up. . . ."[27]

Churchill's machinations went virtually undetected by contemporaries, who were too busy debating the propriety of Repington's presence at headquarters or the means by which his dispatch had slipped past censors. Margot Asquith, however, was quite explicit that "our *wonderful* Cabinet" had been "smashed! . . . by the man whom I always said *would* smash it—Winston."[28] But everyone had grown so weary of Margot's effusions that no one seems to have taken at all seriously her version of the events of May 1915. Yet Churchill's role, as she professed so emphatically, was the decisive one.

It would be foolhardy to deny that Winston Churchill, throughout his career, was not only ambitious but frequently ruthless in his attempts to realize those ambitions. But in May 1915, it was obvious

[23] Hobhouse to Buxton, June 10, 1915, Buxton Papers.
[24] Arnold Bennett's Journal, May 21, 1915.
[25] Royal Archives, G.V., CC4/132.
[26] Major Gerald French (ed.), *Some War Diaries . . . of the Earl of Ypres* (London, 1937), pp. 202–203.
[27] Blake (ed.), *Haig*, p. 93.
[28] Margot Asquith to Haldane, May 18, 1915, HP 5911, ff. 39 ff.

that he was motivated by considerably more than the prospect of personal gain. Even Hobhouse, who thought Churchill's behavior "treachery and certainly disloyal," had to admit that, in the light of circumstances, it was "justifiable."[29] One can imagine how much Asquith's lackadaisical approach to urgent problems must have galled Britain's greatest wartime leader, who already displayed the enormous appetite for work and capacity for service that became legendary later in his distinguished lifetime. Never by any stretch of the imagination a party man, Churchill did not hesitate in 1915 to sacrifice the Liberal Party on the altar of national victory. As was so often the case, his impatient pursuit of goals rebounded to his disadvantage as a politician. Precisely what Churchill expected to achieve for himself in 1915 remains open to speculation. Rumors circulated that he had set his sights upon "a new ministerial office, a sort of Department of Public Safety," which would have allowed him to exercise an overriding control over all wartime operations.[30] Others hinted that Churchill, at the age of forty-one, coveted nothing less than the premiership, a prize that eluded him until his sixty-sixth year. In any event, he had come to identify a more vigorous war effort with increased powers for himself.

Repington's article, for which Churchill had furnished the impetus and possibly the information, was followed by other, equally direct assaults upon Asquith's leadership. It was common knowledge that A. J. Balfour, though a top-ranking Unionist, cooperated intimately with the Government on military matters. The political correspondent for the *Daily News* failed to appreciate the significance of his remarks when he wrote on the 19th that Balfour

has been, for a year now, a member of the Defence Committee, in which capacity he has enjoyed what amounts to Cabinet responsibility for all naval and military decisions. Indeed, he has belonged to the inner Cabinet, and has assisted the Chancellor of the Exchequer continuously in the endeavour to adjust labour conditions in the munitions areas. Mr. Balfour has a room at the Admiralty where he works assiduously, and all the important decisions of Government are known to him.

According to H. A. Gwynne, editor of the *Morning Post,* who obtained his information from Churchill's close friend, F. E. Smith, Churchill and Lloyd George had hoped to work with Andrew Bonar Law, the

[29] Hobhouse to Buxton, June 10, 1915, Buxton Papers.
[30] Fitzroy, *Memoirs,* II, 594.

Unionist leader, and had settled for Balfour only because "A. B. L. did not like the thing from the beginning and would have nothing to do with it."[31] Balfour, who had lost the Unionist leadership four years earlier, had less to lose from a coalition and immeasurably more to gain. Hobhouse told Buxton that, by the spring of 1915, "Ll. G. and A. J. B. had resumed their colloquy of 1909, never long interrupted." Not only was Balfour provided with a seat on the Defence Committee and a room at the admiralty but, Hobhouse revealed, Balfour had also been taken "against the wishes of the Cabinet and without their knowledge . . . to the Board of Trade Committee on Supplies. He thus knew of the difficulties at the Dardanelles, and the quarrel between W. S. C. and Lord Fisher." Using the information that his confederates placed at his disposal, Balfour seized the occasion of Fisher's resignation to "put a pistol at [the] P[rime] M[inister]'s head, threatening debates and disclosures at W[ar] O[ffice] and Admiralty." Hobhouse reported that Asquith's initial reaction had been to resist such blackmail, but that ultimately, "advised by Ll. G., I think, who *alone* was consulted, I know," Asquith agreed to reconstruct the Government on a broader basis.[32]

Regardless of Balfour's ultimatum, the party truce that had existed since the early days of the war was strained to the breaking point. But Asquith remained justly confident that in all other cases he could depend upon the Opposition front bench to restrain critics of the Government. The Unionist "shadow cabinet" met on the 14th at Lansdowne House to consider a proposal by Lord Robert Cecil that the Opposition move "for a Committee on the state of the Nation, with closed doors, in order to discuss freely the action of the Government in regard to several matters in the conduct of the war which are giving rise to much anxiety"; its members rejected this strategy and decided instead to "personally urge" the Government to exert greater effort, and to promise Unionist support in the unlikely event that Asquith deemed it "necessary to employ compulsion . . . either for the army or for the production of munitions of war."[33] Opposition backbenchers, who had never taken kindly to the political truce to which they were committed by their leaders, demanded a more aggressive policy. Reping-

[31] Gwynne to Leo Maxse, May 17, 1915, Maxse Papers.
[32] Hobhouse to Buxton, June 10, 1915, Buxton Papers.
[33] Chamberlain's diary, May 14, 1915 [copy], Chamberlain Papers.

ton's disclosure justified the worst of their fears and—in the words of Professor W. A. S. Hewins, chairman of the Unionist Business Committee—made them more determined than ever to "carry the matter through." On the morning of Monday, the 17th, Hewins put down notice of his intention to raise the question of munitions in the House on Wednesday.[34] Needless to say, his opportunity never arrived. By that time, the Government he sought to indict had resigned as the prelude to the formation of a coalition.

It had been so long since Asquith had shown his mettle that contemporaries found in difficult to believe that he was acting from strength, not weakness. But his response to the political crisis revealed him the astute tactician and resourceful fighter he was. "Had the Prime Minister waited," H. W. Massingham wrote in the May 29 *Nation*, "the gust of poison gas which threatened Lord Kitchener would have been swept down the wind, the personal trouble at the Admiralty settled to the national satisfaction by the retention of Lord Fisher and the dismissal of Mr. Churchill, and a deficient organization of warlike supplies changed and extended." Massingham might have added that Asquith could also have saved Haldane. But it did not serve Asquith's purposes to wait. Instead he seized the initiative and attempted the coup that Lloyd George brought off with more durable success nineteen months later.

Churchill, who never underestimated his adversary's capabilities, subsequently described Asquith's performance in May 1915 as "the convulsive struggles of a man of action and of ambition at death-grips with events."[35] Haldane confirmed to Edmund Gosse on the 25th that Asquith was "struggling hard. But it is on his own account, not mine. . . ."[36] Asquith played every card in his hand with consummate skill, causing maximum anxiety among his opponents by his solitary deliberation. He perceived and exploited the differences among them, and the Government that emerged on the 26th was testimony to his powers over them. He kept his Liberal colleagues no less than the leaders of the Opposition in the dark, and infuriated the King by spending the "supremely critical day" of the 16th on the golf links, unavailable for consultation.[37]

[34] This entry is dated May 15 in Hewins's manuscript diary (Hewins Papers) and May 18 in the published version, *Apologia of an Imperialist*, II, 30 ff.
[35] *Great Contemporaries*, p. 123.   [36] Gosse Papers.
[37] Stamfordham to Esher, May 16, 1915, Esher Papers; this was repeated in Esher's diary for that date, but omitted in the printed version.

Of course Asquith consulted Bonar Law directly and through Lloyd George, but he recognized the weakness of the Unionist chief's position. Acting in concert with such senior colleagues as Austen Chamberlain and Lord Lansdowne, Bonar Law hastened to the Government's rescue ostensibly to avert any "controversial discussion" that might put off the Italians.[38] But as A. J. P. Taylor has so persuasively argued, Bonar Law, aware of strong backbench attempts to force his hand, was acting to "thwart this pressure."[39] He feared that an assault upon the beleaguered Government would bring it down, presenting him with the awesome task of forming the first Unionist ministry in a decade; this, he was convinced, could serve neither party nor national purposes. He had no doubt that, in the event of a General Election, the Unionists would be returned with a working majority, but he knew that a Unionist Government would not only widen and expose the ideological cleavages within the party—particularly over the vexing problem of national service— but would also make it difficult to implement the stringent policies that wartime exigencies demanded. The nation, particularly the working classes and Irishmen, would more readily accept from familiar Liberal hands the bitter medicine that Britons would have to swallow if the war was to be won. Besides, Bonar Law was by no means reluctant to allow the Liberals to bear the disapprobation that would attach to such measures.

Like most leading Unionists, Bonar Law believed that coalition would give the Liberals an easy way out of their difficulties at the same time that it compounded the difficulties that beset the Unionists. Two months earlier he had endorsed a memorandum written by H. A. Gwynne to the effect that whatever the "shortcomings" of the current ministers, "with a Unionist Opposition we can stir them up—and stir them up with some effect, but given a Coalition Government we should get callous and careless." And, according to Gwynne, Bonar Law had brushed aside overtures from Lloyd George and Churchill.[40]

---

[38] Bonar Law to Asquith, May 17, 1915, quoted in Robert Blake, *The Unknown Prime Minister* (London, 1955), pp. 246–47; Blake explains that "Bonar Law had agreed with Asquith and Lloyd George to write such a letter in order that Asquith could show it to his colleagues and make the situation clear to them." According to Chamberlain, before Bonar Law had the opportunity to present this letter, he received an invitation to Downing Street to discuss Cabinet reconstruction. Chamberlain's diary, May 17, 1915 [copy], Chamberlain Papers.

[39] "Politics in the First World War," in *Politics in Wartime* (London, 1964), pp. 19–20.

[40] Gwynne to Maxse, May 17, 1915, Maxse Papers; Gwynne's memorandum of March 26, 1915, is among the Bonar Law Papers.

Walter Long, who took the local government board in the first coalition, insisted to Gwynne on May 20 that he "loathe[d] the idea of a Coalition Government."[41] Lord Lansdowne, who entered as minister without portfolio, found the situation "intensely disagreeable."[42] Lord Curzon, who became lord privy seal, and Lord Derby, who later became Lloyd George's war minister, expressed identical sentiments. And Lord Charles Beresford, one of the Liberal Government's most implacable enemies, contemplated the "fatal effects" of coalition,[43] which his wife had hitherto seen as the work of "our worst enemy . . ., A[rthur] B[alfour], who is always at the A[squith]'s and now has a room at Whitehall."[44] Few of the Opposition leaders were enthusiasts for coalition and most were dead set against it. Yet on May 17, Bonar Law decided to join Asquith. For one thing, he had little choice. As Austen Chamberlain counseled him that evening: "If our help is asked by the Gov't. we *must* give it. God knows each one of us would willingly avoid the fearful responsibility; but the responsibility of refusing is even greater than that of accepting. . . . We cannot shirk this job because we don't like it or because we think the risks to ourselves too great."[45] For another thing, Bonar Law had personal reasons to accept. His control over the party was being challenged by rebellious backbenchers on the one hand and, less obviously, by Balfour on the other. Had Hewins been incited by Balfour, who threatened Asquith with such a prospect? Was Balfour, who had played no part in the Lansdowne House discussions, making a bid to re-establish himself in the Unionist hierarchy, possibly as leader? If Bonar Law disowned his backbenchers, would they ally themselves with his predecessor? The materials are not available—and possibly do not exist—which might answer these questions; but it appears probable that Bonar Law, in his decision to enter a coalition, was reacting to a threat considerably more dangerous than that which Hewins represented.

The motives behind Asquith's bid to Bonar Law are easier to ascertain. The Prime Minister hoped to recapture lost authority, moral and political, as the head of a national administration. His idea of "broad-

---

41 Gwynne Papers.
42 Sir Almeric Fitzroy's diary for May 20, 1915, *Memoirs*, II, 594.
43 Beresford to Bonar Law, May 17, 1915 [copy], Gwynne Papers.
44 Lady Charles Beresford to Gwynne [April ?], 1915, *Ibid.*
45 Chamberlain to Bonar Law, May 17, 1915 [copy], Chamberlain Papers.

based government" was to commit the Unionist leaders to his defense, and he gave little thought to the Labourites and Irish Nationalists, whom he did not expect to accept his invitation. He candidly admitted to Lord Stamfordham that "very few" of the Opposition leaders ("always excepting Mr. Balfour") were of the caliber to "add to the strength of his Government": Bonar Law, he professed, "is an untried horse. Lord Curzon has the brains and the gift of speech but is not popular with his own party or with the Government. The *Pall Mall's* suggestion of Derby he brushes aside."[46] Asquith remained, as A. M. Gollin has described him, "a man convinced of his own power" and of his singular ability to preside over the discordant factions of any ministry.[47] In a sense the Liberal Government, with its heterogeneous elements, was already a coalition. He had neither regard nor respect for Bonar Law and, with Margot, never tired of the jest that the Unionist chief had been fashioned not by God but by Glasgow. He might have paused to reflect that Sir Henry Campbell-Bannerman too was a Glaswegian who had put him in his place a decade earlier.

There are numerous indications that Asquith also conceived of coalition, at least at first, as a means to relieve himself of Lord Kitchener. His memorandum of May 17 cited both the munitions shortage and Fisher's resignation as reasons for his decision, thereby giving credence (despite his tortuous phraseology) to "the more than plausible parliamentary case in regard to the alleged deficiency of high explosive shells."[48] In his interview with Lord Stamfordham two days later, Asquith gave equal weight to the two developments. Bonar Law returned from his Downing Street conference on the 17th to tell Chamberlain that both Lloyd George and Asquith considered it "absolutely necessary to get rid of Kitchener," and that the Prime Minister intended to substitute Lloyd George at the war office.[49] The latter confirmed this on the 19th in a conversation with Lord Riddell.[50] J. A. Pease, who held the portfolio for education in the outgoing Cabinet, reported Asquith's complaint that Kitchener had not only "ignored French's

---

[46] Lord Stamfordham's memorandum, May 19, 1915, Royal Archives, G.V., K770/3.

[47] *Proconsul in Politics*, pp. 260–61.

[48] Copies of Asquith's May 17 memorandum survive among the Kitchener Papers, the Asquith Papers, the Harcourt Papers, and the Samuel Papers.

[49] Chamberlain's diary, May 17, 1915 [copy], Chamberlain Papers.

[50] Riddell, *War Diary* (London, 1933), p. 89.

demands for more high explosive supplies," neglecting to bring them before the Cabinet, but also had refused to "allow civilian help" to straighten out the mess at the war office.[51] Margot Asquith, who spent a "sleepless night of misery" after her husband informed her of his plans, wrote a distraught appeal at 6:30 the next morning to Lord Haldane, whom she mistakenly presumed to have retained some influence over Asquith: she begged him to acquaint "not only Ll. George but Henry" with the fact that "there [will] be a scream all over, from the King to the Navvy, . . . when the public learn that K. has gone."[52]

Asquith, a master at the art of finding excuses for inaction, did not require Haldane or anyone else to point out the dangers of Kitchener's removal. Rather than employ his newly founded coalition as a means to solve the problem at the war office, he employed it as a means to share that problem. He convinced himself, and ultimately his colleagues, that any gain in efficiency would be outweighed by the loss that the Government would suffer in public confidence. Asquith had been afforded an unusual opportunity to realize the lofty goals he had enunciated in his circular memorandum; he passed it by in favor of the path of least resistance and greatest personal security. By returning Kitchener, bedecked with the Order of the Garter, to an office for which he had revealed himself singularly ill-equipped, Asquith acknowledged the fact that the formation of the 1915 coalition was, first and foremost, a stratagem to prolong his lease on Downing Street. He had taken refuge behind Kitchener's massive index finger that protruded from recruitment posters,[53] and it is symbolic that he was not evicted from the premiership until a higher authority had first removed Kitchener from the scene.

If Asquith was responsible for the retention of an unfit secretary of state for war, others must share the blame for permitting him to con-

[51] Conversation of May 17, 1915, quoted in Addison, Four and a Half Years, I, 78–79.

[52] May 18, 1915, HP 5911, ff. 39 ff.

[53] The few letters from the Asquiths that survive among the Kitchener Papers reveal the extent to which Asquith had come to depend upon his war minister as the protector of himself and his policies. On August 18, 1915, Margot warned Kitchener of a plot to impose conscription, and she urged him to stand by "Henry, Grey, Crewe, Arthur Balfour, McKenna and Runciman" to "beat Curzon, F. E. Smith, Winston and Ll. George. . . ." Two months later, Asquith—sounding remarkably like his wife—found himself "in a most critical situation" on the same issue, and reminded Kitchener that "so long as you and I stand together, we carry the whole country with us. Otherwise, the Deluge!" ("Most secret"), Oct. 17, 1915.

tinue as Prime Minister. It was difficult to find anyone, at this point, who commanded the confidence of both the nation and a majority of parliamentarians. "The real difficulty," Balfour wrote to Lord Esher, "is to find the man. I look round all the conceivable alternatives, and I find him not!"[54] David Lloyd George could think of three alternatives to Asquith, including himself, but he supplied logical arguments why each was unacceptable: the Liberals, he explained to Bonar Law,

would not stand a Unionist Prime Minister, having regard to the relative numbers in the House; . . . [Sir Edward] Grey's eyesight put him out of the question, apart from the fact that he had even less push and drive than the present Prime Minister; and lastly, that he himself could not think of taking the position as he would be too much exposed to jealousy and criticism.[55]

Lord Salisbury and Lord Robert Cecil confessed that they too could think of no one with whom they might replace Asquith; the former held vain hopes that a means might be found "to plant out Asquith without superseding him (which is impossible) and at the same time to get things into the hands of the younger men of the front benches— I mean comparatively younger." Salisbury proposed to entrust "the conduct of . . . War business" to an inner cabinet, "and Asquith would only come in with the rest of the Cabinet to satisfy or reject . . . decisions."[56] Such schemes were by no means the idle pastime of disgruntled Unionists. Augustine Birrell, a Liberal elder-statesman who served as Irish secretary in both ministries, doubted whether "a big, loosely constructed Coalition Cabinet will command confidence, and [whether] it will . . . feel any in itself." He would have preferred "a *War Committee* of 6 or 8 men—of both parties— . . . leav[ing] the rest of the Cabinet alone to meet once a *fortnight*."[57]

Birrell's reaction was typical of that of most of his fellow Liberals, who could not understand why Asquith had decided to go this far if he went no further. And they strongly resented the fact that they were presented with a *fait accompli*. "All the other political parties have been consulted in more or less adequate form before or after this new

[54] May 15, 1915, Esher Papers.

[55] Chamberlain's diary, May 18, 1915 [copy], Chamberlain Papers.

[56] "It would be the former," Salisbury confidently predicted, "for they have not got it in them to reject." Salisbury to Lord Robert Cecil, May 19, 1915, Cecil Papers.

[57] Birrell to Sir Matthew Nathan, under-secretary for Ireland, [May 24], 1915, Nathan Papers.

and unprecedented step," the *Daily News* complained on May 29. "The
Liberal Party alone has been offered, so far as we are aware, no opportunity of expressing its opinion on a change which manifestly affects
it more nearly and directly than any of the other parties." The Cabinet
was kept as ignorant as the party rank and file. Charles Hobhouse
professed to be the first to receive a copy of Asquith's May 17 memorandum, and he identified Reginald McKenna, who was with him at
the time, as the second. McKenna, accompanied by Walter Runciman,
"went to consult Grey and found he knew nothing of it. . . ." At this
point they were joined by Haldane. "Have you heard the news?" they
asked the lord chancellor. "No—from the Dardanelles?" "No—from
Downing Street." Haldane, informed of the Prime Minister's request,
"turns his usual ghastly colour and nearly collapses."[58] Although others
might have been impressed by his long and intimate association with
Asquith, Haldane, better aware than they of its political value, must
have suspected the fate that lay in store for him.

In the days that followed, the mechanics of reconstruction put the
finishing touches to Liberal unity and revealed the events of May 1915
in their true light. Birrell took pity upon the Prime Minister, who
"spends his time poleaxing his friends and interviewing his enemies,"[59]
but Asquith displayed masterful control of the situation. He entered
into immediate negotiations with "the two villains of the piece,"
Churchill and Lloyd George, who, "with the help of their Tory friends,"
began the task of allotting places in the new ministry.[60] Lord Riddell,
proprietor of the *News of the World* and a confidant of Lloyd George,
designated Grey and Lord Crewe members of the "inner conclave,"[61]
but there are good reasons to doubt that this was the case. Runciman
repeated to McKenna on the 19th Grey's complaint that neither he
nor Haldane had yet "seen or heard from the P.M."[62] Grey's health
would have excluded him from these proceedings and it is especially
obvious that he was not a party to the supplanting of Haldane. Riddell
was more justified in his assertion that by the 22nd McKenna had dis-

58 Hobhouse to Buxton, June 10, 1915, Buxton Papers.
59 Birrell to Nathan, [May 22, 1915], Nathan Papers.
60 Hobhouse to Buxton, June 1, 1915, Buxton Papers.
61 Riddell, 93; a report in the May 29 *Nation*—probably by Massingham—was
emphatic that Grey "was not a member . . . [of the] small committee of Conservatives and Liberal leaders [who] . . . determined . . . who should come in and who
should go out. . . ."
62 May 19, 1915, McKenna Papers.

placed Churchill at the bargaining table, for by this date it was evident that Churchill exerted little if any influence while McKenna was a power to be reckoned with. Birrell reported an early encounter with McKenna, "the new Chancellor of the Exchequer, always great at a plot."[63] And Lord Fisher congratulated Mrs. McKenna "on our dear Reggie *going up higher*' when the intrigue was under weigh [sic] for him to 'go out'!"[64]

The retention of McKenna—indeed his promotion from the home office to the chancellorship of the exchequer—attested to the powers that Asquith continued to command. The *Scotsman*, which considered this "one of the oddest results of the upheaval," marveled that "the most abused and vilified Minister of recent days" had weathered the crisis so well. McKenna was as much the object of scurrilous press attacks as Haldane. Yet, with the Prime Minister's personal backing, he survived and prospered. "Lord Haldane was not qualified to fight a personal battle for himself," Lloyd George remarked with a touch of sarcasm. "Mr. M'Kenna was. So Lord Haldane was driven in disgrace into the wilderness and Mr. M'Kenna was promoted to the second place in the Government."[65]

The same rule applied in other cases. Those who enjoyed Asquith's favor and who could count upon support from one source or another made the transition from the last Liberal Government to the first coalition. Liberal membership in the finished Cabinet bore a striking resemblance to the way that Asquith had rated his colleagues on February 26, 1915 ("like a Tripos at Cambridge") in an exercise to amuse his young confidante, Venetia Stanley: Crewe, Grey, and McKenna had topped that list, followed by Lloyd George, Churchill, and Kitchener; then, in descending order, came Harcourt and Simon, Haldane, Runciman, Samuel, Pease, Beauchamp, Emmott, Lucas, and McKinnon Wood.[66] It is noteworthy that the undated jottings on Cabinet reconstruction that are preserved among the Asquith Papers begin with the assumption that those furthest down the February 26 list—Wood was an exception—would not receive office in the coalition. The Prime Minister explained to Lord Stamfordham on May 19 that "Harcourt's health is not good: he manages his office well but is no use in the H. of

---

[63] Birrell to Nathan, June 1, 1915, Nathan Papers.
[64] May 29, 1915, McKenna Papers.   [65] *War Memoirs*, I, 138.
[66] Quoted in Jenkins, *Asquith*, pp. 340–41.

C. or with regard to *the War*. . . . Harcourt would like a Peerage and in any case would not have gone on after this Parliament."[67] But Harcourt was not nearly so easy to dispose of. By the third of four calculations, he was salvaged from the losers' column and assigned the office of works. Like McKenna, he was a dependable "Asquith man," and an astute strategist with an important segment of the party behind him.

Like McKenna and Harcourt, Birrell was regarded by most observers as a likely casualty. The Irish secretary in the last Government, he was in the eyes of many Unionists the personification of the Liberal commitment to Home Rule. How could they accept him as a colleague and, for that matter, how could he affiliate with Bonar Law, Carson, and Long? Yet Birrell too retained office, and the Irish office no less. Again the Prime Minister's backing was all-important. Asquith had omitted "our dear Birrell" from his parlor game with Miss Stanley on the grounds that he was "in a class by himself." Equally important was the fact that Birrell enjoyed the confidence of the Irish nationalists, who could not afford to lend their own names to the new all-party Government. He confessed that unlike "some of my poleaxed friends," he would have been glad to retire, but that a Unionist or a lukewarm Home Ruler at the Irish office would have been a red flag to the Irish. "My position is odd," he explained to Sir Matthew Nathan on the 22nd. "They can't touch me. It is not the strength of the garrison, but the invulnerability of the position." Birrell acknowledged how dependent he was upon Asquith's support, though he knew that "a Prime Minister making up a new combination is as untrustworthy as a Young Woman making up her mind whether she will have diamonds or rubies in her engagement ring."[68]

Sir John Simon was another who had aroused fierce enmity, but who survived to take his place—a better place—in the new Government. Walter Runciman's departure too had been mistakenly forecast. The *Daily Express* in its first report of the political crisis on the 18th confidently predicted the displacement of eight ministers of whom only three were absent from the new Cabinet. The *Daily Mail*, reserving its prognoses until the next day, miscalculated on Birrell and Harcourt. On the 20th it ruefully admitted that the only certainty was that

[67] Lord Stamfordham's memorandum, May 19, 1915, Royal Archives, G.V. K770/3.
[68] Nathan Papers.

Asquith and Grey would remain at their respective posts. This, of course, back-handedly raised the question of Lord Kitchener. Lord Riddell heard from one of his many contacts on the 20th that Bonar Law was "strongly opposed to Kitchener," whom he wanted out of the war office and out of the Cabinet.[69] Chamberlain and Balfour attempted to mollify Bonar Law and urged him to take the new ministry of munitions— or ministry of supply as it was often called during this formulative period—leaving Kitchener titular authority. Meanwhile the North-cliffe papers, *The Times* and *Daily Mail,* along with J. L. Garvin's *Pall Mall Gazette,* unleashed a campaign to evict Kitchener from the war office. Colonel Repington, who spoke with more than personal authority, revealed that his "main hope" was to "welcome" Lloyd George to Kitchener's place.[70] But the campaign against Kitchener boomeranged and, if anything, made him more a public hero. Copies of the North-cliffe papers were burned on the London Stock Exchange, and the *Express* admonished its neighbors along Fleet Street that "attacks on Lord Kitchener . . . help Germany." The opportunity was lost, and the minister who should have been the first to be sacked was permitted to remain and to cause further mischief.

By creating an unwieldy coalition with twenty-two places, two more than the Government it had replaced, Asquith was able to accommodate most of his former colleagues and an array of prominent Unionists. There were in fact only two major casualties, one more apparent but both very real: the first was Lord Haldane, excluded entirely from the new formation; the second was Winston Churchill, who remained in a decidedly minor capacity.

Various accounts have been provided of Churchill's removal from the admiralty in May 1915; none make it clear why the politician who seemed in virtual control of the situation on the 14th had become its victim within a week's time. The half dozen letters between Asquith and Churchill that exist among the Asquith Papers testify to a steady weakening of Churchill's position: on the 17th he offered suggestions for the composition of the new Cabinet; on the 21st he begged for "any office—the lowest if it is of use in this time of war. . . ." The usual explanation is that the Unionists, who had never forgiven Churchill his apostasy in 1904, demanded his demotion if not his exclu-

---

[69] Riddell, p. 91.
[70] Repington to Lloyd George, May 20, 1915, Lloyd George Papers.

sion from Asquith in 1915. Even in the unlikelihood that such feeling might have persisted among responsible Unionists, other factors were vastly more important.

Churchill had made an unsuccessful challenge and, for this, he took the consequences. Clearly Asquith possessed a freer hand in dealing with him than with either Balfour, who stood well beyond his reach, or Lloyd George, who had fortified his position with support from Radicals, Unionists, and above all, press magnates. Churchill, who had been elevated at Asquith's discretion, had no reserves of power to sustain him. Increasing doubts about the Dardanelles venture, with which the Churchill name was readily identified, may also have played a part. It also appears that Churchill's position was seriously weakened by the fact that the intriguers dissolved their alliance as soon as they had achieved their primary object, the disruption of the *ancien régime*. Lloyd George, Balfour, and Churchill all favored a more vigorous prose- cution of the war, but they differed considerably on the lengths to which they were prepared to go. There is evidence that once Balfour had finished playing both ends against the middle, he began to play the middle against each end: in a letter to Lord Robert Cecil on May 17, he cautioned against revealing too much to Lloyd George. Churchill, the least adept at the political game, was easy prey for older, more cynical hands. This would have been neither the first time nor the last that he was treated ungratefully by Lloyd George, or that Balfour betrayed an ally or a principle for political advantage.

What is less open to conjecture is the fact that Churchill's difficulties, which ejected him from the admiralty and nearly kept him out of the first coalition, had little if anything to do with pressures applied to Asquith by the Unionists. When it suited his purposes, the Prime Minister easily withstood any such pressures. Roy Jenkins and others have made patently clear that by this time Churchill hardly enjoyed a filial relationship with Asquith. He was thrown over in May 1915, like Haldane, not to appease the Unionists so much as to facilitate Asquith's strategy. As Bonar Law's ultimatum to Asquith on May 17 would imply, the Opposition made only those formal demands that Asquith had indicated a willingness to entertain. The Unionist leaders could not have seriously opposed Churchill's retention of the admiralty out of support for Lord Fisher, for they did not hesitate to assent to Churchill's replacement by Balfour, whom Fisher had labeled every bit as objectionable. Nor could they fault his performance as first lord—the Dardanelles affair was something else again—which had been so much more to their liking than it had been to that of most Liberals.

Historians have by and large failed to consider that the Liberal rank-and-file, let alone the Liberal leaders, had more reason to be incensed against Churchill than their counterparts across the House. Lord Beauchamp, among those deprived of office, informed Lord Stamfordham that the "feeling among his colleagues is that [Churchill] is primary cause of trouble and should be first to go instead of others who will lose their seats in Cabinet."[71] The political correspondent for The Times reported on the 22nd that Liberal M.P.s, "look[ing] upon Mr. Churchill as the author of all their party ills," were "petitioning their chiefs to exclude [him] from the new Ministry altogether." Liberals had reasons of their own to remember with distaste Churchill's part in the Ulster crisis on the eve of war, and many of them had never forgiven his eagerness to apply troops as an antidote to industrial unrest. Many Unionists had since come to appreciate Churchill's aggressive naval policy, particularly in the days when the Government had seemed to waver between war and neutrality; but what Unionists hailed as vitality, Liberals often condemned as irresponsibility. In addition, Liberal resentment of Churchill was aggravated by persistent rumors of his role in the press intrigue. W. M. R. Pringle, a lifelong Asquithian, warned the Prime Minister that

a number of your supporters have been driven to the conclusion that the present crisis has been brought about by the actions of Mr. Churchill. I do not only refer to his differences with Lord Fisher but we believe that he was privy to the intrigue which resulted in the Repington disclosures.

In these circumstances we regard his presence in the Government as a public danger. It is only fair therefore that you should know, before any arrangement is concluded, that the attitude of a considerable number of members will be determined by this conviction.[72]

In any event, Asquith—who offered his party only a twenty-minute explanation of his decision, ex post facto—was not likely to have been influenced by the sentiments of backbenchers. If he subsequently cited pressures from one source or another, this was a convenient way for him

[71] Stamfordham to the King, May 19, 1915 [cypher telegram], Royal Archives, G.V., K770/4.
[72] May 20, 1915, Asquith Papers.

to dignify and obscure his intentions. From the moment that the culprit was known, he was determined to rid himself of Churchill. But how? A general reconstruction promised an easy solution. With the Unionist leaders inside the Government, Churchill would have no one to champion or exploit his cause. Lord Derby hit the mark when he put down the whole affair to the fact that "Asquith was afraid of sacking Winston."[73] The King expressed satisfaction that "the Prime Minister is going to have a National Govt., only by that means can we get rid of Churchill from Admiralty."[74] According to reports that reached the attentive ear of Lord Fisher, it was Balfour who pointed out to Asquith the risk of leaving Churchill outside the coalition where he might provide a magnet for disaffected politicians of both camps: "It's a wonderful story that Winston was cast out by the Prime Minister from the Cabinet and brought back into it by Balfour."[75] Instead Churchill was retained, but he was relegated to the chancellorship of the Duchy of Lancaster, a ministerial back-kitchen well out of harm's way. Lloyd George told Lord Riddell on the 23rd that he had "fought" to get Churchill something better, and intimated that Asquith had been the stumbling block.[76] And the fact that Churchill pleaded his own case to the Unionist leaders, seemingly above the Prime Minister's head, suggests that they were not responsible for his demotion. The following autumn, Churchill resigned his sinecure and took up the command of a battalion in France, where he waited out the lifetime of the Asquith coalition and the frame-of-mind for which it stood.

Lord Haldane was entirely another matter. Unlike Churchill, he posed no threat to Asquith's leadership, nor did he exert any appreciable influence over the war effort. Why then was he dropped from office? There are a number of interdependent explanations which elucidate Asquith's strategy at this juncture and in the months that followed. Aware of the gathering forces of discontent in political society and beyond, Asquith was attempting to secure his position. Haldane's portly figure was an obvious piece of ballast to be jettisoned if he was to obtain sufficient buoyancy to ride the crest of the wave. Personal allegiances never mattered quite so much to Asquith as his determination to reach the top and remain there. Churchill, not without bitterness,

---

[73] Derby to Gwynne, May 22, 1915, Gwynne Papers.
[74] King George V to Queen Mary, May 19, 1915, Royal Archives G.V., CC 4/132.
[75] Fisher to McKenna, May 22, 1915, McKenna Papers.   [76] Riddell, p. 94.

likened him to the proverbial "man in the 'howdah': wherever the elephant goes, he will go." Lloyd George, who repeated Churchill's remark to C. P. Scott with gleeful malice, compared Asquith to "Palmerston in his later days: nothing to him matters so much as that he should stay where he is. . . ."[77]

Whether the retention of Haldane would have weakened Asquith's hand in dealing either with the Unionists or the country remains debatable. But his presence in the coalition would not have strengthened Asquith's position and that, after all, was the object of the exercise. The Prime Minister conceived of coaltion as a means to saddle his critics—and potential critics—with ministerial responsibilities that would make it inconvenient if not impossible for them to plot against him. He explained to Lord Stamfordham that "not in all cases" were ministers selected "for their fitness for office" and that certain ones were instead chosen because "they are safer *in* than out of office!"[78] Haldane, who neither rendered material assistance against intriguers nor was himself capable of intrigue, had no place in such an assemblage. He could be depended upon to take his dismissal gracefully and not to become the focal point for controversy. It was easier to dispense with Haldane, whose loyalty could be taken for granted, than other Liberals, who might take advantage of the divisions within the party.

It was an unsavory business. Loulou Harcourt, a veteran of the power struggles of the 1890s, could philosophize that as "a cook cannot make omelettes without breaking eggs, so a Prime Minister cannot make a coalition without breaking colleagues."[79] But others were less jovial. "Of all the detestable features of this detestable business," Herbert Samuel wrote to Charles Hobhouse, whom he succeeded as postmaster general, "the replacements of Liberal ministers by their own colleagues are the worst."[80] Walter Runciman contemplated the "queer unpalatable prospect for those of us who remain in this mixed company," and consoled himself that "at the worst it cannot last long."[81] And Augustine Birrell, who deprecated the "twopenny halfpenny coalition," acknowl-

---

[77] Memorandum of Sept. 3, 1915, Scott Papers, Add. MSS. 50, 901, f. 202.

[78] Lord Stamfordham's memorandum, May 22, 1915, Royal Archives, G.V., K770/11.

[79] Harcourt to Buxton, June 3, 1915 [copy], Harcourt Papers.

[80] May 26, 1915, Samuel Papers.

[81] Runciman to Samuel, May 26, 1915, *Ibid.*

edged that Asquith "had parted (in circumstances which *never* can be reported favourably upon) with one or two of his closest friends, and he has a Cabinet composed of warring, uncongenial, and it may be traitorous elements."[82]

Historians have accepted uncritically Asquith's statement that Haldane's exclusion, like Churchill's transfer from the admiralty, was a concession "insisted on by Mr. Bonar Law and his friends."[83] It is of course possible that such a demand was made in conversation, but not a scrap of written evidence survives. Austen Chamberlain, on the other hand, was explicit that it was Asquith who first proposed Haldane's removal from the woolsack when he met with Bonar Law on the 17th.[84] Perhaps the Prime Minister merely anticipated the Opposition's terms. In any case, the Unionist leaders were given an indication that their objections to Haldane would not be ignored. They received so few concessions with which they might appease their followers that they could not afford to forego this one. It was not for another decade, until Grey and Asquith had published their memoirs, that the story became current that Asquith had yielded to unremitting Unionist pressure. Sir Robert Perks, who had known Asquith and Haldane since their Liberal Imperialist days, confessed he "did not know till I read Grey's book . . . that the Tories had made it a condition that Haldane should not join the Coalition Government. I have seen H. many times since, and he has not said a word of this."[85]

Lord Morley, who remained a keen observer of the political scene, told J. H. Morgan, a journalist friend, that Asquith had acquiesced to Haldane's exclusion "without a murmur."[86] Members of Asquith's family, admittedly closer to the Prime Minister, have described the intense grief with which he sacrificed his friend. How can these conflicting accounts be reconciled? Like any successful Prime Minister, Asquith was quite capable of divorcing the political from the personal. He was genuinely distressed by the departure of Haldane, with whom he shared so many memories, and by the satisfaction it would give their mutual enemies. Yet he had few political reasons to mourn his loss. Vaughan Nash, assisting in a secretarial capacity at Downing Street, confided

[82] Birrell to Nathan, June 12, 1915, Nathan Papers.
[83] *Memories and Reflections*, II, 101–102.
[84] Diary for May 17, 1915 [copy], Chamberlain Papers.
[85] Perks to Rosebery, Oct. 18, 1925, Rosebery Papers.
[86] Morgan, "The Riddle of Lord Haldane," *Quarterly Review* (Jan., 1929), p. 171.

to Sidney Webb "that Asquith and other members of the Cabinet found Haldane woolly-headed and troublesome."[87] Undoubtedly Haldane had in the course of time offended certain colleagues whom Asquith valued or wished to cultivate: McKenna and Lloyd George got on poorly with him, and Kitchener, upon whom Asquith leaned, resented his military advice and his intimacy with Sir John French. And Haldane had never been popular among the Radical backbenchers, whose support Asquith wanted desperately to retain: the exclusion of Haldane might please them; it was certainly not something many would take to heart.

The only prominent politician to speak out strongly on Haldane's behalf was Churchill, who acknowledged that he was "so short of credit at the moment that I can only make an encouraging signal."[88] In a speech at Dundee on June 5 he paid warm tribute to the former lord chancellor and lamented the nation's loss. But Churchill had always acted chivalrously toward Haldane, whom he regarded as "one who has always given me the greatest possible encouragement and help."[89] They had had their differences and moved in different social circles— Haldane never attended weekend parties aboard the admiralty yacht *Enchantress*, a good index to Churchill's friendships—but Churchill respected the services he had performed. Earlier that spring, Churchill had replied to Haldane's critics while others in higher places remained conspicuously silent: "Yes—Winston's speech was splendid," Haldane wrote to his sister on May 8. "Had the P.M. or Grey said something of this sort six months ago, much trouble might have been saved."[90] Churchill told Lord Riddell on July 6 that "Asquith had acted very wrongly in shedding Haldane . . . and that he should have been left in his position as Lord Chancellor."[91] This was precisely the treatment Churchill accorded Lord Simon a quarter century later, despite the latter's record as an appeaser.

J. L. Garvin, a confederate of the intriguers, broke the story of the Cabinet crisis in the late night edition of the May 18 *Pall Mall Gazette*. "The whole method and temper of Cabinet administration in wartime is the question at stake," he informed his readers. But Garvin did not

[87] June 14, 1915, Beatrice Webb, *Diaries*, I (London, 1952), 38–39.
[88] Churchill to Haldane, May 21, 1915, HP 5911, f. 50.
[89] Churchill to Haldane's mother, June 8, 1915, HP 6082, f. 15.
[90] HP 6012, f. 95.   [91] Riddell, p. 111.

intend to drive Haldane from office. "I wanted a coalition but never dreamed of one like this," he assured Haldane on the 26th. "I deplore your departure and when assured at first that you did not wish to remain Lord Chancellor I hoped at least you would remain as Minister for Education."[92] From whom had Garvin heard that Haldane wished to vacate the woolsack? However self-effacing, Haldane had never contemplated retirement from public life. When Asquith's memorandum reached him on the 17th he dutifully submitted his resignation, hoping in vain it would not be accepted. The next day he made first mention of the crisis in letters to his mother and sister, whom he advised he would not be able to get down to Cloan that weekend. To the latter he revealed that he suggested to Asquith "that it may be wise to use my office in order to bring in [Sir Edward] Carson," the Ulsterite leader.[93] It was understood that the lord chancellorship was one post that the Opposition would probably claim. Yet Haldane never expected to stand down in favor of a fellow-Liberal as ultimately proved the case.

It has been suggested that Haldane sought to ease his burdens for medical reasons. But he was healthier at this time than he had often been in recent years. Margot Asquith, writing to him on the 18th, assumed that Grey would retire on grounds of ill health and that he would remain. That certainly would have been a more logical arrangement. The foreign secretary, his eyesight failing, was incapacitated for long stretches of time and despondent. Haldane, on the other hand, looked forward to judicial work and assorted projects for postwar reconstruction.

Haldane informed his mother on the 19th of the virtual certainty of a coalition: "I do not know what will happen as regards myself, but I have thought it right to give H. H. A. complete freedom."[94] Both the next day and the day after he reported that, to his knowledge, nothing had been settled, though the feeling grew that he would not be included in the new Government. On the 22nd he "regard[ed] it as certain that I shall go," but he trusted "that it is not permanent."[95] Others, too, anticipated his exclusion. The *Daily Mail*, which had predicted it from the start, asserted on the 21st that "Lord Haldane goes out by the unanimous wish of both parties." The *Nation*, more sympathetic to him, foretold his retirement on the 22nd, but mistakenly expected the same for Harcourt. Haldane's fate does not seem to have

[92] HP 5911, f. 104.   [93] HP 6012, ff. 98–99.   [94] HP 5993, f. 191.
[95] HP 5993, f. 197.

been settled until late on the 23rd. Margot Asquith wrote to Haldane at five o'clock the next morning and to his mother and sister later that day. "I cannot write for indignation!" she prefaced her four-page letter to him. She recounted that her husband had wept when he told her the news that the Unionists refused to serve with Haldane. "I shall never forgive them—*never*. That you should leave Henry's Cabinet—that 8th rate men like Bonar and Austen and Long should be *Kept* is to me unthinkable. Will it mean that we shan't see much of you? No! Don't say that."[96] To Haldane's sister, Margot wrote that "some neutral judge" would become lord chancellor, and that she had tried to get Lord Crewe to refuse to join the coalition without Haldane.[97] To Haldane's mother, she proffered assurances that "Henry and Grey fought like Cats and Lions" for Haldane ("that noble angelic man") but to no avail.[98]

But speculation continued. On the 25th Haldane told his mother that "the fight is still going on, but I shall be well content to be out if that has to be."[99] That morning's *Times* took for granted his imminent departure (it said the same about Harcourt) while the *Manchester Guardian* expressed doubts "whether Lord Haldane will go after all." The *Scotsman* too came round to the view that "the general expectation of [Haldane's] retirement is not to be too readily taken as accurate." Yet it was on this day that Sir Stanley Buckmaster, solicitor-general in the last Government, received Asquith's invitation to become lord chancellor in the next.

It would have been one thing for Haldane to cede the woolsack to Sir Frank Finlay, Sir Edward Carson, or some other Unionist lawyer; it was quite another for him to make way for a Liberal and a relatively minor one at that. At one point Asquith thought of Lord Sumner, a distinguished judge with Unionist proclivities, whose name he put on the back of an envelope and mentioned to Lord Stamfordham on the 22nd. But the Prime Minister was reluctant to allow this prize to fall into Opposition hands. Even before he spoke to Stamfordham, he had offered the post to Sir John Simon, who regarded it as a political cul-de-sac and preferred "the sack rather than the wool-sack."[100] Simon wrote to Haldane on the 25th to express relief "that it is not I who

[96] HP 5991, ff. 54–55.   [97] HP 6025, ff. 91–92.   [98] HP 6082, f. 8.
[99] HP 5993, f. 201.
[100] Simon to Buckmaster, May 18, 1915, quoted in Heuston, *Lives of the Lord Chancellors*, p. 265.

takes your place (though I know Buckmaster feels as I do and never dreamt of displacing you). . . ."[101] What was the point of displacing Haldane who, as the *Scotsman* pointed out, had "ministerial and legal qualifications incomparably greater than those of his successor"? If Asquith had been strong enough to insist upon a Liberal, why had he not insisted upon the one best qualified? The *Scotsman* cited Buckmaster's appointment as incontestable proof that the Unionists had entertained no designs upon the office and that Haldane had retired of his own accord. Rumors abounded that the Prime Minister had deliberately planted a complaisant nonentity upon the woolsack who would "keep it warm" until the propitious moment when he would exchange the premiership for the lord chancellorship in a Lloyd George Government.

Out of office Haldane became, to his own amazement, "more popular than I ever was with the Liberal Party." Unable to appreciate the necessity for the Prime Minister's drastic step and frustrated by the want of information, the Liberal rank-and-file identified with Haldane's plight. Like them, he was the victim of unseen forces and frontbench treacheries. Some two-hundred Liberal and Irish M.P.s, many of whom had been bitter critics of his army estimates, presented him with an address that lauded his services to the nation. Simon assured Christopher Addison at lunch on the 26th that there were those "inside the Cabinet [who] feel as strongly as we do outside about the dismissal of Haldane. . . ." He related that negotiations between the parties nearly broke down two nights before "when the Prime Minister at last put his foot down" and declared his minimum terms on a take-it-or-leave-it basis. ". . . I only wish," Addison recorded in his diary, "as did the others, that the P.M. had put his foot down about [Haldane] as well."[102]

Haldane could console himself not only with his new-found popularity, but also with the Order of Merit which he received from the King when he surrendered the Great Seal. Letters of commiseration came in great number from many of the leading lawyers, soldiers, and statesmen of the realm, each of whom received in reply a humble letter that discussed national rather than personal problems. Among those who wrote was Lord Curzon, who begged to "be allowed to retain undiminished your private friendship" and who deplored the loss to "the government of one of its main sources of intellectual strength at

[101] HP 5911, ff. 76–77.   [102] *Four and a Half Years,* I, 82.

a moment when concentration rather than dissipation is the need of the hour."[103] More surprisingly, Haldane received a warm letter of tribute from Sir Max Aitken, later Lord Beaverbrook, whose subsequent affiliation with Bonar Law kept him from publicizing his sympathy.

Others might have been vindictive, but not Haldane. He was annoyed that the Unionist leaders had yielded so easily to backbench prejudices they knew to be unfounded; yet he did not blame Asquith for yielding in turn to the Unionist leaders. He reasoned that nothing mattered nearly so much as the preservation of national unity. What wounded him was Asquith's failure to commiserate with him.

The fact that Haldane took for granted that his membership in the coalition would impair its effectiveness in Parliament and the country does not necessarily mean that this would have been so. The press attacks to which he had been subjected in recent months made him more acutely self-conscious than ever. Public opposition to him was in fact greater in the months after he left office than it had been before. But popular sentiments hardly worried Asquith, who had formed a coalition as insurance against a General Election and whose preoccupation was parliamentary attitudes. True, Mrs. Emmeline Pankhurst, the redoubtable suffragette, was violently anti-Haldane,[104] but Asquith had never paid heed to her. And the politicians and journalists who persecuted Haldane during the early months of 1915, were unappeased by his departure, and refused to support the coalition whether or not he belonged. They were of course jubilant to witness the disruption of the Liberal Government for which they believed themselves in some measure responsible; but they took little satisfaction in what had replaced it. In the opinion of Leo Maxse, any government headed by Asquith and dominated by anticonscriptionists was not a National Government. He berated the Unionist leaders for falling into the Prime Minister's trap and refused to give the events of May 1915 more than cursory attention in the *National Review*. Lord Willoughby de Broke, among the most intractable of diehard Tories and equally fierce in his denunciations of Haldane, thoroughly agreed with Maxse. He came away from a party caucus at the Carlton Club convinced that once again the Unionists had been betrayed by their front bench: "Nobody

103 May 26, 1915, HP 5911, f. 95.
104 Mrs. Pankhurst to Lloyd George, [Dec. 10, 1916], Lloyd George Papers.

could tell me that our leaders had extracted any pledge from Asquith beyond asking for a certain number of seats in the Cabinet."[105]

Haldane's exodus saved neither the Government from further censure nor, for that matter, him from further vilification. In fact, it was after he left office that he suffered some of the most savage attacks. Nearly two months later he received, at the instigation of the *Daily Express*, over 2,600 abusive letters in a single day, providing a full-time job for his kitchenmaid, who attacked them with a scullery knife.[106] And in July 1915 Leo Maxse, relentless in pursuit, threatened to publish a volume facetiously titled *Viscount Haldane, O.M.: a Study in Responsible Statesmanship*. So long as Asquith presided over affairs of state, and so long as the systems of voluntary recruiting and "business as usual" survived, the agitation against Haldane continued. It made little difference that he no longer held the seals of office, for he remained nonetheless a convenient scapegoat for the ideals and causes that had come to be identified as "Haldaneism." In December 1916, when Lloyd George dispossessed Asquith from the premiership, the *Daily Mail* ("The Paper that is Combing Them Out") celebrated the ejection of "the Haldane gang."

Even if Haldane might have thought that the attacks upon the Government would cease with his departure, Asquith labored under no such illusion. But the creation of a coalition made it virtually impossible for future attacks to enjoy the backing of the Opposition leaders, who were now pledged to the Government and to its leader. Backbench criticism could easily be discounted, but frontbench criticism was another matter. Asquith had not been alarmed, he assured Lord Stamfordham on May 19, when W. A. S. Hewins put down a motion to debate the shells shortage, for this "was fortunately made by a private member and so the Prime Minister was able to refuse to discuss it: but if the front opposition bench had moved it, discussion must have followed."[107] Haldane was sacrificed not to silence enemies, who remained vocal nonetheless, but for more subtle reasons. His place in the Cabinet was necessary if Asquith was going to achieve what he

[105] Willoughby de Broke to Maxse, June 5, 1915, Maxse Papers.

[106] Haldane's *Autobiography* (p. 283) fails to make clear that this incident followed his resignation and in no way precipitated it.

[107] Lord Stamfordham's memorandum, May 19, 1915, Royal Archives, G.V., K770/3.

described to Herbert Samuel as a "balance."[108] This in itself is a concept that merits investigation.

Obviously the balance to which the Prime Minister referred was not numerical: Liberals outnumbered Unionists three to two in the coalition. Nor could Asquith have meant a balance of power, for the key ministries remained secure in Liberal hands and great care was taken to keep Bonar Law, a tariff reformer, at a safe distance from the treasury, the war office, or the newly created ministry of munitions. Asquith's insistence upon filling these strategic offices with Liberals had nearly brought the plan for coalition to ruin, yet he remained adamant. At one point he proposed to combine the duties of the chancellorship with those of the premiership rather than let the former fall to Bonar Law. Curiously enough, he raised no particular objection to letting Balfour take the treasury, and it was Bonar Law who vetoed this arrangement by telling Lloyd George that while the Government might regard Balfour "as one of the Opposition, the latter looked upon him as much more belonging to the Government!"[109] It becomes evident that Asquith was seeking to strike a balance within the new Cabinet between the intraparty advocates of laissez-faire principles (Balfour among them) and those politicians who favored a more active and far-reaching intervention on the part of the state. He remained justly confident that his office and prestige would be sufficient to tilt that balance in the direction of the former.

Advocates of Organization, regardless of their party affiliation, looked to the coalition to carry through legislation that neither party could undertake single-handedly. They expected immediate steps to clamp down upon resident aliens, to prevent neutrals from delivering classified commodities to enemy ports, to regulate profits and wages at least in the munitions industry, and to implement schemes for national service. By and large, they were thwarted by Asquith, who astutely held such decisions at bay. He had presided over a change in personnel—a diverting game of musical ministries—not a change in policy. For as long as he remained at the helm, he retained all he could of the old system.

Why had he not retained Haldane with it? For one thing, Haldane's reputation and personality threatened to disrupt the forces that Asquith

[108] Samuel's memorandum, May 26, 1915, Samuel Papers.
[109] Lord Stamfordham's memorandum, May 25, 1915, Royal Archives, G.V., K770/12.

wanted to hold together. For another, Haldane represented no segment of public or party opinion that had to be taken into account. In addition, a careful examination of events provides indications that Haldane, despite appearances, no longer fit comfortably within that system. He had modified his stand against compulsory service and, given the opportunity, might have thrown in his lot with the supporters of Organization. His various proposals for postwar reconstruction were a marked departure from traditional Liberal thought. He had, in short, revealed the tendencies that would eventually take him beyond Liberalism and into the first Labour Government.

CHAPTER VIII

RETURN JOURNEY

*Now that you are disentangled from the party machine on suspicion
of intellect, I hope you will give the country a bit of your mind. . . .
You have only to let yourself go to be a much greater power outside
the Cabinet than you were as a purple patch on that fearfully inadequate
body. They are dear creatures, and to know them personally is to be
hopelessly incapacitated from sentencing them as they will be sentenced
at the bar of History; but their attempt to enlist you was an attempt to
mix up the Old Bailey with the Judicial Committee, or to make an
Ecclesiastical Commissioner of Martin Luther. You remember St. Luke's
story about Peter when the Lord sank his boat by the miracle of the
fishes. Well, I have an improbable vision of Asquith falling on his knees
and saying "My dear Haldane: depart from me; for I am a sinful man."*
— BERNARD SHAW*

Lord Haldane's relationship with Asquith after May 1915 provides
a useful postscript to the making of the first wartime coalition by
further reflecting the deterioration of Liberalism of which the Cabinet
crisis was not a portent but a confirmation. The problems that befell
them and their friendship provide a valuable index to the political
realignments of the postwar decade.

All the more pity that the subject has been treated more with sentiment than objectivity. Major-General Sir Frederick Maurice, Haldane's
official biographer, was profoundly indebted to Asquith, who had come
to his assistance in May 1918 when he had backed into a political
hornets' nest by challenging the veracity of the Lloyd George Government's army statistics. He categorically denied that May 1915 had

* Letter to Haldane, August 3, 1915, HP 5912, f. 85.

marked a parting of the ways between Asquith and Haldane, telling his readers that in the research for his two-volume biography he uncovered "no trace" that his subject "ever bore Asquith any grudge," and, to the contrary, "abundant evidence that [Haldane's] affection for his old friend and ally" remained undiminished.[1] Yet Maurice would not have had to look beyond the papers that the Haldane family placed at his disposal to find ample indication that Haldane's relations with Asquith were, if not estranged, equivocal.

The *New Statesman*, eager to claim Haldane as a wholehearted convert to socialism, was no closer to the truth when it declared that to the end of his days he "never ceased to blame Asquith for dropping him on the formation of the first Coalition Government. . . ."[2] Haldane, who gave Asquith the benefit of any doubt, was not a person to indulge in rancor and recrimination. He cherished too many fond memories of past associations ever to regard Asquith with anything but warmth. Yet at the same time, he realized how little he and Asquith had come to have in common, socially and politically. He was profoundly disappointed to see his friend cling to office rather than principles, something the Asquith of Hampstead days would never have done. The Webbs, who came to dinner at Queen Anne's Gate on July 22, deduced from the conversation that their host "had broken with Asquith" once and for all. "The country is being governed by three men: Balfour, Kitchener and Lloyd George," Haldane told them, "and Balfour is the real Prime Minister."[3] He could more easily forgive Asquith's treatment of himself than Asquith's ready acquiescence to political pressures (what Roy Jenkins has described in his biography as "the speed with which Asquith allowed solutions, which were not his own, to be imposed on him").

Haldane had sufficient reason to take offense. His injury was compounded by Asquith's failure at the time of the Cabinet crisis to offer a personal explanation or a few words of consolation. It was from colleagues that Haldane learned of Asquith's decision to reshuffle the ministry, and from the press that his services had not been retained. Lady Asquith has ascribed her father's silence "not to lack of feeling,

[1] II, 6–7.   [2] August 25, 1928.
[3] *Diaries*, I, 42; this entry is dated July 23 in the printed version. In the original diary, Mrs. Webb added: "The breakdown of British war administration is due to Kitchener's ignorance of civil life and to Asquith's apathy and rooted disinclination to trouble about anything until it becomes a public scandal." XXXII, Passfield Papers.

but to its intensity": the Prime Minister "was a shy man of strong emotions, who often (to his detriment) left the deepest things he felt unsaid."[4] Yet Asquith did not take advantage of the passing weeks to rectify the situation. When Haldane appeared as guest of honor at the National Liberal Club on July 5, Asquith, who was expected to attend, sent a written testimonial that was read for him. Sir Arthur Acland was impressed by Asquith's "fine letter [which] carries one back to days far away,"[5] but Haldane remained untransported.

Haldane often suspected, not without reason, that he was being patronized. He went to lunch at Downing Street on October 12 and reported to his mother, almost with surprise, that the Asquiths had "made themselves very agreeable."[6] On a subsequent occasion he found them "affectionate" and confessed, indicating a prior apprehension, that he "was glad I had gone."[7] Yet his visits were few and there is no indication that he returned their hospitality. His head was not turned when Margot, inviting him to her stepdaughter Violet's wedding on November 30, 1915, professed, much to his amusement, "that she and the P.M. want 'their oldest friend'! to sign the register."[8] When he learned on December 12, 1916, that Asquith had been deposed from the premiership, he wrote a heartfelt note of sympathy. And yet he could write the same day to his mother that Asquith and Grey "are only having what another of their colleagues encountered at an earlier stage."[9] It was not that Haldane was insincere, but only that he realized, as Maurice and others have failed to do, the distinction between his relationships with Asquith, past and present.

Haldane's pride had been wounded by his exclusion in 1915. But this in itself did not turn him against either Asquith or Liberalism. It was Asquith's indifference to Haldane's programs more than to his political fate that widened the gulf between them. Haldane, who reserved his holiday weekends for his mother at Cloan, refused the occasional invitations he received to the Wharf. After tendering excuses for a

[4] *The Times*, Nov. 2, 1964.
[5] Acland to Haldane, July 7, 1915, HP 5912, f. 76.
[6] Oct. 13, 1915, HP 5994, f. 113.
[7] Haldane to his mother, Aug. 3, 1916, HP 5996, f. 49.
[8] Haldane to his mother, Nov. 30, 1915, HP 5994, f. 185.
[9] HP 5996, f. 167. "Personally," Margot wrote cattily to Mrs. Haldane on the 28th, "I feel proud to be in the same boat as your Richard, only I wish I had half his or H.'s [equanimity]. Grey has shown no grandeur of character or courage over Richard and has not helped H. much either." HP 6082, f. 67.

Sunday in April 1917, he received word that "the old P.M. . . . wanted particularly to see me" and he agreed to join Asquith for lunch the following Wednesday. He arrived at Cavendish Square brimming with ideas for educational reform and curious to know what Asquith had in mind. He found to his dismay that he was one guest among many and that "it was impossible to get any good done. The old relation[ship] will not easily be restored," he sadly admitted. "I think time has changed the outlook on life of the ex-P.M. and that he is no longer keenly interested." Repeated indications that Asquith was not in any sense "an enthusiast for reform" convinced Haldane that he had to "pursue my own path."[10] It was a path that led him into temporary collaboration with Lloyd George and eventually into the first Labour Government, where he found the vindication that Liberalism denied him.

Haldane had experienced no comparable falling out with Grey, whom he regarded as a fellow-victim of events.[11] The foreign secretary was too broken a man, physically and politically, for anything more to be expected of him. Haldane visited Fallodon in early June and came away feeling greater pity for his host than for himself. It took little to discourage Grey, perpetually office-weary, with public life, and the events of May 1915 were more than sufficient. He gave Haldane the distinct impression that if the news from the front were more encouraging, he would seize the occasion to withdraw from the Government. Time and again he reproached himself for his failure to accompany his friend into retirement.

Grey's distress convinced Haldane that loss of office had its compensations. He realized that had he continued upon the woolsack he could neither have influenced policy decisions nor "have rendered material help in any departments that count."[12] That would have been unbearably frustrating. The ceremonials of the lord chancellorship had impinged upon his projects for judicial and educational reform to which he could now devote his full energies. He "would not have *refused* to

---

[10] Haldane to his mother, April 21, 25, 27, 1917, HP 5997, ff. 140 ff.

[11] Perhaps Haldane gave Grey too much the benefit of the doubt. The draft copy of Grey's autobiographical *Twenty-Five Years* that survives among the J. A. Spender Papers reveals the disquieting fact that it was Spender, not the author, who was responsible for the book's tributes to Haldane's war office work. Add. MSS. 46, 389, ff. 110 ff.

[12] Haldane to his mother, June 6, 1915, HP 5994, f. 1.

continue to serve," he told Lord Rosebery. "But in my heart I welcomed the decision." And "no longer a servant of the Crown," he absolved himself of the King's Pledge and "ceased to confine myself to soda-water."[13] It amused him almost as much as it galled his critics that after the coalition Government voted to pool and equalize ministerial emoluments, his judicial pension of £5,000 exceeded the salary that was paid to his successor.[14] Nor was he sorry to be far removed from political doubledealing and party strife; he heard of "great unrest in the Liberal Party" and of a "movement to substitute Ll. G. for H. H. A.," but assured his sister that he was "keeping aloof" despite what she might hear to the contrary.[15]

Those who had long taken for granted that Haldane's removal would precipitate the collapse of the Liberal edifice, could not believe that their victim, out of office, was out of power. His speech at the National Liberal Club on July 5 was widely interpreted as a move to tilt the political balance and possibly to insinuate himself back into office. He had not come, he told his sympathetic audience, "to talk on personal matters." Instead he appealed to the nation for self-restraint and cautioned "that the public should not be led astray by this craving for scapegoats." The case to which he referred was not his own but that of General von Donop, the master-general of the ordinance, who was permitted by Lloyd George, the new minister of munitions, to bear the blame for the munitions shortage. Haldane praised von Donop as a trustworthy and resourceful public servant, and recalled that a Cabinet committee had been created the previous autumn ("of which my learned friend Mr. Lloyd George was a member") that had placed sufficient orders, but that the munitions manufacturers had proved unable to meet their quotas.[16]

To many politicians and journalists it appeared that Haldane was being used to strengthen Asquith's (or Kitchener's) hand against the Unionists and Lloyd George, equally formidable threats. Lloyd George was "furious with Haldane," whose speech he took as "public evidence

[13] June 9, 1915, Rosebery Papers; Asquith, who had taken the vow of abstinence less seriously, thought that Haldane's teetotalism had "led to a notable diminution in his energy and buoyancy." Jenkins, p. 362n.
[14] Haldane to his mother, June 8, 1915, HP 5994, ff. 5–6. The lord chancellorship, among the most lucrative of appointments, had paid an annual salary of £10,000. It was reduced during wartime to £4,286.
[15] June 13, 1915, HP 6012, f. 106.
[16] Glasgow Herald, July 6, 1915; also the Nation, July 10, 1915.

of a secret intrigue."[17] He promptly attacked Haldane in the House of Commons. Haldane learned from Margot that Asquith and Lloyd George had exchanged strong words, each suspecting the other of disloyalty. Sir Henry Wilson, writing to Leo Maxse from the front, agreed that the "Old Firm" was attempting to restore Haldane in either an "executive or consultative" position; he was relieved after reading the National Liberal Club speech and "Squiff's fulsome letter," to hear that Lloyd George had "fallen rather heavily on the old fat liar and this is all to the good."[18] Lord Northcliffe, who prophesied that Asquith's premiership would not survive the summer, saw Haldane as the ringleader of "a conspiracy to accomplish L. G's downfall," and denounced him in *The Times* and *Daily Mail*.[19] "Much controversy rages round my head," Haldane recounted on the 8th, citing a particularly "foolish article" in *The Times* which he attributed to the pen of Northcliffe himself. He noted that the *Morning Post* had published an interview with "one of the great munition manufacturers . . . [who] entirely confirms what I said to the public," and he vowed that he would continue "to defend helpless officers who are unjustly attacked while I have a breath left in my body."[20] A day later he sent home a cutting from the *Daily Mail* regarding an "Anti-Haldane League," dedicated "to prevent him from forcing his way into the Cabinet. The difficulty," Haldane explained to his mother, "is that he does not want to go into it."[21]

Haldane encouraged false suspicions by lending his services to the new Government as an intermediary between Lord Kitchener and Sir John French, whose relations Asquith's daughter has compared to "those between a dog and a cat: Kitchener was the dog who did not bother about the cat until he had to do so; French was the cat which arched its back and spat."[22] Haldane, eminently qualified to deal with the problems of the Territorial Force, found French "as affectionate as a brother," and Kitchener "very friendly and confidential, and would, I think, like to have had me continue as his colleague." He made two brief visits to the front: one in late July, when he induced French to return with him to placate Kitchener; the other in early October.[23]

---

[17] Diary for July 9, 1915, Riddell, pp. 112–13.   [18] [n.d.], Maxse Papers.
[19] Diary for July 8, 1915, Riddell, p. 112.
[20] Haldane to his mother, July 8, 1915, HP 5994, f. 45.
[21] HP 5994, f. 47.   [22] *Winston Churchill*, p. 326.
[23] Haldane to his mother, July 24, Aug. 1, 1915, HP 5994, ff. 71, 81; also Gosse's note of August 2, 1915, Gosse Papers.

Sir Henry Wilson confirmed rumors that "old Haldane was out here," though he was unable to tell Maxse "what the old devil was at." At least, he consoled himself, "I got the chance of being rather rude to him which pleased me!"[24]

The military setbacks that autumn, which ultimately brought the supersession of French by Haig, also brought Haldane's name back into prominence. At a time when the air seemed to be clearing, there were new charges that Haldane had reformed the British fighting forces into impotence. It did not go unnoticed that he was occasionally in the vicinity of the war office, where he went by invitation of the general staff to discuss administrative problems. A puerile attack was made upon him in the House of Commons on October 27, which John Dillon put down with Gaelic pugnacity.[25] In early November, rumors began to circulate that Lord Kitchener was being pressured to resign so that Haldane could return to the war office: Lord Milner reported "great excitement" on the subject in his diary on the 6th. Haldane heard them too, but told his mother that however loudly war office officials might cry for "Uncle Richard, . . . he cannot go and the P. M. must just try his best" to work things out. "It is all very stupid."[26] On the 21st he wrote his sister that the "bad state" at the war office continued, as did "a strong movement . . . for my return." He remained aware, however, that "I won't do at present at all events."[27] Colonel Repington, "as attached as ever and thoroughly ashamed of *The Times* and other attacks," called upon him on December 15 and proclaimed "that the way to save the situation is obvious: Lord K. to leave the war office and I to return there, the only fit man in the country, he says. But he agrees that it is out of the question." Still, Haldane concluded, "I wish I had been there, all the same."[28]

By this time it was not Lord Kitchener from whom Haldane yearned to save the war office, but rather Asquith, who was substituting during Kitchener's extended visit to the Mediterranean. The Prime Minister was grateful for the opportunity to pry into war office files, which the

24 Oct. 10, 1915, Maxse Papers.
25 Mrs. Haldane expressed gratitude to Dillon, who replied: "My speech was quite unpremeditated—and was simply an explosion of bottled up indignation over the abominable and unscrupulous attacks on Lord Haldane by a poisonous crowd of men and newspapers—who have been in very large part responsible for the coming of the present war. . . ." Nov. 26, 1915, HP 6082, ff. 39–42.
26 Nov. 8, 1915, HP 5994, ff. 149–50.   27 HP 6012, f. 115.
28 Haldane to his mother, Dec. 16, 1915, HP 5994, ff. 209–10.

imperious Kitchener had placed off limits to his civilian colleagues. What Haldane deplored was the fact that Asquith, at Lloyd George's prodding, was also tampering with bureaucratic procedures. He was flattered to hear that Asquith had been "extolling" his mother "to the people about at Grillions," but told her that the Prime Minister's "opinions about yourself are sounder than his opinions about War Office organisation."[29] He went to see Asquith and "strongly remonstrated" that proposed changes "would paralyze the General Staff in Ordnance questions"; but Asquith had already "let himself be overpersuaded," leaving Haldane to "wish he were less hasty in such difficult matters."[30] Haldane's fear was that General von Donop, whose powers had been eroded, would resign (Lloyd George dismissed him in December 1916) and that there would be a "row" when Kitchener returned. Above all, he regretted the "tearing up [of] the organisation of the War Office" by Asquith and Lloyd George which, so far as he could tell, was "both unnecessary and mischievous."[31]

Haldane's comings and goings did not go unnoticed by his proclaimed enemies, who again hoped to use him to obtain the prize that had eluded them in May: the removal of Asquith and Kitchener. It was widely known that the Asquithian Liberals, with Kitchener's invaluable assistance, were obstructing the passage of national service and that opinion within the Cabinet was bitterly divided across party lines. The Milnerites, who kept close contact with Geoffrey Robinson of *The Times*, believed that Asquith and his "system" would have to be destroyed quickly if the war was to be won: "Squiff, Grey, K.," Sir Henry Wilson wrote to Leo Amery, "even the Bosh could not carry that load. . . ."[32] The conscriptionists along Fleet Street, led by Lord Northcliffe, calculated that by bringing into further question Liberalism's preparations for war—military and diplomatic—they would force the issue of compulsion and, most probably, Asquith's resignation.

In mid-December, Northcliffe and Robinson "got wind of" information that "a ministerial intrigue of a most mischievous character" was afoot to abrogate the naval blockade of Germany. The "arch-conspirator" was identified as Lord Haldane, and it was said he had the staunch

[29] Nov. 24, 1915, HP 5994, f. 175.

[30] Haldane to Sir Charles Harris, Nov. 25, 1915, Harris Papers.

[31] Haldane to his mother, Nov. 29, 1915, HP 5994, f. 183.

[32] Dec. 18, 1915, quoted in Gollin, *Proconsul*, p. 322, and described as "a concise and accurate summary of Milner's feelings."

cr. Radio Times Hulton Picture Library

Haldane, Secretary of State for War, at Hendon

support of such veteran Liberals (and anticonscriptionists) as Walter Runciman, Sir John Simon, and Lord Crewe; Sir Eyre Crowe, permanent undersecretary at the foreign office, was implicated, as was Sir Edward Grey, who was held to be "particularly lachrymose on the subject of the starving German women and children." Northcliffe, who was secretly sending money into Germany to sustain two widowed aunts, was not averse to capitalizing upon the suspected humanitarianism of others.[33] Yet on this occasion his charges were unfounded. His informant was presumably Leo Maxse, who was making similar imputations at this time in the *National Review* and in a rash of letters to journalist and politician friends. Bonar Law heard from Maxse that Haldane would supplant Kitchener at the war office, and from John Baird, his parliamentary private secretary, that Haldane was slated for the foreign office.

[33] See Pound and Harmsworth, pp. 491–92.

Lord Robert Cecil replied to Maxse that "no hint of Haldane's activity has reached me."[34]

Those who for one reason or another cocked a watchful eye for Haldane's political re-emergence knew perhaps better than he that he retained too many commitments and contacts to withdraw from public life. On July 14, after making certain that no journalists were within earshot, he vowed to a deputation of M.P.s who presented him with a petition of esteem and appreciation that he would accomplish "a good deal for them in education and social reform."[35] Like many of the signatories, he eventually found himself outside the ranks of Liberalism. His path was indicated as early as June 14, when he canceled an engagement at Grillions with Edmund Gosse to resume his periodic dinners with the Webbs. A month later he expressed to Mrs. Webb keen interest in Leonard Woolf's blueprint for international government, published as a supplement to the *New Statesman*. She noted a profound change in her friend, who had become "far more anxious to raise the standard of education among the whole people than he was in old days," and was quick to perceive that this not only marked the resumption of past activities, but also was a means by which Haldane hoped to re-establish his reputation and career.[36]

During the spring of 1916, as Asquith's premiership entered its final phase, Haldane began to make common cause with an erstwhile educational reformer, David Lloyd George. Often disdainful of one another as colleagues, they now found vital areas of agreement. And Lloyd George could freely consult Haldane, even pay gracious tribute to him, without compromising himself. At a dinner party in early April, Haldane and Lloyd George "made out a plan which Ll. G. has undertaken to put through. He and I," Haldane informed his sister, "have made an alliance on education once more."[37] The following month, Lloyd George came to him with a scheme for half-time education for youths between fourteen and eighteen, and invited him to take a room at the education office. Haldane was gratified to be asked advice and optimistically viewed these overtures, for which he gave Lloyd George personal credit, as "a

[34] Dec. 6, 1915, Maxse Papers.
[35] Haldane to his mother, July 15, 1915, HP 5994, f. 57; the address bore over 200 signatures.
[36] Unpublished diary, May 4, 1916, XXXIII, Passfield Papers.
[37] April 5, 1916, HP 6012, f. 126.

slight sign of [the Government's] recovery from timidity."[38] Asquith did not attend their conferences and left the question of education, like so much else, to others. Haldane, by no means oblivious to Lloyd George's faults, was impressed by his boundless energy and his concern for problems of postwar reconstruction. He was convinced that, more often than not, the scrapes into which Lloyd George got himself and the Government could have been averted "had H. H. A. been firm and taken trouble."[39]

Haldane proceeded cautiously, unwilling "to deflect the movement [for educational reform] by a controversy over myself." He outlined his strategy to his mother on May 22: "I shall be quiet for a little before intervening again publicly, but I shall watch [for] my opportunity." Meanwhile, he stood by nervously, "prepared with full material."[40] Several weeks had passed before he proceeded to act. On July 12 he spoke on national education in the House of Lords, where he had not ventured a scheduled address since his departure from office. "The opening of the campaign to which I hope to devote the rest of my life went off well," he reported to his mother. "The Lords were very sympathetic and my reception was admirable, notwithstanding the Duke of Buccleuch's foolish attempt to upset me. He went on his back and I do not think I turned a hair."[41] The incident to which Haldane referred, and his imperturbability, made more of an impression than the speech itself. The seventh Duke of Buccleuch, who sought to avenge the 1911 Parliament Act, ejaculated protests that Haldane's "past conduct" showed him unfit to address the British nation. Lord Knutsford "felt so indignant" that he went to see the Duke the following morning and made him feel "a little ashamed of himself." Knutsford also intervened to prevent "that irresponsible Willoughby de Broke" from joining the fray.[42] Haldane was warmly applauded by his fellow-peers, not because they embraced his proposals, but because they were as embarrassed as he by the outburst. "This is only the first round," he promised his sister. "Letters are pouring in, some of them from Unionist peers. Also of course threats of assassination, but I think the tide is turning."[43]

[38] Haldane to his mother, May 24, 1916, HP 5995, f. 163.
[39] Haldane to Gosse, June 20, 1916, Gosse Papers.
[40] HP 5995, ff. 159–60.   [41] July 13, 1916, HP 5996, f. 17.
[42] Knutsford to Haldane, July [13], 1916, HP 5913, ff. 44–47.
[43] July 13, 1916, HP 6013, ff. 142–43.

The newspapers, he calculated, "are now with me by 3 to 1," though *The Times*, much to his disappointment, remained "on the fence," and the *Morning Post* saw "no reason why the House of Lords should listen to him on any subject but the confession of his own sins." Haldane was proud to have rendered service to a worthy cause. And now, he was convinced, the Government would no longer be able to resist pressures "to publish the Berlin papers."[44]

On both counts, he suffered profound disappointment. Grey and Asquith refused to release documents concerning the 1912 Anglo-German negotiations while the war continued. At the same time, the Government proved less receptive to his proposals for education than he had hoped. On August 27 he wrote a "very private" letter to Gosse, enumerating his difficulties with Lord Crewe, the president of the board of education and Asquith's political lieutenant: "I will not go on," he proclaimed, "but will conduct an independent campaign unless I am given a sufficiently free hand."[45] A month later he reported the last in a series of interviews with Crewe and Asquith in which he received assurances that his "education organisation . . . will not be meddled with again."[46] Yet Haldane had come to despair of Asquith's capacity for social reform.

Still, Haldane had grave misgivings when Asquith was overthrown in early December. Although he counseled the King to grant the new premier a dissolution upon request when the Crown privately solicited his legal advice, he was not being disloyal to Asquith but loyal to the principles of constitutional democracy. He could not help feeling that Asquith's humiliation was "the result of [his] being too easy" and he found it "a comfort to be out" of political life at such a time.[47] When Lloyd George formed his coalition ministry, Haldane could only express the fervent "hope that he will do better than I expect."[48] On the next day he met Lord Buckmaster, newly displaced from the woolsack, to whom he described Asquith as "a first class head of a deliberative council, . . . [who] is versed in precedents, acts on principles, and knows how and when to compromise." Lloyd George, on the other hand, "cares nothing for precedents and knows no principles,

[44] Haldane to his mother, July 14, 1916, HP 5996, ff. 19–20.
[45] Gosse Papers.   [46] Haldane to Gosse, Sept. 15, 1916.
[47] Haldane to his mother, Dec. 4, 1916, HP 5996, ff. 157–58.
[48] Haldane to his mother, Dec. 6, 1916, HP 5996, f. 163.

but he has fire in his belly and that is what we want."[49] On the balance, Haldane did not suppose "that the new Government will make as much difference, one way or the other, as people think." What bothered him most was the fact that it was so obviously "low class," a strange complaint from a future Labour lord chancellor.[50] He forgot this objection once the new Government had become "firmly rooted," and had indicated, with thè appointment of H. A. L. Fisher, vice-chancellor of Sheffield University and a former Oxford don, its dedication to educational reform: "The new P. M. is certainly more energetic than his predecessor," he wrote approvingly to his mother on January 19, 1917.[51]

Lloyd George's courtship of Haldane continued after the death of the first coalition and the birth of the second. The new Prime Minister, who had the attention span of a butterfly, appreciated Haldane's ability to work caterpillar-like at detailed problems of organization. In addition he recognized Haldane's value as a link with the Webbs and other socialist intellectuals, including R. H. Tawney and Harold Laski, whom he could meet at Queen Anne's Gate. Lloyd George's visits buoyed Haldane's hopes of restitution. The Prime Minister was "very friendly indeed" when he came to dine in mid-April 1917 and told Haldane in parting: "You must come in. All the difficulties must be put aside for the nation wants your brains badly." Haldane, deeply moved, related to his mother that he "simply smiled" and replied that "I would help as I was doing from outside."[52] In June Lloyd George named him chairman of a committee on the machinery of government, which subjected departmental institutions and procedures to scientific analysis and issued its report, as a basis for bureaucratic reform, in January 1919.[53] The assignment was arduous and time-consuming, but one to which Haldane came naturally. He welcomed it not only as a sign of confidence in himself, but as the prelude to his return to office. "Ll. G. I am told (I have not seen him) is not only very friendly but declares that I have been horribly used and that he will set things right," Haldane wrote to his sister, announcing his chairmanship:

He is to get Balfour's assent to publishing the Berlin documents. . . . He wants to form a progressive Cabinet after the war. The desire is said to be that I should enter it in some large capacity. The first step is to get the

[49] Buckmaster to Maurice [n.d.], quoted in Maurice, II, 45.
[50] Haldane to Gosse, Dec. 7, 1916, Gosse Papers.   [51] HP 5997, f. 14.
[52] April 17, 1917, HP 5997, ff. 132–33.   [53] See Heuston, pp. 227–28.

misrepresentations killed and for this it is better that for the present I should preside as quietly as possible over this committee. But I am to be consulted about many things. I have stipulated that I must have a voice about the Army reconstruction in view of peace.[54]

Time passed and Haldane, determined "to wait until the mountain comes to Mahomet,"[55] heard nothing further of efforts to clear his name and restore him to Cabinet rank. Had he taken the Prime Minister too literally, or had Lloyd George made promises that he never intended to keep? Perhaps Lloyd George had underestimated the opposition to Haldane that persisted within the coalition. Bonar Law advised Christopher Addison "that some of his people did not like the idea of Haldane helping in Reconstruction," to which Addison, refusing to "be a feeble imitator of Asquith," replied with an invitation for Bonar Law to "send the objectors along to me [as] I should welcome the opportunity of enlightening them about Haldane."[56] Edwin Montagu remonstrated to Bonar Law in terms nearly as strong. By August 23 Haldane had given up waiting to be summoned back to office and was hard at work on a philosophical treatise, which would, "quite as likely as not, never see the light. For I know," he told Gosse, "I am a bad writer and should draw but few people with it." He did not sound entirely convinced, nor did he convince his friend, when he expressed gratitude to "British Philistinism" for exiling him to the "peace and comfort" of his library and for excluding him from the company "of the colleagues of L. George."[57]

Whenever Haldane began to despair of Lloyd George, he reminded himself of the alternatives. He considered it "courageous" of the Prime Minister, paying tribute to the army and navy, to have alluded to his prewar military reforms: "It was," he boasted to Gosse, "almost if not quite the part of his speech most loudly applauded by the H. of C."[58] Asquith, not to be outdone, followed with a laudatory statement which, Haldane noted, was delivered "in private." He described to his mother how Asquith "reproached Lloyd George for not having named me, but as someone who was there observed, he himself said nothing."[59] In addition, Lloyd George continued to flatter Haldane with requests

---

[54] June 13, 1917, HP 6012, ff. 196–97.
[55] Haldane to his mother, June 19, 1917, HP 5997, f. 214.
[56] Diary for July 30, 1917, Addison, II, 425.   [57] Gosse Papers.
[58] Oct. 31, 1917, Gosse Papers.   [59] Nov. 2, 1917, HP 5998, ff. 100–101.

for assistance and social favors. The Prime Minister and Lord Derby invited him to dine on February 7, 1918 "with the heads of the Army," and asked his advice "on points of great importance and secrecy, and afterwards the P. M. drove me to Downing Street to consult further there. It was like old times."[60] Three weeks later Haldane reciprocated by inviting Lloyd George and the Webbs to "a frugal but interesting little dinner party of four," after which Lloyd George remained and took a long walk with his host, "guarded by a vigilant detective who followed." Haldane continued to be impressed by the Prime Minister's ideas for reconstruction and his "courage over the prospects of the war."[61]

Haldane remained in contact with Asquith, who sent him copies of his published writings and to whom he sent congratulations upon his son's engagement. Yet he had no desire to bring back his old chief. He "deplore[d]" proposals for an Asquith-Lansdowne coalition, for which Margot was known to be "intriguing busily" and for which many of "the old lot" hoped. "It is in detail," he professed, "that the present Government is unsatisfactory. On the main ground we should change them for something much feebler."[62] He was appalled to learn that Margot, "up to her elbows in intrigues," had gone so far as to invite their common enemy, H. A. Gwynne of the *Morning Post*, to Cavendish Square to solicit his support against Lloyd George. Haldane was confident that the plot would fail if for no other reason than that "the Liberals are too pacifist . . . to get a vote of no confidence in Ll. G."[63] Lord Morley, who came to lunch on May 8, the day before the Maurice debate, agreed that any change in leadership was unthinkable. Haldane said as much that afternoon in the House of Lords, where he denounced "the madness of upsetting the Government with a great battle pending. I hear," he recounted to his sister, that "20 Cavendish Square is 'much upset' by my language."[64] Yet he insisted that he had done no more than he thought necessary. After his speech in the Lords, Haldane retired to Cloan, where he fell gravely ill. Gosse wrote saccharine letters that kept his friend abreast of political developments in London, where his defense of Lloyd George against Asquith remained

[60] Haldane to his mother, Feb. 8, 1918, HP 5999, f. 50.
[61] Haldane to his mother, March 1, 1918, HP 5999, ff. 86–87.
[62] Haldane to his sister, Feb. 13, 1918, HP 6013, ff. 11–12.
[63] Haldane to his sister, Feb. 18, 1918 (1:15 a.m.), HP 6013, ff. 13–14.
[64] May 9, 1918, HP 6013, f. 31.

a topic of conversation. Elizabeth Haldane, reporting her brother's recovery to Gosse on the 18th, wrote perceptively of his prospects and his relations with Asquith:

He has felt so long that there was a dividing line between him and H. H. A. that I don't know that this is as trying as it might have been. But it is always hard to differ from old friends, though really one has felt far away from the atmosphere of No. 20 [Cavendish Square] for so long. What R.'s future is it is difficult to say but it may be a very important one and anyhow if he lives it will be a useful one. He has powers of a kind not possessed by any of his former colleagues and I realize how valuable his life is.[65]

For the duration of the war, Haldane busied himself with committee work, fulfilling his promise to H. A. L. Fisher to "let the new Government have unbroken approval."[66] He devoted time and effort to the future of the coal mines, the principles of governmental organization, higher education, and technical training. He helped Lloyd George grapple with Irish problems and persuaded him not to enforce conscription there. On at least one occasion his intervention in the House of Lords saved the Government from embarrassment and possibly defeat. As victory appeared imminent, he grew disturbed that Lloyd George did not speak with greater moral authority in international affairs. Yet he scoffed at the suggestion that he might remedy the situation by taking a hand in the peacemaking. He was a good deal more impressed when members of the United States peace commission intimated that, had time permitted, the Americans would have sent for him to help prepare their army. Balfour, who knew of the Americans' high regard for Haldane, suggested him to Lloyd George in 1919 as a possible ambassador to Washington.

Nor was there time for British voters to adapt to the conditions of peace before they were called to the polls to return a new Parliament. Supporters of the Lloyd George coalition were rewarded with the "coupon" (disparagingly titled by Asquith who was denied it) from which the election took its name. Trevor Wilson has brilliantly demonstrated[67] that the coupon was Lloyd George's device to save the Liberal Party from annihilation. But those who were saved were predominantly Lloyd George Liberals and no longer Liberals per se. Margot Asquith,

[65] Gosse Papers.　　[66] May 28, 1918, Fisher Papers.

[67] "The Coupon and the British General Election of 1918," Journal of Modern History, xxxvi; also The Downfall of the Liberal Party, pp. 135 ff.

anticipating her husband's defeat, wrote distraught letters to Haldane's relatives, alleging that he, like everyone else, had been mesmerized by the Welsh Wizard: "I never understood why your brother took suddenly to Ll. G.," she complained to Elizabeth Haldane on December 2,

except that Ll. G. is a *really* charming man—a man and woman charmer.... But then Lord Haldane said he was the only possible P.M. and raved about him in [the] H. of Lords. We were all stunned. No one was as ill-treated as your brother. All revengeful people will have the pleasure of seeing H[enry] ill-treated now! and by his own Liberal M. P.s in [the] H. of C. which your Richard never was. The deserters from Montagu down have been *quite* worth watching! The elections are so grotesque that I hope the Tory [Party] will come in or the National Party. Winston tells my friends that H[enry] is crushed for ever. I would rather be crushed than elevated by the Northcliffe Party anyhow.

She closed with the admonition that Lloyd George "has the soul of an auctioneer and people who adore him may gain this world but they lose their souls."[68] Margot, in her grief, took a more realistic view of the situation than even her husband, who as late as the 18th denied to A. G. Gardiner of the *Daily News* rumors ("A tissue of absurdities") that things were not going well.

Haldane's sister believed as her brother did that the time would soon come when he, by virtue of his unique position, would save the Liberal Party by mediating between its warring leaders. But the General Election of 1918 left Haldane nothing to mediate between. From the 425 Liberals who stood, 136 "couponed" Liberals were returned as opposed to 20 some odd Liberal independents. Haldane was particularly shocked by the outcome at East Fife, where Asquith, opposed by a recalcitrant Unionist, was defeated. He had trusted that Asquith, with or without Cabinet office, would long continue to participate in public life. "I did not expect it of my Countrymen," he wrote to him as soon as the results were known. "But it must be accepted calmly. This has been an entirely unreal contest in which the silent voter has given an uninformed vote. There is no doubt that new schools of thought have been growing up, but that is not sufficient explanation."[69]

Where did Haldane stand in the wake of the Liberal debacle? There no longer remained the slightest hope that Liberalism, or even one of its varieties, would build a new society. Lloyd George, whom he and

[68] HP 6027, ff. 234–37.   [69] Dec. 29, 1918, Asquith Papers.

many progressives had looked upon to head a postwar Radical-Labour alliance, had thrown in his lot with the forces of conservatism. Financial exigencies and political considerations soon led him to sacrifice the social programs he had discussed so often with Haldane. In the summer months of 1919, Lloyd George (and Churchill on his behalf) resurrected his 1910 proposals for a fusion of the traditional parties against the emergent forces of labour and socialism, not by any means identical. This settled the matter for Haldane. Like Asquith, Lloyd George no longer provided an agency to effect the designs to which he had dedicated himself.

Others, cut adrift, shared his perplexity and concern. William Wedgwood Benn, the Liberal whip, requested an interview in November and informed Haldane of widespread "despair about the prospects of Liberalism." He asked Haldane to address a committee newly formed to plot a new course for the party. Haldane was honored to think that in their time of need the Liberals "seem to have resolved to turn to me." He accepted the invitation, through he expressed "fear [that] H. H. A. will not be pleased."[70] His message to this private assembly of Opposition Liberals is not known, but it is significant that Wedgwood Benn eventually followed Haldane into the Labour Party.

At what point did Haldane cease to be a Liberal and become a Labourite? In an age when party labels counted for little, the question is not only futile but irrelevant. Given his personality and the political context in which he operated, the transition was easy and logical. It was not a conversion, for his methods and ambitions remained precisely the same. Nor was it formal, for party membership was not required for participation in Labour councils or indeed in the first Labour Government. It required no deliberation for Haldane, long recognized as a Liberal with vaguely collectivist principles (and collectivist friends), to become a vague collectivist with liberal ideals. He would have fit comfortably into today's Liberal Party, which admirably fulfills many of the functions he advocated for Liberalism in his day. He might even have found a place in the post-Churchillian Conservative Party. As G. P. Gooch wisely observed of his friend: "Though Lady Violet Bonham Carter referred to him as Comrade Haldane, he was no more and no less a Socialist after he changed his party label than before."[71]

[70] Haldane to his sister, Nov. 19, 1919, HP 6013, f. 73.
[71] *Under Six Reigns*, p. 190.

A member of an earlier generation with an undue respect for political nomenclature, Haldane hesitated to publicize his growing affiliation with Labour. Tactical considerations influenced his decision: he had no wish to stigmatize the fledgling movement with his unpopularity. Social bias also played a part: he was often embarrassed by the gaucheries of Labour leaders and disturbed by their disregard for traditional procedures. Through the Webbs he gradually widened his circle of Labour Party acquaintances. C. P. Scott, who came to see him on December 16, 1917, discovered that Haldane was serving as "chairman . . . of a little advisory committee to the Labour Party, under [Arthur] Henderson's auspices, who meet at the Sidney Webbs' house and of which the Webbs were the most active members."[72] In June 1918 his friends induced him to attend a Labour reception, where he was warmly welcomed; but he disclaimed "any plans with [Labour] at present . . . except *ab extra*."[73] Lord Birkenhead, who became lord chancellor in 1919, felt "no passion for the judicial seat" and gladly let Haldane fill in for him whenever possible. This raised speculation in the press that Haldane yearned to be back upon the woolsack, possibly as a Labour chancellor, which he emphatically denied to his mother as "very foolish."[74]

Increasingly sympathetic to Labour, Haldane nonetheless looked forward to Asquith's return to Parliament after the 1918 General Election. He came to realize at this time the fundamental incompatibility of his two devotions. Asquith spoke glowingly of him at a Reform Club luncheon on January 15, 1920, but failed to provide any indication (Haldane looked desperately for one) that he had given thought to Britain's social needs. Sir Charles Firth wrote on January 21 to describe Oxford's preparations for the Royal Commission on the Universities: "Several people here have expressed a wish that you were its chairman instead of Asquith," he told Haldane. "My impression is that Asquith's views on higher education are those prevalent at Balliol in 1870, and that he has learnt nothing about it since."[75] Haldane's Labour friends vowed that if Asquith stood in a by-election at Spen Valley, they would oppose him "hotly." Sir John Simon, who contested the seat as an Asquithian Liberal, was presently defeated. It was instead the Lanark-

---

[72] Memorandum by Scott, Scott Papers, Add. MSS. 50, 904, ff. 197 ff.
[73] Haldane to his sister, June 13, 1918, HP 6013, f. 36.
[74] Oct. 28 and Nov. 3, 1919, HP 6002, ff. 125, 135–36.
[75] HP 5914, ff. 206–207.

shire constituency of Paisley that Asquith chose in January 1920 for his comeback.

Asquith's official biographers, J. A. Spender and Cyril Asquith, accepted at face value Margot's word that Haldane, among other renegade Liberals, endorsed the Labour candidate at Paisley. This was a mindless distortion. Disappointed by Asquith's refusal to diverge from old lines, Haldane nonetheless hoped to see him restored to an active political life. The controversy arose from the fact that Haldane philosophized during an interview that Liberalism was a spent force and that it was "with Labour that the hope lies for tomorrow." This was interpreted as a rejection of Asquith's candidacy. "What a strange man your son Richard!" Margot wrote from Paisley to Mrs. Haldane, denouncing him for "choos[ing] this moment to stick a knife into Henry. What odd people God makes! To think that your son and Ll. George should hunt in couples!" Even Grey, she added, was "utterly sad" at the betrayal.[76] The *Glasgow Herald* took great delight in reporting Haldane's "*Et Tu Brute.*" The *Scotsman* snidely referred to him as "a distinguished seceder." Haldane, who had not applied his remarks specifically to events at Paisley, was annoyed when others did. It is difficult to see how the coincidence could have escaped him. In any event, he immediately attempted to remedy the situation by declaring that were he a voter at Paisley, he would support Asquith, "whose commanding parliamentary gift and great experience is needed in the House of Commons." He boasted to his mother that he had paid "a tribute of affection . . . to my old friend and colleague . . . without qualifying a word I have said before."[77] The *Glasgow Herald*, perceiving as much, concluded that this personal espousal did "not atone for his rejection of Liberalism as a creed."

The electors of Paisley went to the polls on February 12. Haldane wrote his mother that day:

I hope Asquith gets a seat. But I do not feel that it will do much good. Parties will have to be re-cast and their scope enlarged before a proper alternative government can be formed. . . . Meantime Margot is tiresome because she is ignorant. She has done much to make it difficult in the years gone by for Asquith to rise to the occasion.[78]

It was a fortnight before the ballots were counted and Asquith was declared the victor. Haldane was relieved, but he refused to take the

[76] Feb. 7 and 9, 1920, HP 6082, ff. 116, 118–19.
[77] Feb. 9, 1920, HP 6003, f. 41.   [78] HP 6003, f. 45.

Paisley returns as a sign "that the main current of political thought either is or will be deflected."[79] In this respect he was a good deal more realistic than those who hailed Paisley as a new Midlothian and who waited in vain for a Liberal renaissance.

Haldane had traveled too far to maintain pretenses, even to himself. He was now fully committed to the defense of Labour against, if need be, both Lloyd George and Asquith. Lord Loreburn, more bitter as the years passed, looked with suspicion upon "Haldane's manifest efforts" to win the confidence of Labour politicians: "He is obviously trying to get into the limelight. He can't be without it."[80] Such criticism did not deter Haldane, who received a procession of Liberals who agreed that "Asquith has had very little to say to the nation." He took it upon himself to caution Labour politicians against a premature challenge to Lloyd George, who was waiting "to entrap them in an election in which he will claim Asquith on his side." And on February 24 he came to Labour's rescue in the House of Lords. "I am not a member of the Labour Party and do not intend to be," he affirmed to his mother. "But they are in earnest and have great ideals. . . ." That evening he met Asquith at dinner and enjoyed a "pleasant and affectionate talk, our divergence notwithstanding."[81]

Further contacts with Labourites allayed Haldane's anxieties and mollified his prejudices. He attended "a really remarkably high toned meeting" in mid-March at which he saw evidence that "the old spirit is being displaced by the new, which, so far as the bulk is concerned, is quite moderate." He was delighted to receive many letters of gratitude and a flood of invitations. "How it will develop I know not," he confessed to his sister. "I have no machine and I have burned my boats. Full steam ahead."[82] Sir Robert Perks, a friend since Liberal Imperialist days, met Haldane on July 2, 1920, and described his "interesting talk" to Lord Rosebery:

He says he is spending much time with the Labour leaders, "trying to understand their views." He finds them "most reasonable and anxious to understand their employers' position." He expects to see a coalition of "modern Liberalism and Labour." I asked him if he was to be the Labour Government's Lord Chancellor, whereat he blandly smiled.

[79] Haldane to his mother, Feb. 26, 1920, HP 6003, f. 60.
[80] Loreburn to Bryce, Feb. 1, 1920, Bryce Papers.
[81] Haldane to his sister, Feb. 19, 1920, HP 6013, f. 85; also Haldane to his mother, Feb. 20 and 25, 1920, HP 6003, ff. 54–55, 59.
[82] March 16, 1920, HP 6013, f. 87.

He has no confidence in Asquith's leadership—and bemoans the absence of any prospective leader.[83]

In the summer of 1921, Grey—now dignified as Viscount Grey of Fallodon—approached Haldane with proposals for a new political grouping. The idea had originated with Lord Robert Cecil, who wanted to join Grey in forming a new Opposition to which moderate Unionists and Labourites might adhere. Haldane was under the mistaken impression that Grey had not yet consulted Asquith. Grey struck him as "evidently attracted," despite his near blindness. Haldane, however, eschewed the idea, pointing out "how enormous was the work to be done" and concluding that it was probably too late to begin. "I doubt whether it will come to anything," he told his sister, "but we shall see. I will not join unless the thing is made very real" and education received sufficient prominence.[84]

The same criterion prompted Haldane to withhold his support from Asquith, who invited him on January 10, 1922, to join a Liberal demonstration at Central Hall, Westminster, at which he and Grey would speak. Offended by the official tone of the letter, and dismayed by Asquith's reluctance to elaborate upon policy, Haldane replied with a polite but stiff refusal:

My public life has for long past been bound up with the cause of education, more than with anything else. It is now so bound up more than ever. . . . Three years ago . . . I came to the conclusion that whichever of the existing parties was really most in earnest about the general enlightenment of the people would in the end get their confidence. I observed then, as I observe now, the almost complete lack of harmony between my strong conviction on this subject and the programme of official Liberalism. Sir Donald Maclean alone seems really to care about the matter. In the official programme, and even in your own speeches, I can find no response about the thing I care for before any other at this moment, and regard as the key to reform generally. That is why I am driven to seek it where I see a chance of finding it. And that is why I feel I ought not to accept an invitation which in other aspects I much appreciate. For I am with you in all else.[85]

Asquith promptly defended his party's attitude toward education by citing a speech he had made at Bristol nearly a year before. But Haldane remained unconvinced and brought the dialogue to a close by repeating that education "demands so real and great a place in any

[83] Rosebery Papers.   [84] July 5, 1921, HP 6013, ff. 115–16.
[85] Asquith Papers.

political programme" that he found Liberalism sadly deficient.[86] Relations were further strained when extracts from this correspondence found their way into the press. Each disclaimed responsibility and blamed the other for the leakage.

Haldane's Liberal friends henceforth saw little of him upon their platforms or even in their drawing rooms. Perks offered the diagnosis that "too much Einstein seems to have made him ill,"[87] alluding to the fact that Haldane was busily applying the theory of relativity to philosophy and had played host at Queen Anne's Gate to its distinguished formulator. Margot came closer to the mark when she ascribed Haldane's distance to his infatuation with the Webbs. He was spending more and more time in their company and that of other Labour leaders. In the autumn of 1922, Bonar Law withdrew his support from Lloyd George and the coalition crumbled. A General Election in November returned a Unionist majority, as expected, with Labour winning more seats than the Asquithian and Lloyd George Liberals combined. Asquith held Paisley, for which Haldane wrote him a letter of congratulation. But the Liberals, in Haldane's opinion, remained 'in a hopeless position. . . . I first saw things going wrong in 1909," he reflected. "I could then, I think, have averted the split with Labour. Now [it] is too late. . . ."[88]

A year later there was another General Election, the second of three within a two-year period. At last Haldane came out openly as a supporter of Labour and campaigned actively on behalf of Labour candidates. In the returns that were announced on December 8, the Unionists lost heavily to both the Liberals and Labour, but retained more seats than either in the new House. Stanley Baldwin, reluctant to form a minority government, was willing to allow Labour to show its mettle. Asquith agreed, consoling himself that the Labour experiment, which would come sooner or later, could never be conducted under "safer conditions." This opened the way for the King to send for Ramsay MacDonald when Parliament met early in the new year.

In the interim, MacDonald withdrew to Lossiemouth to ponder the composition of the first Labour Government. He annoyed some of his closest followers by being virtually incommunicado during these fateful

---

[86] Jan. 19, 1922 [copy], HP 5915, f. 143.
[87] Perks to Rosebery, July 7, 1923, Rosebery Papers.
[88] Haldane to his sister, Dec. 7, 1923, HP 6013, f. 165.

weeks. One of his few contacts was Haldane, comparatively close by at Cloan. On December 20 Haldane revealed to Sidney Webb that he was in close communication with the next Prime Minister, who had promised to break journey at Cloan on his return to London. "I think I can be of more use to your cause outside any government than within it," he explained, offering to advise the Defence Committee as Lord Esher had done. "If I were younger I should be more willing to join if asked, but am now too set in legal and other endeavours. Moreover I am pretty clear that there would be division of Labour opinion over my presence. You must avoid this."[89] MacDonald, in a letter to Haldane on the 23rd, would not hear of these disclaimers. He suggested that Haldane take the portfolio for education, but mentioned the secretary-ship of state for India and the lord chancellorship as other possibilities. At Cloan on January 4 they discussed the situation and it was agreed that Haldane would return to the woolsack, relieved of sufficient judicial duties to permit him to take a hand in defense and other administrative matters. As late as the 10th, Haldane articulated fears that MacDonald's supporters would balk at the arrangement; but the next day it was publicly announced that he would occupy the woolsack. "My relations with Ramsay are wonderful," he told his sister on the 15th, the day that Parliament convened. "I think he has opened the whole of his mind to me and he has consulted me about every appointment. How can I shape his policy? I will have to try, but I am doubtful of my own capacity. However I am on excellent terms with the Labour leaders."[90] That evening, at MacDonald's request, he entertained his colleagues at Queen Anne's Gate. Refreshment consisted of orangeade and lemon-ade, and the "unofficial cabinet meeting" that followed was reassuringly sober ("a remarkable display of competence and also of conservatism"). Elated, Haldane affirmed that he had "never attended a better cabinet meeting."[91]

It was not until the 23rd that the first Labour Government took office. The previous evening, Haldane wrote touchingly to Asquith, with whom he had formally severed the last of his political ties. It was a letter to an old friend and not to a present adversary, sufficiently emotional to be dated with the wrong year:

My mind goes back to the evenings before either of us could contemplate Parliament for ourselves, evenings in which we were nonetheless concen-

[89] [copy], Passfield Papers.   [90] HP 6013, ff. 170–71.   [91] HP 6007, f. 84.

cr. Radio Times Hulton Picture Library

The Labour Lord Chancellor in Procession

trated on ideas. And I think of old days at Cloan and at Ambleside, or in London.

Nor do I forget how you stood by me, or how you fought for me over the Chancellorship in 1905, or how you put me there in 1912. Believe me, I am not oblivious of these things.

Now it is a new period, and our adventure is both difficult and uncertain. It is not without misgiving that I face it. But I do not consider that I have [the] right to stand aside in this hour.

None the less, the old sense of personal affection and of gratitude remains with me. If not for you I should not have been where I am—Whatever that may stand for.

And so I shall continue to the end to describe myself as

Yours ever affectionately,
H. of C.[92]

Asquith replied with equally warm allusions to the many memories they shared. In his diary, he acknowledged the receipt of Haldane's "very nice and really touching letter," but could not resist gloating that the "misgiving" Haldane expressed was more than justified: "He and the

[92] Asquith Papers.

poor ex-Tory Lord Parmoor will have a hellish time in the House of Lords."[93]

Haldane, who was of course accustomed to being outnumbered in the upper house, did not have an easy time of it; nor had he expected to. "A difficult adventure this," he wrote to Sir John Simon, an old colleague, the day after he took office. "But it is a question of the practicability of introducing a new spirit into the administration of public affairs. Whether there will be success in this adventure remains to be seen. But I felt bound to try to help, although not anxious to enter on office again."[94] Haldane had known how little any Government could accomplish without a parliamentary majority. He had anticipated the heavy demand upon his fund of knowledge by his new colleagues, of whom only Arthur Henderson had ministerial experience. What he had not expected was the infidelity of certain Labourites to Beatrice Webb's principle of "work, work, work." He found many Labour politicians "too socially disposed," particularly MacDonald, to whom "social life is a novelty." The Prime Minister's predilection for "great dinner parties" and country weekends left him inadequate time to supervise ministers and civil servants.[95] Haldane had had the same complaint of Asquith. He regretted too that MacDonald drove the Liberals away instead of making overtures to them. On several occasions, one regarding the appointment of magistrates, tempers flared and Haldane threatened resignation. Yet he remained in office the full nine months, performing his judicial work, advising on matters of defense, helping out at the foreign office, and taking consolation in the fact "that as we near the precipice, Ramsay and the Labour Party generally are clinging to me more and more."[96]

When he came to look back upon his second chancellorship, Haldane had no regrets. His presence had conferred a measure of respectability upon the first Labour Government that had helped to allay fears of Bolshevism. He had also prevailed upon his colleagues in a number of instances to proceed with greater tact and moderation. He regarded these nine months as a gestation period which produced a Labour

---

[93]Asquith, *Memories*, II, 209. Parmoor, lord president in the first Labour Government, had written to Haldane on May 26, 1915, to express "real regret on public and private grounds" at his exclusion from office. HP 5911, f. 93.

[94] Jan. 24, 1924, Simon Papers.

[95] Haldane to his sister, April 7 and 10, 1924, HP 6013, ff. 175–76.

[96] Haldane to his sister, Oct. 3, 1924, HP 6013, f. 184.

Party with the maturity and public confidence to wield full parliamentary powers. He did not deny that mistakes had been made. Yet Labour remained, he wrote in January 1925, "the party that is most in contact with the democracy of this country." This was an implicit indictment of Liberalism which, by extending the suffrage and literacy, had benevolently created the conditions with which it was not equipped to cope. The traditional parties had failed to achieve "the closest contact with [the] people" and to bridge "the gaps which separate class from class unjustly." It was a failure Haldane had shared and for which he had done a decade's penance. Only Labour recognized, however dimly, the potential of the great nineteenth-century franchise reforms and the moral obligations these imposed upon political leadership. As a result, he prophesied, Labour "will prove in the end to be the party that has really averted upheaval in this country. It may progress slowly but seems to me to be progressing surely."[97]

For personal reasons, too, Haldane was glad to have joined the Labour Government. His mother, in her final year, was able to see him fully vindicated and restored to dignity upon the woolsack. He knew how much this meant to her. And he had returned, however briefly, to the corridors of Whitehall, where he had always found the air more invigorating than that of the courtroom or library. He was able to harangue the chiefs of staff with his monologues, regale a new generation of politicians with his after-dinner reminiscences and cigars, instruct trade unionists in Cabinet etiquette, and draft innumerable memoranda. For these opportunities he was supremely grateful. These contacts continued after he left office in November 1924, for he remained leader of the Labour peers and, in addition to other assignments, assumed the chairmanship at Baldwin's invitation of a subcommittee of the Committee of Imperial Defence.

In the years that remained to him his health declined rapidly. Sir Robert Perks, out for a Saturday morning motor ride on July 2, 1925, "nearly ran over a bent, contemplative figure crossing Birdcage Walk and, on looking up, . . . saw it was the Labour Lord Chancellor."[98] In October 1926 Haldane again exchanged letters with Asquith, offering welcome assurances that "changes in outward relations . . . [had not] transformed the old inwardness."[99] These were the letters of old men

[97] Maurice, II, 180–81.
[98] Perks to Rosebery, July 3, 1925, Rosebery Papers.   [99] Asquith Papers.

who dwelled upon a remote past that they could remember with greater affection than the events of more recent years. Understanding one another perfectly, neither made an effort toward more formal reconciliation. On August 19, 1928, Haldane died, six months after his friend. He was buried to the doleful strains of the Black Watch pipers down the hill from Cloan beside the family chapel at Gleneagles. Even now he did not rest easily, for that night his grave was desecrated by a local madman, convinced that the former lord chancellor had been buried alive.

What conclusions remain to be drawn from a public life linked so inextricably to the declining fortunes of the Liberal Party? However troubled, it was not without its satisfactions. However frustrated, it was not without its achievements, though these tended to be obscured by the partisan animosities that enveloped them. Here was painful demonstration of the prolonged crisis of confidence in Liberalism to which Liberals themselves succumbed during wartime.

Lord Haldane's tribulations were those of a party and ideology in distress. His weaknesses, even at their most personal, were ones he shared with his political generation. His failures no less than his attainments were a reflection of the order to which he belonged.

His was a useful life, not only for what it accomplished but also for the directions in which it pointed. He fell from office, like Asquith and Lloyd George after him, because Liberalism lacked the cohesion and strength to sustain him. The Liberal politician who suffered most dramatically and perhaps most unjustly as a result of his party's breakup, Lord Haldane eventually outdistanced Liberalism. In this respect he showed greater sensitivity of purpose than most of his colleagues who survived the upheaval of May 1915 and who allowed him to be their scapegoat.

SELECTED BIBLIOGRAPHY

PRIVATE PAPERS

Of primary importance to this study were the papers of Lord Haldane, his sister, and mother in the National Library of Scotland, Edinburgh. But the papers of contemporary politicians and journalists yielded much of value; these collections, in public and private depositories, include:

H. H. Asquith Papers [Earl of Oxford and Asquith], Bodleian Library, Oxford.
A. J. Balfour Papers [Earl of Balfour], the British Museum, London.
Arnold Bennett's Journals, City Museum, Stoke-on-Trent.
R. D. Blumenfeld Papers, courtesy of Sir John Elliot.
Andrew Bonar Law Papers, Beaverbrook Library, London.
Sir John Brunner Papers, courtesy of Sir Felix Brunner.
Viscount Bryce Papers, Bodleian Library, Oxford.
John Burns Papers, the British Museum, London.
Sydney Buxton Papers [Earl Buxton], courtesy of Mr. and Mrs. J. Clay.
Sir Henry Campbell-Bannerman Papers, the British Museum, London.
Lord Robert Cecil Papers, the British Museum, London.
Joseph and Sir Austen Chamberlain Papers, the University Library, Birmingham.
Geoffrey [Robinson] Dawson Papers, selection courtesy of the Hon. Mrs. Cecilia Dawson.
Sir Charles Dilke Papers, the British Museum, London.
Viscount Esher Papers, courtesy of the Hon. Christopher Brett and Mrs. Brett.
H. A. L. Fisher Papers, Bodleian Library, Oxford.
A. G. Gardiner Papers, courtesy of Mr. and Mrs. Patrick Gardiner.
Edmund Gosse Papers, the Brotherton Collection, the University Library, Leeds.
Sir Edward Grey Papers [Viscount Grey of Fallodon], the Public Record Office, London.
H. A. Gwynne Papers, courtesy of Vice-Admiral I. L. T. Hogg, C. B., D. S. C.
Lewis Harcourt Papers [Viscount Harcourt], courtesy of Viscount Harcourt.
Sir Charles Harris Papers, courtesy of Mr. Alan Harris.
W. A. S. Hewins Papers, the University Library, Sheffield.

Earl Kitchener Papers, the Public Record Office, London.
David Lloyd George Papers [Earl Lloyd George of Dwyfor], Beaverbrook Library, London.
Reginald McKenna Papers, the Library, Churchill College, Cambridge.
Leo Maxse Papers, the County Record Office, Chichester.
Viscount Mersey Papers, courtesy of Viscount Mersey.
Viscount Milner Papers, the Bodleian Library, Oxford.
Viscount Morley-Andrew Carnegie Correspondence (microfilm copy), the Bodleian Library, Oxford.
Sir Matthew Nathan Papers, the Bodleian Library, Oxford.
Viscount Northcliffe Papers (copies), courtesy of Sir Geoffrey Harmsworth.
Earl Roberts Papers, the Army Museums Ogilby Trust, London.
Earl of Rosebery Papers, the National Library of Scotland, Edinburgh.
Royal Archives, Windsor, by gracious permission of Her Majesty, Queen Elizabeth II.
Herbert Samuel Papers [Viscount Samuel], House of Lords Record Office, London.
C. P. Scott Papers, the British Museum, London.
Sir John Simon Papers [Viscount Simon], selection courtesy of Viscount Simon.
J. A. Spender Papers, the British Museum, London.
George Sydenham Clarke Papers [Baron Sydenham of Combe], the British Museum, London.
Beatrice and Sidney Webb Papers [Baron and Lady Passfield], the British Library of Political and Economic Science, London.

OFFICIAL PAPERS AND DOCUMENTS

Parliamentary Debates (Hansard).

Cabinet Papers, 1906–1915, Papers of the Committee of Imperial Defence, 1905–1914, Minutes of the War Council, August 5, 1914–May 14, 1915, and reports from the Prime Minister to the Sovereign, 1905–1916; these have been made available at the Public Record Office, London, by gracious permission of Her Majesty, Queen Elizabeth II. In certain cases I have quoted Cabinet Papers from the extensive collection in the Harcourt Papers.

SERIAL PUBLICATIONS

Newspapers and journals have been consulted not only for editorial opinion, but also as a source of information. They include:

Blackwood's Magazine, Daily Chronicle, Daily Express, Daily Mail, Daily Telegraph, Daily News, Evening Standard, Fortnightly Review, John Bull,

Manchester Guardian, Morning Post, Nation, National Review, Pall Mall Gazette, Scotsman, The Times, Westminster Gazette.

PUBLISHED SOURCES

Addison, Christopher: *Four and a Half Years.* 2 vols. London, 1934.
—— *Politics from Within.* 2 vols. London, 1924.
Amery, L. S.: *My Political Life.* 3 vols. London, 1953.
Arnold-Forster, H. O.: *Military Needs and Military Policy.* London, 1909.
—— *The Army in 1906.* London, 1906.
Arnold-Forster, Mary: *The Rt. Hon. Hugh Oakeley Arnold-Forster.* London, 1910.
Asquith, Earl of Oxford, and: *Fifty Years of Parliament.* 2 vols. London, 1926.
—— *Memories and Reflections.* 2 vols. London, 1926.
Asquith, Countess of Oxford, and: *Autobiography.* 2 vols. London, 1920, 1922.
Baker, H. T.: "Lord Haldane." In the *Army Quarterly.* October, 1928.
Beaverbrook, Lord: *Men and Power.* New York, 1956.
—— *Politicians and the War.* Garden City, N. Y., 1928.
Beer, Samuel H.: *British Politics in the Collectivist Age.* New York, 1965.
Begbie, Harold: *The Vindication of Great Britain.* London, 1916.
Blake, Robert (ed.): *Private Letters of Douglas Haig.* London, 1952.
—— *The Unknown Prime Minister.* London, 1955.
Blumenfeld, R. D.: *R. D. B.'s Diary.* London, 1930.
Bonham Carter, Violet: *Winston Churchill as I Knew Him.* London, 1965.
Brett, M. V. (ed.): *Journals and Letters of Reginald, Viscount Esher.* vols. II and III. London, 1934, 1938.
Briggs, Asa: "The Political Scene." In Simon Nowell-Smith (ed.): *Edwardian England, 1901–1914.* London, 1964.
Buchan, John: *Comments and Characters.* London, 1940.
Chamberlain, Sir Austen: *Politics from Inside.* New Haven, 1937.
Churchill, Winston: *Great Contemporaries.* New York, 1937.
—— *The World Crisis.* 3 vols. London, 1923–1931.
Colvin, Ian: *Carson, the Statesman.* New York, 1935.
Cramb, J. A.: *Germany and England.* London, 1914.
Dangerfield, George: *The Strange Death of Liberal England.* London, 1935.
Dean, Joseph: *Hatred, Ridicule or Contempt.* New York, 1954.
Ellison, Gen. Sir G. F.: "Reminiscences." In the *Lancashire Lad.* Monthly issues of 1935–1936.
Fischer, Fritz: *Germany's Aims in the First World War.* New York, 1967.
Fitzroy, Sir Almeric: *Memoirs.* 2 vols. London, 1927?
French, Maj. the Hon. Gerald (ed.): *Some War Diaries . . . of the Earl of Ypres.* London, 1937.

Gardiner, A. G.: *Prophets, Priests and Kings*. London, 1914.

Gollin, Alfred M.: "Asquith: a New View." In Martin Gilbert (ed.): *Century of Conflict*. London, 1966.

—— *The Observer and J. L. Garvin*. London, 1960.

—— *Proconsul in Politics*. London, 1964.

Gooch, G. P.: *Under Six Reigns*. London, 1959.

Guinn, Paul: *British Strategy and Politics, 1914–1918*. Oxford, 1965.

Grey of Fallodon, Viscount: *Twenty-Five Years*. 2 vols. New York, 1925.

Haldane, Gen. Sir J. Aylmer L.: *The Haldanes of Gleneagles*. Edinburgh, 1929.

Haldane, Elizabeth: *From One Century to Another*. London, 1937.

Haldane, Louisa K.: *Friends and Kindred*. London, 1961.

Haldane, Viscount: *An Autobiography*. London, 1929.

—— *Before the War*. London, 1920.

—— *Great Britain and Germany*. New York, 1912.

—— *The Meaning of Truth in History*. London, 1914.

—— "Some Recollections." In the *Atlantic Monthly*. October, 1919.

Hale, James Oron: *Publicity and Diplomacy*. Gloucester, Mass., 1964.

Hamilton, Gen. Sir Ian: *Compulsory Service*. London, 1911.

Hamilton, Ian B. M.: *The Happy Warrior*. London, 1966.

Hankey, Lord: *The Supreme Command*. vol. I. London, 1961.

Harris, Sir Charles: *Lord Haldane*. London, 1928.

Heuston, R. F. V.: *The Lives of the Lord Chancellors, 1885–1940*. Oxford, 1964.

Hewins, W. A. S.: *Apologia of an Imperialist*. 2 vols. London, 1929.

Hirst, F. W.: *In the Golden Days*. London, 1947.

The History of the Times, IV (2 vols.). London, 1952.

Houston, Henry J.: *The Real Horatio Bottomley*. London, 1923?

Horner, Frances: *Time Remembered*. London, 1933.

Howe, Mark D. (ed.): *Holmes-Laski Letters*. vol. I. Cambridge, Mass., 1953.

Hurwitz, S. J.: *State Intervention in Great Britain: A Study of Economic Control and Social Response, 1914–1919*. New York, 1949.

Hyde, H. Montgomery: *Lord Reading*. London, 1967.

Inge, W. R.: *Diary of a Dean*. New York, 1950.

Jenkins, Roy: *Asquith*. London, 1964.

Lloyd George, David: *War Memoirs*. 2 vols. London, 1934?

Lockhart, J. G.: *Cosmo Gordon Lang*. London, 1949.

Louis, Wm. Roger: *Great Britain and Germany's Lost Colonies, 1914–1919* Oxford, 1967.

Lyman, R. W.: *The First Labour Government*. London, 1957.

McKenna, Stephen: *Reginald McKenna*. London, 1948.

Magnus, Sir Philip: *King Edward the Seventh*. London, 1964.

—— *Kitchener: Portrait of an Imperialist*. London, 1958.

Marder, Arthur J.: *From the Dreadnought to Scapa Flow*. Vol. I. London, 1961.

Marwick, Arthur: *The Deluge*. London, 1965.

Markham, Violet: *Friendship's Harvest*. London, 1956.

Maurice, Major-General Sir Frederick: *Haldane*. 2 vols. London, 1937–39.

Masterman, Lucy: *C. F. G. Masterman*. London, 1935.

Midleton, Earl of: *Records and Reactions*. New York, 1939.

Morgan, J. H.: "The Riddle of Lord Haldane." In the *Quarterly Review*. January and April, 1929.

Mowat, C. L.: *Britain Between the Wars, 1918–1940*. London, 1955.

Nicolson, Sir Harold: *King George the Fifth*. London, 1952.

Ogg, David: *Herbert Fisher*. London, 1947.

Oliver, F. S.: *Ordeal By Battle*. London, 1915.

"The Paradox of Lord Haldane." In the *New Statesman*, August 25, 1928.

Petrie, Sir Charles: *The Life and Letters of Austen Chamberlain*. 2 vols. London, 1939–1940.

Pound, Reginald, and Geoffrey Harmsworth: *Northcliffe*. London, 1959.

Pringle-Pattison, Andrew Seth: *Richard Burdon Haldane*. London, 1928?

Repington, Charles à Court: *Vestigia*. Boston, 1919.

Riddell, Lord: *More Pages from My Diary*. London, 1934.

——— *War Diary*. London, 1933.

Roberts, Lord: *Fallacies and Facts*. London, 1911.

Sommer, Dudley: *Haldane of Cloan*. London, 1960.

Spender, J. A., and C. Asquith: *Life of Lord Oxford and Asquith*. 2 vols. London, 1932.

Stansky, Peter: *Ambitions and Strategies*. London, 1964.

Stewart, A. T. Q.: *The Ulster Crisis*. London, 1967.

Taylor, A. J. P.: *England, 1914–1945*. Oxford, 1965.

——— *Politics in Wartime*. London, 1964.

Trevelyan, G. M.: *Grey of Fallodon*. Boston, 1937.

Webb, Beatrice: *Diaries* (edited by Margaret Cole). 2 vols. London, 1952, 1956.

——— *Our Partnership*. London, 1948.

West, Sir Algernon: *Private Diaries*. London, 1922.

INDEX